Gui

Behind The Iron Curtain

Sir Bernard Pares, the distinguished Russian historian and analyst, helps us to understand the aims and policies of modern Russia by exploring her past history.

With warmth, humanity and understanding, he analyzes the country, the people and—under the Soviets—education, political development, social institutions, religion, the family, industrial and agricultural planning, her record during World War II, and the years immediately following.

In his *Epilogue* (part of which is reprinted from *A History of Russia* published by Knopf in 1948, and part of which was written especially for this edition revised by the author just before his death in 1949), Sir Bernard Pares evaluates Russia's internal situation and her position as a world power.

Here is a significant and provocative book that will give you the background to evaluate and understand the forces that have shaped and are shaping the politics and policies of Russia today.

Other MENTOR Books of Interest

RUSSIA

by

BERNARD PARES

A MENTOR BOOK

Published by THE NEW AMERICAN LIBRARY

To SAMUEL N. HARPER
Comrade of Travel and Study

This is an original MENTOR BOOK, first
published in 1943, revised and brought up to date
by the author in 1949.

THIRTEENTH PRINTING, APRIL, 1959

MENTOR BOOKS are published by
The New American Library of World Literature, Inc.
501 Madison Avenue, New York 22, New York

PRINTED IN THE UNITED STATES OF AMERICA

CONTENTS

I

THE COUNTRY

RUSSIA IS A COUNTRY COVERING ABOUT ONE-SIXTH OF THE LAND surface of the world. That, of itself, makes it impossible to ignore it—least of all at a time when force is the dominant factor.

Its history has been one of continuous colonisation—for the most part less by governments than by peoples, prompted by a desire to escape the close attention of governments. Russia has been the classical land of evasion, a feature which even pervades the Russian language—there is no word for "the" or for "a"; "is" and "are" are usually omitted; the reflexive is the same as the passive—and, just like the language, the colonisation has at different times sought out the lines of least resistance.

In early times even European Russia could not for the most part have all been properly included in Europe, which in the south was for generations bounded by the higher western bank of the Dnieper; outside that line were fluid nomad peoples, of Asiatic origin and successively on the move.

In European Russia, as it is now, the mountains are all on the circumference—in the east the Urals, which are not very high; in the south-east, the far higher Caucasus; the natural boundary on the south-west, which even up to the latest annexations still lay outside the Russian State, is the Carpathians, from which in early history much of the Russian or eastern branch of the great Slavonic family migrated on its march of eastward colonisation. The bulk of present European Russia is a vast plain resting on a granite foundation, with a wide central plateau, which forms the main basis of Russian history; this plateau is only slightly elevated, but with the clear crisp air it makes one feel quite high up: I have had that feeling when standing all night in the Kremlin.

The most definite thing in Russian geography is the rivers, and they are also the most regular in their behaviour among all the citizens of Russia. They originate in great reservoirs of marsh: there is a greater proportion of marsh in Russia than anywhere else in Europe. It was not difficult, even in early Russian history, to connect them by "portages," so that light boats could be carried from one water system to another. The rivers flow quietly onward through a crumbly soil, which assists their power of fertilisation. In a present-day Russian railway guide, something like a third will be taken up by the water routes. Moscow owed her importance largely to the fact that she controlled the head waters of the various systems, which were at first her refuge from invasion and later the roads of her imperial advance. The rivers of Siberia, which are even greater than those of European Russia, nearly all flow northwards into the Arctic Ocean —which very much tends to limit their usefulness, but here, too, the process of colonial advance, easy enough in almost unpopulated country, was in advance from one river system to another. It was just in the most confused and disorderly period of Russian history that this advance eastwards took the biggest dimensions.

The Russian rivers were the main roads of Russian history. Between them lay vast hinterlands of forest or marsh, or both together, in which the harassed population might find a refuge. One river after another would light up into a history of its own: the Dnieper system with its capital at Kiev, the Volga system with Moscow, the Volkhov-Neva road, first with Novgorod the Great, now almost a village, but once the greatest merchant city in Russia, and later, near the end of its course to the sea, with St. Petersburg, planned by Peter the Great as his window opening on Europe. The main rivers—Dnieper, Don, Volga—through most of their way flow from north to south, and by a curious "tilt of the earth"—as it has been described by Russian scholars— the western bank, the line of defence against the invading nomads, is generally considerably higher than the eastern— almost like a series of steep ramparts against Asiatic invasion. The lordly rivers of Siberia flow northwards through vast park-like tracts of virgin forest, almost uncharted and unexplored. At Krasnoyarsk a piece of this virgin forest was left untouched as the park of the new town.

As the rivers were the only lines of light on the map, they were practically the only centres of traffic; so much so, that the early Scandinavian Vikings, advancing along the great water road of their time, described Russia as Garderyk, or the Kingdom of Towns. An ancient monkish chronicler, in his just claim that early Russian history belongs to Europe, tells how the waterway of Volkhov-Dnieper is only the eastern link to a vast belt of water communication completed by the Baltic, the North Sea, the Atlantic, the Mediterranean, and the Black Sea. And the Vikings, who were the first founders of the Russian State and not long afterwards accepted Christianity, did indeed traverse this rounr route, and the easiest part of their navigation was through that eastern link formed by the rivers of Russia, which were also the eastern belt of Europe and Christendom, and were defended by them against the nomads who unceasingly poured in from Asia.

The northern mass of European Russia was, and largely still is, thick forest. It was through unending forest that Napoleon marched to Moscow in 1812. Silver birches, pines and firs; firs, pines and silver birches. It is far easier to lose one's way in a square half-mile of these forests than in a square mile of our smaller ones. The passer-by turns down a twig here and there as he goes, to help any waylaid wanderer to find an exit. Here, Russian peasantry, seeking shelter in the woods from the invading nomads, blended with the primitive Finns, who racially belong to Asia, and formed the Great-Russian family, perhaps now the largest national block in the world. Even well into the nineteenth century the majority of Russians lived in forest.

Agriculture was hard in these surroundings and in this climate—far harder than on the wonderful southern soil from which they had been driven. The great water-roads had fostered that vast and broad sociability which is today the charm of Russia for every Western visitor, and it was this that has given the guarantee of State unity. It was not natural that the dominion over any of these great water-roads should have been for long divided. But here in the remote backwoods, near the head waters of smaller, tributary rivers—each of which in that time of divisions might form a separate little principality united to others only by a loose family tie—it was fear and caution that prevailed. The lonely worker in the forest, as he blazed the roots of trees to obtain a short-lived stimulus from the poor clay soil before moving on further, did not know what danger of man or beast might spring out on him from behind any tree. It was the forest that made that constant wariness which is the chief characteristic of the Great-Russian peasant, as also it made that world of fancies and musings in which he is absorbed, especially in the long winter nights. It was first the forest that made the Russian peasant, or the Russian peasant soldier, the champion evader in the world.

He has a native instinct for the slightest gradation of cover. So one thought as one saw him crawling forward on his belly into No Man's Land when on the attack. A soldier, guiding me at night through the same "interesting" region

—that was their word—kept turning from right to left and back without any apparent reason. "Why do you do that?" I asked. "I feel it in my legs," he said simply, and I think I know what he meant.

South of this great mass of forest which covers most of the north of European Russia and most of Siberia, lies another great belt of almost treeless plain. It is the famous "black soil" formed by the attrition of glacial action, which provides the greatest granary in Europe, the long-sought goal of German ambitions. It is called Ukraine, or Borderland, and its people speak a strong variant of Russian. They have not the Finnish admixture of the north; and, indeed, the early Russian State, of which Kiev was the capital, was based on this part, though it covered a lot of the north, and its reigning family later migrated thither, ultimately to centre itself at Moscow. In this great plain, reeds grew high enough to give cover to man and horse, but it is a land of vast horizons, and it was over this most fertile country that the nomads, in their time of predominance, advanced on Europe. History long eschewed the forest world, but was early at work on the black soil, and it was therefore a land of constant struggle and combat and deeds of daring, such as filled up the lives of the free Cossacks who escaped hither from the serfdom which grew up in the north. Here the fighting man had his value—and this life of adventure has contributed greatly to Russian poetry and to that spirit of daring in thought and action which is another of the great charms of Russia. The Ukrainians have never had a real State of their own. A legend says that when the Creator distributed his gifts to others, he left them out, but in the end he comforted them with the gift of song; and, indeed, the folk song of Ukraine, deeper than the German and more melodious than the Great-Russian, is probably the most beautiful in the world.

Yet forest and plain, traversed alike by the great rivers, were designed by nature to be one great State. There are no natural boundaries to divide them; and economically they are vital to each other and interdependent. Moscow, at the head waters, stands almost at the junction of the two. And over them alike, in the absence of mountains, flows evenly with only gradual variation, the same stern climate, becoming more and more continental as it approaches the great block of Asia, with sharper extremes of heat and cold. The deserts of Central Asia send their harsh and blasting winds into European Russia, and it is only in the north-west, which originally was not inside the Russian frontiers but later housed the artificial capital of Peter the Great, that there penetrate feeble off-shoots of the beneficient and moderating sea-winds of Europe. The good that they do here, by the way, is little enough, and the damp and dreary climate of Leningrad is far more trying to the health than the strong and stimulating air of Siberia.

The Russian climate is a stern one, with long months of winter and, in the north, of darkness, when no agricultural work can be done. Yet the frosty sky is bright and blue and the hard, powdered snows make a merry road to anywhere. Then comes the sudden spring, when all movement seems forbidden, while the great snows and the great river ice melt; and then wild flowers break out everywhere, so that to the Russian peasant it can seem no mere fiction that death is followed by resurrection; and Easter, like so many saint's days that mark in his calendar the changes of the seasons, seems indeed also a great feast of Nature. It is not long before the summer becomes hard and brazen and dry, and gradually breaks in heavy thunderstorms. The early autumn is wonderfully even and beautiful, and everyone and everything again recover their balance. Then another period of cold rain and broken roads till King Frost resumes his cheery rule.

The Russians do not disregard their climate as we do; they defend themselves against it. The houses, even of the peasants, are terribly overheated. Even the trains have double doors, so that the passengers, after fastening themselves well up, can pass by gradations into the could outer air; and foreigners will probably find that they have to show something like the same respect for the climate as the Russians.

The potential wealth of Russia was always prodigious: there can hardly be any country which could be richer or any where the natural resources have been more neglected or wasted. In the earliest times Constantinople was so dependent on Russian supplies that it made the most precise trade treaties by which the Russian traders obtained unusual privileges and facilities: they carried thither in small ships down the Dnieper waterway the forest wealth: furs, honey, wax—and slaves. In the Middle Ages Novgorod the Great possessed vast reserves of forest wealth, coveted by the German cities of the Hansa League. Peter the Great, in his masterful way, did all he could to develop this wealth; but after him Russia had to wait for further development till the economic revolution initiated by the emancipation of the serfs in 1861, which was led into profitable channels by three notable Finance Ministers

—Vyshnegradsky, Witte and Kokovtsev—who brought the country to its highest level of prosperity in the period before the Great War.

Russians were always talking of their "inexhaustible treasure house" and dreaming hazy dreams about the future, but ordinarily the country was content to jog along on a level which quite often sank below that of starvation. Famine would come almost periodically for three years at a time. The country was divided into the producing provinces in the south and east and the consuming provinces in the north. Even more than half-way southward from Petersburg to Moscow there will hardly be a week of summer without one night of frost. The black soil of the south is twice the size of France, and as good as the best land in France or Belgium, but it has to supply the poor clay soil of the north. It takes no more than a breakdown of transport to produce a famine. Western Siberia is one of the greatest areas for farm products in the world, and cold storage made them invaluable to Western Europe, yet an idiotic internal customs duty was laid on them to hamper their competition with the producers of European Russia. It was only the railway building of Witte that made these supplies readily available.

Yet agriculture is far and away the most important industry of Russia. From unknown antiquity up to 1906 northern Russia was farmed on the primitive principle of communal land tenure, which till the eighteenth century prevailed all over Europe, but was abandoned then because it was a hopeless obstacle to initiative and improvement. In Russia it was preserved even after the emancipation of the peasants in 1861 because it offered a lazy and inadequate substitute for poor law relief. The land belonged to the village community as a whole, and each member was therefore supposed to be assured of "a bit of bread"; but for the sake of fairness—a very strong instinct in the Russian peasantry—it was divided up into innumerable cumbrous strips, constantly diminished in width by the rise of population; I have frequently met peasants who had one hundred and fifty scattered over many square miles, and probably the man had only one horse—some had none. I have stretched my legs across a strip so narrow that an ordinary plough had no room to turn around on it. Then, as the State balance chiefly depended on the export of grain, huge amounts were sent abroad which were sorely needed at home; a correspondent of *The Times* once wrote that our food supply was largely dependent on the mortality of Russian children!

Yet, however ill-managed in the past, the output of Russian agriculture was very impressive. Before the south was developed, the flax of the north had a special importance for British traders, particularly of the "Russia Company" endowed with great privileges by John the Terrible, and supplied rigging for the English Navy. The Russian rye crop is of special interest to Germany. The black soil yields great quantities of wheat. But there are lots of other crops in that part. I remember looking out of a train at dawn and seeing a vast unbroken stretch—there are no hedges in Russia— of sunflowers, grown for their seeds and oil, making their morning bow to the sun. Another district, in the north, is devoted mainly to medicinal herbs. There are extensive cotton fields in Russian Central Asia, which began to be properly developed during the American Civil War, and now, thanks to long-pursued work of irrigation, are of growing value. Russia gets tasteful wines from Crimea and the Caucasus and has also a variety of agreeable mineral waters. She has her own tobacco from Crimea, Caucasus and Turkestan, where she also grows some rice.

Agriculture does not create large sums of floating capital, for which reason the shrewd Witte (1892-1903) created a very large gold reserve. Russia always carried on mainly by foreign loans—principally French ones during the period of the Franco-Russian Alliance (1894-1917). Witte used this cleverly to the profit of Russia by encouraging foreign capital to set up its factories in the country, so that it should spend its money there and provide wages for Russian labour. Capital was to be obtained primarily for the development of the vast natural resources: it will be clear from this alone, how great was the importance of the public scrutiny of the State finance, and therefore of the principle of national representation.

These natural resources seem illimitable. After agriculture comes the vast mileage of virgin forest, whose great belt extends all through northern Russia and northern Siberia. There was reckless wastage. On either side of the great Trans-Siberian Railway, the finest achievement of Witte, the forests were blazed by the contemptuous use of wood fuel, in a country overrunning with petroleum. The forests only began to be really profitable in the period of the Duma, the first Russian Parliament (1906-17), and the railways only began to give a profit in the same period.

Fisheries are among the great treasures of Russia—on the northern and Siberian coasts and on the magnificent rivers —rich in a great variety of fish, many of which are unknown to us. They give the impression of astonishing profusion. At Ormsk, on the Irtysh, sitting waiting for a boat beside the town pier, I saw two fishermen, in Biblically primitive costume, holding the two ends of a net, walk several times into the river and literally scoop the fish out, as if there were hardly room for them there. When I expressed my surprise to a Siberian business friend, he was only surprised at my surprise. When the coarse salmon go down the broad Amur, one of the biggest rivers in Siberia, they say it almost looks as if you could walk across their backs. The cormorants of the Arctic seem to be engaged in one continuous meal.

I am looking at a large economic wall map of the whole State; how tiny little Europe looks in comparison! Almost every kind of metal or mineral leaves its mark on it. Goldfields are sprinkled about over nearly the whole of the vast eastern half of Siberia—on the Lena, in the Altai Mountains, and down the coast as far as Vladivostok. For a long time the working was quite inadequate, but now Russia already apparently takes second place in the world in gold output, and she has other great reserves charted but as yet unworked. The Urals give gold, platinum, a number of curious minor precious stones. It was the discovery of coal and iron in close neighbourhood in the Don basin that attracted the lately liberated serfs and built up a new industrial Russia in the south. There are also big coalfields in the Urals, Central Asia, the Altais, on the Lena and on the coasts of the Pacific and Arctic Oceans, and iron is only less generously distributed. Two big coalfields were discovered in the eight months that I spent in Siberia in 1919. There are also reserves of copper, lead, zinc, nickel and aluminum. Of manganese, mostly in the Caucasus but also in parts of the Urals, Russia has vastly the greater part of the whole world supply.

Everyone knows of Russia's stores of petrol. On the Volga one was always passing the tankers bringing it up from Baku, the main centre of supply; but a so-called "second Baku" is being developed in the Urals, and there are even workings close to the Arctic coast on the Pechora. But enough has been said to show that Russia was already more than ripe for State planning.

Russia has nearly everything that could make her self-supporting; and yet she lived on foreign loans, sought her technical experts from abroad, and had to send thither for spare parts when, as so often, her machinery broke down. It is not surprising that Lenin should have declared her to be a colonial dominion of foreign capital.

II
THE RUSSIANS – AND OTHERS

THE RUSSIANS

THE RUSSIAN PEOPLE, THAT LIVES IN THIS GREAT LAND, HAS the instinct of its greatness—and of the littleness of the individual self.

The Russians have a wonderful physique. Perhaps this is a survival of the fittest, for the nation has lived through numberless famines and epidemics. They are often largely and loosely built: the Great-Russian is broader and stockier than the Ukrainian. What they can stand is surprising: the soldiers used to tell me they couldn't go through more than *four* nights running without any sleep; and a Scottish surgeon, landed in Russia in World War I, said: "I don't think there can be a wound from which the Russian can't recover: you cut off his leg without anesthetics, and he says 'Thank you, Sir.'" There is a fine Russian word for a fine Russian quality—*vynoslivost*, "lasting a thing out," and it applies not only to the man but to the nation, not only to the body but the mind. No counting on quick returns for your labour. On the other hand, in accordance with his climate—the short bright summer and the long dark winter—the Russian is habituated to working in great bursts, if they can be followed by long intervals, and all his intervals are usually very long.

The Russian enjoys space, and what he likes before all things is elbow room—elbow room, with brotherhood with his fellowman, but without compulsion, which he is always seeking to avoid. Russian life is fluid—that is how, quite apart from government action, it has come to spread itself over so great a part of the world. The Russian was always a born wanderer—and that not only the Russian of the ruling classes. He has a wonderful knack of getting on with anybody and loves to add to his knowledge. Even language hardly seems to be an obstacle, and anything distant fascinates him. Maurice Baring tells how he dozed off to sleep while a number of Russian soldiers talked of the Red Sea, the White Sea, the Black Sea, the Yellow Sea—they may have added a few more colours: they got them all mixed up, but they were terribly interested in all of them.

The Russian had enough of compulsion if he stayed near

the centre. It did little for him, and its futility came to a head shortly before the events which led to the Revolution, when the Government itself felt compelled to summon a commission representative of the inhabitants and to set it the ominous problem of "the impoverishment of the central provinces." Villages were electing "walkers" (*hodoki*) who trekked far away into Siberia—hitch-hikers who slept anywhere, got surreptitious lifts on trains, or tramped patiently for uncounted miles, to find some "good land" to which perhaps the village might migrate more or less wholesale later, quite against the law. When the Home Minister of the last Tsar called his attention to this, Nicholas II very sensibly asked how many were doing it and, on being told, he remarked that it seemed wiser to foster the movement than to repress it. But assiduous bureaucratic fostering never drew such sturdy elements as these Pilgrim Fathers, who later in their new homes came to be known as the "old inhabitants" and formed the most conservative element of the Siberian population.

It was in the same way that the population of the capitals was recruited—Moscow and even the originally almost un-Russian Petersburg: and that, not in the manner of Dick Whittington but after careful scouting, like that of Joshua and Caleb. Men of a given village would cultivate a given trade and move to a given quarter where it was centred—gardeners, carpenters, cobblers, cabmen and so on. The village community let them go only on condition that they sent part of their earnings to pay the village taxes, and in old age the city peasant would hand over his job to a son or a nephew and return to his legal share in the village farming. I have seen whole villages which were chiefly supported by their town earnings. In the summer, while the factories might be closed for repair, one might see fellow-villagers at the Petersburg terminus all going home together to take part in the harvesting. A town priest in Moscow once told me that, with the exception of a retired colonel, his parish consisted only of peasants. Again, at a village meeting before the revolution, held miles away from any station—I was the only person present except the local peasants—I found that about forty per cent of them had at one time worked in Petersburg or Moscow.

There is a natural frankness in the Russian's approach to his fellow beings. He has instinctively the sense of a big world and a big Russia, and he wants to be friends. When he meets any decent foreigner, especially an Englishman or American, it is if anything stronger: for they have the inquisitiveness of big children, and like to explore those who seem most different to themselves, and always in the hope of finding points of contact. The more remote the new acquaintance seems, the greater is the pleasure in discovering that he is a fellow man and a good comrade, and the little points of difference will all seem fresh and interesting to him. In World War I, I used constantly to be wandering along various parts of the front line with a single peasant soldier at night, when time and place made the mind more alert, and have often been "explored" and "exploring." There is nothing impertinent and encroaching in this: they don't bother about the details, they want to know what you are like, what you feel and think. I remember a soldier from the Caucasus explaining to me what different peoples live there; he had a few racy words for each— the fierce Georgians who shoot at sight (Stalin is one of them), the commercially-minded Armenian, the middleman Jew, and each description ended with the words "but they're sociable people." Two peasants from opposite ends of Russia, members of the First Duma who had set up house-keeping together, told me that the best thing of all about this institution for them was that they found that there was so much alike in all that they thought and felt and hoped.

The First Duma had the best peasant members: they were really chosen simply as the "best men," without any thought of politics or parties. What delighted talks my American colleague Samuel Harper [1] and I used to have with them: and what an instinct they had for telling a story—colour, life and restraint. One of them, an elderly bearded man—Samuel, you will remember Sharkov—had been given a public flogging for heading a deputation with reasonable peasant complaints to the local Governor. "How many strokes did they give you?" I asked. "Who counted them?" he said carelessly and told us the rest just as if he himself had not been the victim: for instance how the doctor was called in to see what he could stand, and retired saying "you can give some more." "And which party do you think will win?" Harper asked another; for the peasants remained rather demonstratively "Non-Party" and were sizing up all of them. "Every Party has its secret," he said, "and that Party which keeps its secret longest will win, and I think it will be the Non-Party"; and that was just what I have always thought myself.

Peasants show fully as much delicacy of thought for you as the better educated, and there is a keen instinct against exag-

[1] Formerly Professor of Russian History and Institutions in the University of Chicago.

geration. It comes out in all their choice of words, especially their liking for the use of the negative: "not particularly decent," "not a pretty women" or the opposite: "not bad with herself." Also there is a natural dignity—no claim to equality, but the real equality which consists in being quite satisfied with what you are. The peasants are very proud of their class name "the men of the Cross" and they have always had a tremendous loyalty to their class. This makes them perfectly at ease with you—say, in an all-night drive under the moonlight when your driver is also your friend and discusses everything in heaven and earth—and it is just the difference between you that is attractive; for, as Lord Hugh Cecil once said in one of the most Slavophile speeches that I have ever heard in Russia, "The heavenly choir is not a unison but a harmony."[1]

Picture a ragged little caretaker of a peasant court-house, as he put five chairs against a stove for me to sleep on, asking in the closest detail what happened in England if the House of Commons passed a Bill and the House of Lords threw it out. Or again, what they used to ask us in the country parts in 1906 during that critical time that followed the dissolution of the First Duma. "What control has your (English) Duma over your Budget?" they asked. "What control has your Duma over your Army?" (Here I gave an explanation of the Mutiny Act, which was received with lively approval.) I used to feel, as they seated us on the elders' bench on the village green and all gathered round, as if we were talking to a number of brothers in a smoking room, with a common understanding and common reticences, which I think came from the habits of the traditional village commune. And when in the hectic Second Duma, part of the ceiling fell in, fortunately while the hall was empty, a peasant member asked me "How long has your parliament existed?" and then, grimly, "Has the ceiling ever fallen in?" Or picturesque bearded Kirnosov from the Lower Volga, replying to a squire's speech on the rights of property: "We know your idea of property; my uncle (a serf) was exchanged for a greyhound." There was a thrill of reality which went right through the House.

The best summaries in the changing politics were made to me by peasants. Here is one from the Lower Volga, after the suppression of the abortive revolution of 1904-7. This peasant had just given us a most lively picture of the behaviour of all the chief personages in his village—the priest, the doctor, the schoolmistress, the police corporal, all watching to see where the cat would jump next in the capital. "And what's

[1] In the Tretyakov Gallery in Moscow in 1912.

the difference between five years ago and now?" I asked. "I couldn't tell you a thing like that," he said. "Well, have a try." "Five years ago there was belief (in the Government) and fear. Now the belief is all gone, and only the fear remains."

What is the chief difference between those times and the present day? Several years ago I was making my third trip down the Volga. Well, there is a sort of genuine stiffening of what was weakest in the Russian nature, the backbone. There is the same friendly approach, bridging the gap between you at once, but your friend has got more of the sense that he counts. There was never more than a thin layer of gentry along that great river of the Russian people. Now it is all gone, and it seemed to me that the people felt quite at home in managing things for themselves. Not that there was any propaganda in their talk. I think propaganda bores Russians. But there was responsibility and purpose, and with this went a cheerfulness which one could not but be glad to see. Of this new Russia I shall be giving a much fuller picture later.

The language has that which the Russian character seemed most to lack—strength. There are some rather bad consonantal complexities, but they are softened down in speaking and singing: otherwise it is almost as musical as Italian, and Pushkin once wrote a witty skit which might have been either, though the meaning varied absurdly. It has the broad vowels of German or Italian, which make it so musical: when I came back from my first year there, I was taken here for a Yorkshireman—a county where folk-music can still flourish. Russian abounds in open vowels: I think Paul Robeson learnt it for that reason, and he has shown me with his great voice what can be done with them. Also it is very pliable: there are verse effects with unaccented syllables which are perhaps only possible in Russian, Italian or English—say, Edward Lear. This gives a tripping rhythm to their extremely witty political skits, in which puns and double-entendres seem to come up and do service of themselves.

All sorts of nonsense has been written about the difficulties of Russian by people who should have learnt it but didn't; our traders managed quite well with it. It has reasonable modes of expression whose habits can be explained simply enough to any intelligent student, and once you have got them, you will not find yourself let down by constant exceptions. The "slog" or make-up of a sentence is very much the same as in English, only shorter and pithier—and that, I think, is because there is a likeness in the manner of thinking. Anyhow, the language must be simple, if only because of the use which the peasant can make of it. It is wonderful to see what colour and freshness he can get out of his limited vocabulary. Often I have thought, if only I could sit down and write it straight down, to keep all the freshness in it! Even the old annals of the eleventh or twelfth century read with all the freshness and directness of a novel. "Prince," said the men of a great medieval city to an unsatisfactory ruler, "we salute you and show you the way out." We say, "I'll give it you," obviously meaning something very unpleasant. "I'll you" is thought enough in Russian. There is hardly a Russian idiom for which one cannot find an almost exact equivalent in English.

The peasant has an instinctive taste for the equivocal, the non-committal—and no wonder if one considers his long history of instinctive evasion—and the language helps him. I am passing the house of a Land Captain, a small official set up by the Tsar to drill the peasantry. This one felt himself called upon to settle any matrimonial disputes. "What sort of Land Captain is that?" I ask. "He is thought (by whom?) a decent one." "Never mind 'is thought,' " I say. "Well then of course there's not an atom of decency in him," he said. If an outsider cared to ask for his real opinion, he could have it. Again, accompanying a Governor on his local inspection of his province, and being free to do nothing but listen and watch, I could see how the peasants chose the expression which would make him think that everything was in order, so that he might go on and worry someone else. They seemed to have something in common with a class of boys in one of our schools. Or it is like Kipling's "jungle," of which he writes that everything there means something different from what it says. This wiliness, this unwillingness to commit oneself, is one of those peasant characteristics which is very common in other classes, and it is also one of the essential elements in Russian humour.

On the other hand, one has over and over again found among the Russian peasantry an equally strong and instinctive desire for knowledge and culture. "We are people in darkness," they would often say. "In Russia, it is night, darkness," said a Cossack to me as we rode back through the mist from the front in the small hours, not long before the Revolution. "We must have culture," said the leader of a particularly hefty group of peasants from the Lower Volga, stretching himself vigorously. "We are so strong, and full of life. We eat such a lot, we must have culture or we should go wild." And at a pre-revolutionary peasant meeting, one of their first demands was: "We want to have real books," evidently mistrusting those which were supplied to them at the time. One can imagine what a help this was to be to the Soviet Government when it started its signal fight for primary education.

I have written, so far, mostly of the peasants, who are of course the great majority. But the peasant instincts—wariness, hesitations, humour, and above all "back thoughts" (the Russian for *arrière-pensées*) are at the bottom of nearly every Russian. And—peasant or otherwise—the ordinary Russian is always a great big grown up child. I puzzled terribly in my first year in Russia, because everything, in speech or action, happened with such a refreshing suddenness and variety, and I asked myself whether there was not some hidden key, some secret fifth dimension. It was the other way round. They had not been stiffened out like us, they were not "grown up." "We Russians," said a famous Russian friend of England, Paul Milyukov, "are without the cement of hypocrisy," and that is really why every Englishman who goes there is so much charmed by Russia.

I have had the hospitality of all of them, gentry, priests, professional men and peasants, and it has always had the same quality of unbounded kindness and of delicacy of thought. This note never changed. How enthralling they are, those long night conversations, with all sorts of angles focussed on one deeply interesting problem after another. Practically no pretence or snobbery—if there was, it was usually in aliens or officials—but direct intellectual honesty. No awkwardness between old and young, between employer and employed, and every fresh contribution welcomed, especially if it had the nature of a challenge. I remember in 1907 a Socialist tutor in a wealthy household eloquently attacking the conservative or liberal views of the rest of the company, and no one thought of grudging him his evident victory.

It has often seemed to me that a conversation in Russian is less a give and take of argument than a series of dramatised expressions of individual opinion. They are extraordinarily good at this. You do not interrupt, and he won't either when your turn comes. It is like a succession of presentations of different points of view, often very picturesque.

And on the long journeys you will find the same ease of approach in the chance company collected in any railway carriage, and when a fascinating question is stated, each, with what might seem to us a surprising frankness, and without any obtrusion of self, will contribute any experience out of his own life which may bear on the subject. And the conductor will be quite ready to join in, like anyone else. No wonder life is interesting. "When you pass out over the frontier," said Harold Williams, the greatest of all our students of Russia,[1] "don't you feel as if something were being taken out of you?"

Russians are very personal, and Russian humour is often of the kind which we call "leg-pulling." Before 1917, revolutionaries sometimes got engaged as secretaries by foreign correspondents or even by government officials and played their little jokes. The Governor of Kostroma was free and casual and signed his letters without looking through them. His secretary made him responsible for a singular self-revelation: "I ought to say that I am quite unfitted for my post: I drink: I gamble: I take no trouble over my work," etc. The Governor signed this without looking through it, and the Government took him at his word, and dismissed him. Their school-boy pokes were very simple and clever. One of them got on the staff of a prison and, when by good conduct he had earned promotion, he simply unlocked the doors and let his comrades out. There was a certain amount of cheek about this which even the police could not help admiring.

Or, to take an example from a quite different milieu, a Russian army commander of the bull-dog type in the last war was interviewing a German divisional general, who, much to his annoyance, had been kidnapped and brought in by daring partisans. As usual, the prisoner at once began declaiming against the English: "We ought never to be fighting you: we ought to be friends. How long will this horrible war go on?" "Our allies want it to be five years," said the Russian casually, "but we're trying to get them to cut it down to three." "Do you mean it will be like Napoleon's Moscow campaign?" "Oh, no. Moscow doesn't come into it. You'll find our lines of passive resistance on the Volga" (the German groaned); "our lines of active resistance you'll find on the Ural Mountains."

The Russian likes to point his joke with a little flick at the end, and to leave you to think it out. Gogol, in his most humourous and sarcastic play *Revizor*, depicts a ready-witted adventurer who impersonates the traveling Government Inspector in a provincial town. He clears out the pockets of all the local officials, gets engaged to the mayor's daughter, and goes off triumphantly with the best horses. At this moment the arrival of the real inspector is announced. No trouble is wasted on following out the rest of the story, which must have resulted in an anti-climax. The curtain goes down, and as it descends, all the characters fall into a *tableau vivant* of

[1] Later Director of the Foreign Department of *The Times*.

various attitudes of consternation, for which the clever author himself drew the picture.

The Russian mind is quick and lively: what it lacks is balance: it is constantly going off at a tangent. In the Russian, mind and heart work closely together. Intuition is much stronger than reason. The Russian can remain for long sunk in deep prostration, for he is a creature of moods, but he will pass suddenly out of it without any visible transition and he does not ordinarily spoil things by superfluous anticipation as to tomorrow. Friendship, with him, is peculiarly instinctive and personal: it sees, but it does not argue; it does not depend in any way on an estimate of the merits of the friend; it need not necessarily be changed by anything odd or bad that the friend might happen to do. I have always felt with Russians that one begins again where one had left off.

All this will help to explain why the Russians have a special charm for the Englishman. To start with, so many of them speak English so naturally: they are the only foreigners that I know that seem to speak just as if they were Englishmen, with all our intonations, and that is by no means confined to those who have learnt it in childhood: it applies sometimes even to workmen. Then they think so many of our thoughts, which they express in just the same direct way, and above all they exactly appreciate our kind of humour. As Maurice Baring has put it, "there is a sympathy between the natures of the two countries." He doesn't pretend to explain it, but he knows that it is so. The same thing has been noted in turn by Russians. Nicholas Homyakov, the president of the Third Duma, has spoken of "kindred spirits," and adds:

"This 'something' cannot be defined, but it is very easy to see when two persons of different types come together. Is it not this affinity that makes every Russian when he is among Englishmen at once feel at home, though he may not be like them in character, or in beliefs, or in education? You will be told of the corresponding feeling by every Englishman who has lived in Russia, but not by the Frenchman, or the German, or the Italian."

"I think," he goes on, "that the culture of the Englishman finds repose in the primitive natural characteristics of the Russian people, in its native breadth of mind, and in its open and expansive soul. On our side, I own, the alarming indiscipline of the Russian bends before the discipline of mind and will which has grown up with centuries and has entered into the flesh and blood of the Englishman. It fascinates him and draws him to itself."[1]

I have always found this myself. Root instincts of simplicity, humour and enjoyment are shared, and for the rest

[1] "Bases of Anglo-Russian Friendship" in *The Russian Review* (Nelson), Vol. I, No. 2.

the Russian and the Englishman are somehow complementary to each other. The Englishman relishes the feeling of space and opportunity: the Russian welcomes the Englishman's instinct for initiative and enterprise, his plain common sense and his kindly discipline. Sport is another great link, and there is a peculiar zest with which a Russian of any age will set about learning any new English game. I recall an excellent football match, with a bearded goalkeeper at each end. Sometimes it goes too far: "What is Navy Cut?" said a bearded Russian friend to me, looking at my tobacco-tin. "Why, your beard would be Navy Cut if you cut that tip off." He cut it off at once, and said with satisfaction, "Now I am Navy Cut."

Our British trading colony in Russia, whom I have always regarded as peculiarly British—"the hem is stronger than the cloth"—knew exactly how to get on with Russians: good nature and kindly thought will do that for you, and they come natural over there. Some of their elders, who were there throughout the Crimean War, once told me they had no trouble at all, nothing but kindness, as no one seemed to identify our Government with an individual Englishman. Old Sir William Mather, sturdy Manchester Liberal who was the first to start the eight-hour day in his works, always spoke of Russia to me as "my second home": "those days sparkle in my memory," he said. Sir George Buchanan, who—God knows—had a hard enough time there as our Ambassador, spoke of it as "the Russia that I love." Baring saw the true gentleman in the Russian under-dog peasant. I was anxious when I saw so many raw Englishmen poured into Russia at her worst time, but they look back on it as a kind of freemasonry of fellowship. And in the technical service of the Five-Year Plan many an enterprising young Englishman, living and working day by day with the Russian workers, has spent some of the brightest and most stimulating years of his life. All this is an asset. I could always count, in our work of Slavonic Studies in England, that no one who took up the subject would ever give it up.

And it is surprising how thoroughly their quick and friendly minds understand us. I might choose many illustrations in many fields, but I will take our closest and most peculiar one. The Anglo-Saxon is the only foreigner in Russia who finds himself most at home, not in the town, but the country; and here is how Alexis Homyakov, the distinguished Slavophil thinker, gets to the bottom of the genius of our own instinct of home and country:

"Every Englishman is a Tory at heart. . . . The history of England is no mere thing of the past for the Englishman of to-day. It lives in all his life and all his habits, in nearly every detail of his existence. And this historic element is Toryism. . . . He walks through the long aisles of Westminster Abbey, not with the boastful pride of the Frenchman, not with the antiquarian delectation of the German, but with a deep, sincere and ennobling affection. These graves are his own great family; and I am not speaking of the lord or of the professor, but of the workman, or of the cabman who drives about London all day. There is just as much Toryism among the people as there is in the upper ranks of society. Certainly this tradesman or this workman will vote for the Whigs. He thinks that best for his country or for his material interests, but at heart he loves the Tories. He will support Russell or Cobden, but all his sympathies are with old Wellington and Bentinck. Whiggism is his daily bread: but Toryism is all his pleasure in life—his racing, his boxing-match, his cricket . . . his Christmas tree, his merry Christmas games; it is the peace and hallowed joy of his family circle: it is all poetry: it is the fragrance of life. In England every old oak with its spreading branches is a Tory, and so is every ancient church spire, rising in the distance to heaven. Under that old oak many have been happy, and in that ancient church many succeeding generations have prayed."

And again:

"England has grasped the fact that only that is conservative which moves forward, and only that is progressive which does not break with the past."[1]

And I should say here that the appeal of the American to the Russian instinct of friendship is practically the same as our own. We are two kindred peoples, each steering its own course in history, but in Russia we foregather naturally. My own closest fellow-investigator of Russia was an American, the late Professor Samuel N. Harper of the University of Chicago. We lived, travelled and studied together. Together we interviewed every Russian of that time (1906-8) whom we regarded as having significance in Russian public life. We jointly registered each night the results of our investigations, and our notes of the impressions of each of us will be found in the handwriting of the other; and up to his death we had a common language in which we could easily exchange judgments in the fewest of words. To a Russian it seemed quite natural that an Englishman and an American should go about in such close partnership, and they liked to draw us into friendly or even teasing comparisons and contrasts between our two countries which we all equally enjoyed. But this is not an isolated example. I like this of Mrs. Vera M. Dean:

"In many ways, the Russians resemble the Americans more than any other people. Like Americans, they are eager to ask questions

[1] Alexis Homyakov, spokesman of the Slavophils, quoted by his son N. Homyakov in *The Russian Review*, Vol. I, No. 2, pp. 14-19.

and learn new things; they are not afraid to make mistakes; they have an attitude of breezy but not annoying self-confidence, born of the knowledge that they have vast spaces and great material resources at their disposal; and they adapt themselves readily to new and entirely untried conditions." [1]

There have been times when contact with Russia has been much easier for Americans than for us, and then it was they who have rendered much the greater service to our common knowledge.

This helped us to distinguish a little more clearly between what our two countries respectively represented to them. Both represented initiative and character—the matter in which the Russians of that time felt themselves to be most lacking. It is very different now, because the advance which they have made for themselves, the general bracing up of the whole community, is much the most striking of all the differences between pre- and post-revolutionary Russia. But America very rightly represented to them a much more free and open field for enterprise; and of those numberless Russians whom the Revolution has scattered over every country in the world, undoubtedly it is those who have made their new home in America that have found the break easiest and the new start simplest.

In my view, the only foreign countries which have a profound importance in Russia's own development are Germany on the one side, and Britain and America on the other, and the political alignment of the various countries in a second world war was, to me, nothing else than a natural expression of this. France has long since counted for very little in Russia, and Italy not at all, but China does count for much; so,—but on the negative side—does Japan. I have heard Russians distinguish in much the same way, and I can even remember a Russian peasant-driver predicting this alignment to me with some vigour as far back as 1935.

This picture of the Russians which I have given is frankly of the best and kindliest instincts in the Russian nature. They are born, not made: character has to be made, and that the Russian finds the hardest of tasks, and it is just here that he may lean on an English friend and look for guidance, for he is very well aware of his own weaknesses. And in the long run all Russian problems are centred in that of the training of character. The Russian is capable of violent if temporary savagery, of wild excesses—as Dostoyevsky has put it in a memorable essay[2]—of "self-destruction," in which he can

---

[1] *Russia at War*, by Vera M. Dean, pp. 11-12.
[2] "Vlas" in *Diary of a Writer (Dnevnik Pistelya).*

throw recklessly into the bonfire all that he values and reverences most—God, family, self-respect, everything. "This is peculiar to our people in moments when the head is in a whirl," so Dostoyevsky writes. But the impetuous stormy impulse, he adds, is followed by a much more enduring period of self-recovery. For the Russian nature is innately spiritual. A German in drink boasts, a Russian murmurs that he is a miserable sinner.

It would be quite impossible to drive the soul out of the Russian nature, for it is there as the essential part of him. The invisible is always present to him. A lady meets an old peasant woman who has tramped barefoot to Kiev all the way from the Ural Mountains. "And you have come all that way alone?" she asks. "Yes, alone with my soul." And how could she part with it if it is her most intimate companion? It would be quite impossible to make Russian philosophy, so long as it remains Russian, anything other than idealistic. That explains why Marxism, which claims to be rooted in materialism, itself with the Russian becomes a religion. That is the deep mark that he imprints on all his borrowings from secular-minded Germany.

Will this picture help us to guess the future of Communism in Russia? But what do we mean by Communism? Not the unbridled savagery, when the peasant at last saw that his goal was in sight, that all he had got to do was to go and take the land he had always longed for: when every check was removed and every wall, as Lenin had predicted, would fall at a push—though even here there were examples of very remarkable consideration. It was indeed the merit of the Bolsheviks that they again bridled this elemental savagery, though they had a far more persistent savagery of their own. Nor by Communism should we mean Russian Bolshevism with its elemental foundation of age-long repression and bitter resentment, the formulated instinct of the wrath of the people. The early Christians were communists, and so is modern monkhood. A besieged city or a besieged island, like our own in the last war, so full of the best of individualism, was for the time communist; for not private interest could rear itself against the total claim of the community to all life and property within its beleagured bounds. We were all war communists, and most of all the most devoted patriots among us. If we take it in this way, without reference to any particular formula to be imposed, or to the savagery of those who have imposed it there, then the past life of Russia was full enough of the instinct of communism. The Tsardom itself was a perfectly natural and legitimate creation of a great and constant national danger which called imperatively for national defence and a national authority. The village community had to be communist in its long unequal battle with poor soil and climate. The village holding was held in common by all, with periodical re-divisions according to the number of workers, and the villagers would vote on every act in the farmer's year. The whole trend of Russian Orthodoxy is to visualize a great community in which all are equal: its favourite word *sobornost*—"cathedralness" if you like—means union in reverence, in the instinct of the community; and at moments of national danger and distress this sense has always swept everyone in Russia into the community: never have I seen this better in its full beauty than at Easter in the Russian front line in 1915, when, incidentally, it was a Marxist who organised and led the church choir.

The instinct of the community lies very deep in the peasant mind, and he can very well discriminate what this word means to him. Long before the Revolution, in 1908, Harper and I visited a very remarkable revolutionary named Theologov. The son of a priest, he decided to devote himself to the peasants in his own peculiar way. By marrying a peasant girl he became a member of a peasant joint-family—for every worker in it was a member—and he was elected clerk of the village society. He had left his mark on the peasants of his village, and he invited them to make friends with us.

What we can say of the future of Communism in Russia is surely this: that wherever it lies in the instincts of the Russian people it will spread and prosper, and wherever it is in discord with those instincts it will fail. The pride in national planning for the well-being of the community as a whole is a fine and genuine pride, and there is no doubt of the enthusiasm which is inspires, especially among the young. The attempt to take away religion from those who choose to have it is entirely un-Russian; and it is already quite clear that, though religious organizations can be destroyed and religious training abolished, religion at its core, in the human soul, is only made stronger by persecution.

AND OTHERS

The Russian coloniser showed a remarkable adaptability with the more backward peoples with whom he mixed in his wanderings, and this instinct has throughout governed the policy of the Soviet Government. They were many, and they mostly lay to the east of him in his advance into Asia. There are well over a hundred nationalities in the Russian State today.

There were first the primitive Finns of the backwoods who helped to form the Great-Russian blend. They were scattered all over European Russian and gave the names to many Russian rivers and even to the river and city of Moscow. They are also supposed by some philologists to have had something to do with that curious and fascinating feature of the Russian language—the aspects of the verb. There are still little islands of this non-European race between Moscow and the Urals. But there is also a bastion of them, more highly civilised than the Russians, which has lived a life of its own much more to the west, among the granite rocks of present-day Finland. They were for a long time united with Sweden, though possessing their own free institutions. In 1809 they were brought by conquest into the Russian Empire; but the stiffness of their resistance secured for them the right to preserve their national institutions, and there was only union under a common sovereign. This arrangement the last Tsar tried to upset. But in 1918, during the collapse of Russia, they were able to establish their political independence.

Present-day Finns offer almost a complete antithesis to the Russians, having almost the opposite values of character and customs much nearer to those of the Germans. They have all the middle-class virtues. They are scrupulously honest and clean. What one does not seem to find in them is the broad humanity and the fancy and vision of the Russians.

There is a big difference, of which one is immediately conscious, when it is the Russian Government that advances and not the Russian people, and it is still bigger when the advance is not eastward but westward and at the expense of historical peoples of a higher culture. Bismarck, whose whole idea was that Russia should get out of the way of German ambitions by turning eastward, said she should not fuddle her head with Europe and constitutions, she only contracted Nihilism and other contagious diseases. "Let her go eastward," he said; "there she is a civilising force." In the imperialist conquest of the Poles, and still more in that of the eastward German colonies on the Baltic, one felt that Russia had no right to dominate these peoples. The Poles were not made for subjection and have never been able to digest it; the only result is an inner sore which wrenches their whole consciousness and turns nationalism into a fanaticism. Nor had the Russian Government the slightest idea of how to govern the Poles; it could not create anything here, it could only destroy positive values; it attacked the land and it attacked the language, and in each case it suffered signal defeat. The long duel between the two nationalities is not yet over, and it is embittered by the fact that at the very outset of their national histories the Poles accepted Western Catholicism and the Russians Eastern Orthodoxy. Even quite lately, in the still primitive border provinces constantly disputed throughout history and recently again in the last war, where the population is in the main White-Russian or Ukrainian, and certainly not Polish, a peasant might describe himself as Orthodox or Catholic rather than as Russian or Pole.

Equally sharp is the contrast between the Russians and the Baltic Germans. These German colonies owed their origin to that thirst for adventure which survived the crusades and created the nucleus of modern Prussia, and there is no greater contrast than between the Russian and the Prussian. What the German most esteems—especially the Nazi German—the Russian regards with contempt, and *vice versa*. The German Balts had a highly advanced civilisation of their own—with order(discipline, property, learning and literature—which the Russians at one time vainly tried to destroy, especially stirring up the subjugated under-dog population of those parts, the Letts and Estonians; of these the last two never got any recognition of their nationality on the map till the settlement of Versailles in 1919. On the other hand, the Russian Government found invaluable agents for the autocracy in the German and Balts and employed them all over the Empire in the higher civil and military posts, which did not increase their popularity with the Russian population. Bismarck is said to have described the Balts as the best routine officials in the world, and they made the truly awful mistake, which Russians generally avoided, of trying to carry out Russian laws to the letter.

Of the Jewish race something like half lived within the Russian boundaries before 1914. They can claim with reason that they had roots in the Dnieper area before the arrival of the Vikings who made the first Russian State of Kiev. The eastern neighbours of Kiev, the Khans of the Khazars, seem to have practiced the Jewish religion. But in the middle ages most of these Jews belonged to Poland. Here they practically took the place of the middle class, especially between the opposite elements of Polish lords and Russian serfs in the disputed provinces, where they acted as intermediaries with much profit to themselves. It was the partition of Poland at the end of the eighteenth century that brought this mass of Jewry into Russia and created the Jewish question there. The Jews naturally appreciated the advantage of trading over this vast empire, and the Russian Government tried to keep them out by limiting them to the area where they had lived before the Partition. This led to a constant economic warfare in which the Government relied on impossibly harsh laws and the Jews on their arts of evasion. As one Jew put it to me, with excessive frankness, "We are cheats but not rogues." The Jew had to deceive in order to exist, for the laws hardly granted him the right to breathe. Every activity of his was hemmed in with preposterous regulations. He had to buy his way everywhere, and the police were only too glad to take his bribes. The old Government never found a way out of this morass up to the revolution.

These four nationalities—the Finns, the Poles, the Germans and the Jews—officially distinguished from the Russians by an offensive word (*inorodtsy*) which meant "home aliens," were the ones that most caught the eye of western Europe, for they were the most advanced and the worst treated. But there were numbers of others. In the Tartars and kindred races, Russia had a population of something like twenty million Mussulmans, whose affinities drew them to Constantinople just as the Christian subjects of the Sultan looked for help to Moscow. The Tartars were no longer warlike but mercantile, but they had their own centres of civilisation in Bukhara and Kazan and also their own secret methods of communication. The Caucasus, like the Pyrenees, serves as a buttress to relics of ancient races—the Georgians with a great historical and literary past, the Armenians, a trading people who had survived numerous massacres, and several smaller and curious units which had found shelter here. Central Asia contained peoples without a history and without an alphabet. On the far northern shores of the Pacific were the Buryats, also without a life of their own. During the great liberal movement of 1904-7 when the favourite political motto was "The United States of Russia," the gifted Harold Williams, who knew all the languages which he mentions, thus with vision interpreted this formula:—

"The question is whether Russian culture—the sum of spiritual values accumulated by the Russian people during its manifold adventures over European and Asiatic plains—shall so vigorously develop, shall so permeate the political and social structure of the Empire as to exert a constant attractive influence on all the nationalities and infect them with an ardour of co-operative movement—whether the ruling people in fact is capable of creating throughout the Russian dominions a spirit of genuine and quickened imperial patriotism.

"The Russian Empire means not only Pushkin and Tolstoy and Chaikovsky, it means Mickiewicz and Slowacki (Poles) and the Little-Russian (Ukrainian) Shevchenko: it means the Kalevala and Sibelius (Finnish), it means the Russian *byliny* (heroic legends) and the Little-Russian *dumy* ('stories'): and Lettish and Estonian folk songs, and Kirghiz heroic songs about Er Targyn, and the medieval Georgian poem about the man in the Panther Skin, and all kinds of charming products of the young literatures and peoples who are fast learning to express themselves."[1]

For all this huge and vital problem the government of the Tsars had nothing better to offer than a senseless policy of sheer suppression—especially of languages and literatures. Harold Williams, as liberal a soul as ever breathed, loathed it. He also detested the Bolsheviks. But had he lived, he would have had to admit that in this particular matter his dream had come true in the Union of Soviet Socialist Republics of the present day, and he would have been grateful to it for the numbers of new grammars which it gave him to absorb.

III

EAST OR WEST?

ONE GREAT QUESTION RUNS RIGHT THROUGH RUSSIAN HIStory—Tsars or Bolsheviks—and that is because it is one that Nature puts to Russia, and it runs not only through all her story, but through all her thought as well. Russia is at the boundary of Europe and Asia, straddling over half of Europe and an enormous part of Asia. Any line between the two must be imaginary: that adopted by the government of the Tsars did not correspond to our maps. In reality, the two continents are one, divided only by an idea; and the idea has nothing to do with geography—only with civilisation: but that is exactly what makes the question a difficult one.

The first Russia, that of Kiev, was undoubtedly European, and Kiev, even today, feels more European to one than any other of the large towns of Russia. There was no question in those first days. The Russians, of course, are a branch of that Indo-European stock to which most of the other nations of Europe belong. Their parent family, the Slavs, even in the ninth century, extended not only, as now, to the Adriatic, but to the Neighbourhood of Hamburg; Berlin, Dresden, Leipzig

[1] *Cheerful Giver* (Life of Harold Williams by his wife), p. 97.

are Slavonic place-names, and all the Slavonic languages are extraordinarily closely akin. Kiev was a Viking State, defending Christian Europe from the nomads of Asia. Her princes and princesses intermarried with half the thrones of Europe.

All this was broken off short by the Tartar conquest. Already the northern Russians had been blending with the non-European Finnish tribes, which they found in the forests, where they were seeking shelter from the nomad devastations. The conquest itself tore them away from the uniting influence of their great imperial water-road and plunged them into a parochial life of small and divided communities in their new forest home. Quite cut off from their mother Europe, they learned the mind and habits of a subject people, the necessity of guile and manœuvre, of adjournment of all challenge, of a policy of small moves and accumulation of small means, of waiting for life itself to alter all the existing conditions in their favour. No wonder that they became "Asiatised," for in all their own actions they had to follow on the purposes of their Asiatic masters. The very blood became mixed. Even the one great European asset that they retained with unfaltering faith, their Christianity, derived as it was from Constantinople, of itself separated them from nearly all the rest of Europe, and, in the darkness and ignorance into which they had been plunged, itself became another kind of parochialism, cutting them off from their natural fellows.

Yet it is no exaggeration to say that, by stemming the Tartar invasion, far the most formidable of the onslaughts of Asia, and slowly sucking all the life out of the Tartar domination, Russia saved Europe from one of the greatest dangers that ever threatened it and allowed it to grow up in its own way, without such a fundamental interruption as had befallen herself: and when the slow-moving mills of historical processes, far more surely than any military opposition, had so ground down the conquerors' power that it broke of itself, Russia, who had had the hard task of Europe's rearguard, was left with the heritage of leading the counter-stroke of Europe into Asia. In the end this came of itself—very rapidly, and almost imperceptibly. The Russian conquest of Kazan in 1552, the last great Tartar stronghold, opened what proved to be an almost unchallenged road to the Pacific.

Two hundred and forty years of subjection, that is a long break in the initiative and enterprise of a nation—and every one of the other Slavonic peoples, Poles, Czechs, Serbs and Bulgars, has suffered the same temporary elimination. And now the long task of catching up again—to re-attach herself to her natural affinity of race and religion—to Europe. This was an equally hard task, and an equally deep aspiration of the Russian people. The strongest element in its favour was Russian Christianity, which, if one looks right through Russian history, comes out as the most unifying and solidifying factor in it. Even today, there is not one essential difference between the accepted doctrine of the Orthodox Church and that of our own. But politically, even the Church itself had not been wholly able to escape the Asiatic infection. And when Russia could at last turn round and look westward, she found all sorts of new obstacles in her way, sometimes created by religion.

On three sides—north, centre and south—new barriers had arisen, each of which, as it was attacked, seemed only to become more formidable. It was a veritable labour of Hercules, constantly extending and expanding. In the north were the German settlements on the Baltic which, when they at last broke up politically, only opened the door to a terrific struggle with Sweden at her strongest that occupied nearly the whole long reign of Peter the Great. In the south was the last remaining Tartar stronghold in Crimea, and when that began to fall to pieces, it was replaced by the far more formidable barrier of Turkey. But the longest duel of all was in the centre, with Poland, and that bitter feud, with nationality acerbated by religion, has run all through Russian history and is not finished yet. It began with a fight for the mastery of the disputed provinces which have come again into the limelight since the beginning of World War II, but were then united in a vast intermediate State known as Lithuania, stretching at one time almost from the Baltic to the Black Sea. Here Poland was at first the winner. She united "Lithuania" to her under her own crown. She also did all she could to bring the Russian peasantry, who were the chief element in the population of that mixed State, under the authority of the Pope. On this side Russia was at first and for a long time engaged solely in a policy of what we now call "self-determination," very clearly understood as such—to use the language of the time, the reassembling of all Russian population under a Russian sovereign. The life and death struggle came to a long pause with the partition of Poland at the end of the eighteenth century. Poland disappeared from the map. Russia at that time did not annex purely Polish territory, but in this peculiarly shameful deal, she connived at its partition between Austria and Prussia. The Napoleonic Wars engaged Russia much further, making her mistress of Warsaw itself. That was nothing but a source of constant trouble to her, and in the last wars she at first lost not only her hold on the heart of Poland but most of the long-disputed provinces as well.

But it was not only territorially that Russia, throughout this long period, was persistently straining westwards. Against Poland she was at least fighting under the flag of nationality, against Turkey under that of Christendom, but also with a growing interest in the smaller Slavonic nationalities of the Balkans, which ultimately heightened into a national crusade and is commonly described, rather vaguely, by the name of Panslavism. It need hardly be said that Russia's treatment of Poland has proved the greatest discouragement to minor Slav peoples to trust themselves to her. But that was one of the cardinal follies of Tsardom, which was vigorously opposed by most of the Russian thinking public as soon as it found means of expressing itself. In the north, on the Baltic coast, Russia's plea was neither national or religious. It was firstly economic. But it also had a far-reaching political purpose. She was trying to force her way over small peoples, always so far in subjection to others, in order to get an outlet of her own to Europe. This was the main objective of the three most enlightened statesmen of Russian history—John the Terrible, Ordyn-Nashchokin, Minister of Tsar Alexis, and Alexis's son, Peter the Great. There is nothing surprising in the fact that this struggle was completed first of the three, and that Peter, who spent most of his reign on it, was also the outstanding workman in the Europeanising of Russia.

But was Russia to imitate Europe at the cost of her own soul? She was so far behind Europe that she might almost think so. Thinking Russians were poignantly conscious of this backwardness. They were like the schoolmaster close to the Urals who said to me, 'So good of you to be interested in our Asia." It was at once a confession of inferiority and an ironical protest. In this remark we see at the same time the germs of the rival instincts of the Slavophile and the Westerniser, the two great currents of Russian political thought. We English people have never realised how much more Europe is to them than it is to us, and how many painful heart-searchings it has given them.

If there was ever anything like the Renaissance in Russia, it was in the time of Peter's father, Alexis. Then all was happy and confident. Alexis was the most gentle and lovable of Russian sovereigns, and he found no difficulty in blending the new with the old. Sovereign, nobles and people would go forward hand in hand. They need not fear to move, and they need not hurry. They would be in no danger of ceasing to be themselves, and what they chose to absorb from the West they would digest at their own pace. But in the wilds outside the small court circle, the blackness was so abysmal that it would take a revolution to penetrate it, and the revolution came from the throne itself with Peter.

In Russia it was always a question between the slow way and the rapid, the peaceful progress and the storm of change. Klyuchevsky has said of another Russian statesman that he went so fast that he raised a wind against him, and Peter himself was like an elemental convulsion. The easy synthesis of Alexis was smashed to pieces. Everything was to go by order: a wholesale imitation of the West, entirely utilitarian and to the profit of the throne and the State.

There could be no better illustration than his foundation of St. Petersburg. It was not even in Russia but Estonia. It was a marsh—constantly flooded—on which no one was meant to live. It can hardly even be drained properly. It was a few miles from the Finnish frontier—an absurd position for the capital of so vast an empire. The government was thus isolated from the people, and every question had to come to this far corner to receive an official answer. This region could not grow its own food, let alone supply the capital; and the food supply of St. Petersburg had to be a first-class achievement of transport, in a country of which transport was one of the weakest features. No one else had ever dreamed of putting the capital here. Yet, as human labour was the only source, masses of it were worn out in laying solid foundations in the marsh, watch-towers were set up to anticipate the flooding of the great river, and the building of stone or brick houses was stopped all over the empire until that of the new city had got well under way.

All sorts of moral values perished in this process of hurricane change. And the enthroned innovator himself had, so to speak, to feel his way gradually upward from the thing that he wanted to the way in which it could be produced for him. Europe had taken generations to create all these things, and there was no short-circuiting. First the object (say the weapon, for with Peter war came first), then the man who knew how to use it, the trainer for the man, and, last, the civilisation which could have inspired and produced the training. The natural order was completely reversed. And Peter himself, who was essentially an opportunist, was throughout learning his own way upward. And with civilisation throughout went conquest: conquest westward, for which Russia was culturally not qualified. Under Peter's one true successor, Catherine, this contrast became even more appalling. Poland partitioned, the Black Sea won, the door to Europe opened wide—and meanwhile the slough of serfdom more threatening than ever in the rear.

And at that moment blows through the open door the great storm of the French Revolution, and the wars that follow draw Russia into Europe as never before. She partakes in full of its common life. Indeed Russia—though in a curiously negative way, by the strength of resistance in her backward people—proved to be the main factor in the fall of Napoleon. To Europe it looked as if the old had triumphed after all, in the person of Russia. There is something like a paralysis of the intellect that overtakes even such a realist historian as the Frenchman, Theirs, in the contemplation of this awful vengeance of the unknown.

Not so with Russia, where the new ideas already began their counterstroke with the wide-spread conspiracy of the Decembrists. We in England, satisfied with our own Revolution, had looked patronisingly at the first beginnings of revolution in France, and when they went beyond our measure and our interest, we turned aside with instinctive alarm and aversion. For Russia everything was yet to come; and Russians charted the whole story with all its diverse currents with an eagerness and an accuracy such as would never have occurred to us.

In the great slump that followed in Europe, largely under the influence of the Russian imperial power—with the old princes, more obstinately unintelligent than ever, restored everywhere, as if there had been nothing more than a bad dream—Europe was thinking hard, and Russia perhaps the hardest of all. No one with intellect could think that this was to be the end. The reaction was headed by the Russian sovereign and the first Minister of Austria; and as Europe slowly recovered, there came from time to time, again from Paris, minute bells that marked the revival of the challenge. The reign of Nicholas I (1825-55) was nothing else than one long rearguard action against the new ideas, and every assertion of them in Europe was followed by all-round and indiscriminate repression in Russia. As a liberal Russian censor wrote, "When they play tricks in Europe, the Russian gets a smack."

In this atmosphere, more poignant than ever, rose again the old controversy of East and West, this time, of Slavophil and Westerniser. Could Russia produce a soul of her own? It didn't look much like it. Then must she succumb wholesale to imitation of the West? What a complete confession of failure! It began with the publishing of a private letter without the knowledge of the writer. Chaadayev, who wrote it, was isolated from both camps and had leanings toward Catholicism. Russia, he said, as a distinctive moral force, had no past, present, or future; she had no contribution to make to the world. Nicholas I officially declared him to be mad. Both Slavophils and Westernisers were, directly or indirectly, alike pupils of the great German thinkers. The Slavophil Kireyevsky, a most fascinating thinker, found a basis for a cviilisation of Russia's own in her earliest teachers, the old Greek ascetics. Intellect, logic are not everything. In the whole man, heart and mind, intuition and reason should be working in complete harmony. In the West, modern humanism had separated them, but not in Russia. There the corporate consciousness was still entire, as witnessed by Orthodoxy and the village community. By the way, Slavophilism is in no way to be identified with Panslavism: the first is a sincere product of Russian thought; the second is a weapon in the armoury of Russian foreign policy. Belinsky and his Westernising friends would take wholesale from the West, but were anything but clear as to what they wanted to take. Most of them were attuned for secularism and atheism, but, like the Bolsheviks who were to follow them, they turned these into a religion. At bottom, every intelligent Russian is both a Slavophil and a Westerniser, just as, after all, Russia continues to lie between East and West.

The Crimean War was provoked by Panslavism, the imperial demand for an extension of Russian influence. In the end it was a victory on Russian soil of the West, almost at its most inefficient, over Russia, which was worse. It was a war of the fighting man, and on the Russian side, if we leave out the engineer general Todleben, all the distinction that there was went to the Russian peasant soldier. Western lessons were learned, even on the throne, and it was followed by the Emancipation and the other great reforms. But their significance was almost entirely missed abroad, especially in England, who ought to have been the first to give them recognition. Our eyes were blurred by the bogey of Russophobia, an exaggerated fear for our hold on India, just as they are now obscured by an exaggerated fear of Bolshevism. In Russia itself the public mind was confused by the vaguest political theories, which monopolised all our sympathies.

Meanwhile Russia, as usual when humiliated in the West, recoiled into the far easier East, where she absorbed enormous new territories which brought her appreciably nearer to India.

That was quite enough to frighten us, though the methods of advance were very similar to those of our own empire-builders. When the misgoverned Balkans again took fire, we were not able to distinguish between the grasping imperialism of Nicholas I and the national and religious crusade that dragged his unwilling son into war with Turkey; which had to be explained to us too late by Turgenev. This time Russia won, but only to face another galling humiliation from the West in the settlement of Berlin. Alexander II was almost as much blamed by the Slavophils for accepting this as he was by the "Nihilists" for not further revolutionising the structure of the State. There was as yet no clearly formed Liberal public opinion. Of the last five Tsars, it has been the two who made concessions that did not perish by the hands of assassins.

As usual, and with doubly good reason, Russia, that is the Russian Government, retired into itself and sulked—and again set itself to find out what could be made of the easier road eastwards. At home, it was at first a case of just sitting tight. For Alexander III, a strong man with a narrow mind, his course of home policy was permanently set by the murder of his reforming father. Only for the peasants he made an exception; every manifestation of initiative in the educated public was kept under the harrow. Now that the bright hope of liberating the lesser Slav peoples and of perhaps replacing the Cross on Saint Sophia was gone, there seemed less reason than ever for treating the "home aliens" of the Empire with anything like common decency. This was the worst time for the Poles and Germans—later for the Finns, and always for the Jews.

Imperialism instead of constitutions, Asia instead of Europe, those were the watchwords given from the throne to the Russian people. Yet all the time Russia went forward rapidly of herself. However persistently the Government might shut its eyes, the vast economic forces released by the Emancipation were always bringing Russia economically and therefore politically closer into the common fold of Europe. The eastern advance, which went so well with reaction, was at first prosecuted with reservations and restraint, for Alexander was clear that he did not want war. But when his weak-willed son Nicholas II replaced him, all restraint and caution were dropped, and common adventurers took charge of eastern policy. It was not possible to get away from civilisation by plunging one's head into the depths of Asia. In the perpetual search for sea outlets, the head peeped out on the far side, only to receive a crushing blow from that Asiatic government and people which had been most willing to learn all that Europe could teach them.

That was the lesson of the Russo-Japanese War, and it set rolling a great wave of new vigour in the Russian people which, after shaking the very foundations of the throne, at least gave Russia a national representative assembly.

In this bankruptcy of the eastern policy, Russia, of course, turned again towards Europe. In this new period, policy, economics, thought, national aspirations, all combined to westernise Russia, and this time the westernising went deeper than ever before. It ended in her playing an outstanding part in the earlier years of a first-class European struggle. But as so often with her contacts with the West, this one too brought home convulsions on the same world-scale.

In all that follows, Russia does not and cannot escape this constant antithesis of East and West. It speaks a new language, but it is there just the same. Within the new framework, the early Bolsheviks are the new Westernisers—who want to engage Russia in the promotion of revolution all over Europe and in America. Lenin, almost as if without concern, makes enormous sacrifices of territory. Stalin is the national leader of the Soviet home-land, who recovers the lost territory, plants his feet between Europe and Asia—that is, in the centre of Russia—and faces both ways, in home organisation and home defence, against the double menace of Germany and Japan.

IV

WAR AND REVOLUTION
(1914-17)

IT HAS OFTEN BEEN WHAT THE RUSSIANS CALL "A JOLT FROM outside" that has brought about some important move forward in the internal affairs of Russia, and the War of 1914 was no exception. The Napoleonic Wars, as has been mentioned, led up to the first political movement in Russia—that of the Decembrists in 1825. The Crimean War of 1845-6 led directly to the emancipation of the serfs. The Russo-Turkish War of 1877-8 led to the political assassination of Alexander II. The Russo-Japanese War led to the so-called "revolution" of 1904-7 and the institution of a representative and legislative assembly. The war of 1914 was to lead direct to the Revolution of 1917.

Premier Stolypin had said that without a foreign war the revolutionaries could do nothing, and one cannot imagine the regular army of 1914 firing on the police in 1917; but by 1917 the regular army was gone. Its losses for the first ten months of the war were reckoned as 3,800,000, or, to take the reckoning of the Quartermaster-General, Danilov, 300,000 a month; and the officers, who went into action standing, while commanding their men to crawl, were falling at twice the rate of the men. By the end of 1914 the most successful of Russian generals, Brusilov, has written that the regular army was gone already and had been replaced by a "militia of ignoramuses." Hindenburg guesses that the total Russian losses may have been between five and eight millions and adds: "All we know is that sometimes in our battles with the Russians we had to remove the mounds of enemy corpses from before our trenches in order to get a clear field of fire against fresh assaulting waves."[1]

The first mood of the Russian people in 1914 was one of enthusiastic co-operation in the carrying on of the war, and this lasted for a long time. There was an intense devotion to the national army, and especially to the needs of the rank and file. As in the invasion of Napoleon, as in the Crimean War, of which Tolstoy has left so graphic a picture in his sketches of Sevastopol, it was not the generals but the infantry that were outstanding. This is brought out over and over again in the records of the German generals, Ludendorff and Hoffmann: they constantly bear witness to the gallantry of the rearguard actions of 1915 and the complete indifference to losses. General Knox, our senior military attache, breaks out: "I wonder when people will realise that the real hero of the war is the plain infantry private or second lieutenant."

The only way in which the great-hearted Russian public could help its national army was by filling the crying gaps in the Government's own provision for it. This at first was concentrated in the work of the Civil Red Cross. This time its help was welcomed by the Government, and no wonder! The ordinary provision of surgical service for a regiment of four battalions (4,000 men) was five surgeons; and, living at the front for most of the war, I hardly ever found more than three. I saw a regiment lose three-quarters of its men in a few hours. I was present at another action where within the same time every battalion in the front line was reduced from one thousand to a figure between ninety and one hundred. I saw an English surgeon, with one unqualified Russian assistant, deal with three or four hundred cases at a first aid

[1] Hindenburg, *Out of My Life*, p. 273.

point under fire in an action which lasted four days; he had hardly any anæsthetics and no litters; the men lay in the late autumn mud—only a few of them had the shelter of a tent. It was not surprising that most of our wounded had gangrene before they reached the base hospital, and that we were reckoned to patch up for further service in the front line 40 per cent less than the Germans. There were points on the front where anyone with a stomach or leg wound was a lost man, as transport was impossible and the nearest hospital was miles away.

It was with all these needs that the Civil Red Cross coped splendidly. Within little over a month it had organised over a million beds. It brought first aid points up to the regiments and in several cases even into the actual front line. It invented means of transport suitable to the district concerned, when the government equipment had had to be discarded as unusable. The whole of the first year of war was absorbed in this work, and there was no serious criticism till the great retreat of 1915. Yet the Home Minister Nicholas Maklakov, a die-hard reactionary, was always asking the Tsar to dissolve the Civil Red Cross. He looked at it only as a possible organ of revolution. The Tsar sent him to the Commander-in-Chief, the vigorous Grand Duke Nicholas, for his opinion. The Grand Duke, when he had listened to Maklakov's memorandum, apparently said only three words of comment they were the three foulest words in the Russian language, and the Minister was greatly embarrassed as to how to report this "opinion" to the Emperor. The Government was always seeing revolution everywhere, and in the end it succeeded in turning its bogey into a fact. When the Revolution at last came, it was the Head of the Civil Red Cross, Prince George Lvov, who became its first Prime Minister.

The magnificent war effort of Russia was for the most part included in the first fourteen months of fighting, but for one other signal achievement which was to come later. The German generals understood very well the meaning of this war on two fronts, when with admirable dispatch their troops had to be transported from west to east or back. The turning point in the German march on Paris was the detachment of two invaluable corps to stem the chivalrous Russian double advance on East Prussia. They were badly missed on the Marne, and all the same they were too late for Tannenberg. There the Russians had suffered a crushing defeat. Numbers were only an embarrassment and even a waste when sent against an altogether superior artillery. The Russian Commander, Samsonov, when turned on both flanks, himself entered the doomed circle to break the enemy centre by an infantry attack; but he found at once that the huge losses made this impossible. The whole Russian centre, with two corps commanders, had to surrender; and such was the loss of guns that every battery in the Russian army was later reduced from eight guns to six. Yet every military historian regards Tannenberg as having saved Paris (Aug. 26-30, 1915). How different in 1939, when the Poles alone formed our eastern front, and there was no corresponding effort on the western.

The Grand Duke announced the catastrophe of Tannenberg in a bulletin beginning: "God has visited us with a heavy misfortune," and at once sent orders to his southern army which was retreating in front of the massed forces of Austria, to stand where it stood. The Austrians, with something like a million men, were on the point of breaking the Russian centre; but here it was the Russians who outflanked and, closing in on both sides, they drove the enemy in rout not only out of Russian Poland but into and nearly out of Austrian Galicia. Then followed bitter and confused fighting against the Germans in front of Warsaw. Twice the Russians made their plan first, but the Germans were first in carrying theirs out. At one moment, near Lodz, when the Germans had broken through, the Russians in their turn enveloped the intruders, who only got back by desperate fighting. In the winter battle farther north, in February, Hindenburg tried to envelop the Tenth Russian Army, but only succeeded in destroying the greater part of one corps: the rest fought their way out. When a lull at last set in, Russia still occupied more enemy territory than her two adversaries. Yet in the cruel arithmetic of that great struggle, every deficiency of equipment was paid for heavily in human lives. It was at the price of these huge losses that Russia gave us time to organise our own great national army.

As early as November, 1914, the Russian commanders were warned that munitions were running out altogether and that they must expect little more till May. All the same they continued to attack in the Carpathian Mountains with the bayonet, and fought their way clean through this wide range, taking each height one by one. On May 2nd, 1915, Mackensen, sent by the Germans to command there, fell upon the then denuded line and by metal alone wiped it out of existence. Ordinarily, the Austrian infantry did not attack till the Russians were destroyed or gone. By these methods, which became a routine, the whole of the wide bulging front line was driven in at point after point. The German object was to encircle the whole army and destroy it by metal: for this purpose they pushed forward two great pincers on the flanks—in the Carpathians and along the Baltic. The Russians suffered crushing losses—divisions reduced to a few hundred men; they could make no real artillery reply; they retreated slowly, with furious counter attacks with the bayonet at night. Galicia was lost, Lithuania, and Russian Poland, with Warsaw; but the bulging centre was never encircled; as the pincers advanced, it retreated and always got away. The main point was gained; the army was always kept in being, and by the autumn it stood firm on a much better and straighter line running through the famous Pinsk marshes, one of the natural defences of Russia. Ludendorff ends his striking record with a confession of disillusionment and tragical disappointment. The longed-for knock-out blow on one front again escaped him.[1]

For a time it almost seemed as if this gallantry and suffering might bring the attainment of the nation's dearest desire—namely, that at this grievous hour its affairs should be put in the hands of men whom it could trust. The Tsar felt acutely the heavy lot of his army, to which he was passionately attached. After a talk with the President of the Duma, Rodyanko, a fearless and honest old country Tory, he committed its equipment to a commission fully representative of both government and public. He dismissed the reactionary Ministers and summoned the Duma "in order to hear the voice of Russia." All this was anathema to his wife, and to Rasputin who could have no place in a frankly constitutional regime. The aged reactionary Premier Goremykin still remained; it was his creed that Ministers were there to advise the sovereign, but in any case obediently to carry out all his decisions, and Nicholas's final decisions were over and over again those of his wife. Goremykin found himself more and more at loggerheads with nearly all his colleagues in the reformed cabinet.

Things were still going well in the rear when suddenly the Emperor announced his decision to displace the Grand Duke, who was universally trusted, and assume the supreme command. This was really meant as his personal contribution to the army: he was a fatalist and he wanted to share its fate. But this sentimental sacrifice was foolish. The Emperor was no strategist, and he would be personally responsible for all future reverses. On the other hand, he could not govern the

[1] Ludendorff, *My War Memories*, p. 170.

country from headquarters; the tasks of the Ministers would become infinitely complicated, and they foresaw that in practice the Empress would govern in the rear, as in fact she did, though no regular arrangement was ever made. One after the other they tried their hardest to dissuade him, and then all together at a Cabinet sitting, at which he presided; but with the strength of a weak man intent on a personal sacrifice, he stuck to his point. Nearly the whole Cabinet addressed to him a letter making a last appeal. His answer was to prorogue the Duma, to summon the Cabinet to headquarters and to give them a severe scolding. From that time onwards the real government was in the hands of the Empress, and those who had signed the letter were one by one dismissed.

This was the real turning point in the fate of the monarchy. This outcome of a movement which had become nation-wide —Ministers, Duma, army and people—was received with indignation. It is from this point that the police authorities of the time date the rapid growth of defeatism. Growing privations, soaring prices, even violent excesses of military rule, had so far been met with only passive discontent; but if this was what the nation was expected to fight for, then from henceforth nation and dynasty rapidly parted company. The Emperor, except for a few gentle and tender protests, did what he was told by the Empress, and the Empress wholeheartedly did all that she was told by Rasputin. It can definitely be said at this time, when every other country was putting forward its ablest men and when Russia was one of the least fitted to bear the immense strain, she was ruled by Rasputin. "He," says the Chief of Police, Beletsky, one of those who made clumsy-clever attempts to "run" Rasputin, "was the axle on which revolved the destinies of Russia."[1] Rasputin, quite contrary to the current opinion, though absurdly ignorant, was a very shrewd and clever politician, and he also had ideals which if strange were often far-sighted, in some cases anticipating the future; he was all for the peasantry and even stood up for the Jews. But all the time he was constantly making outrageous public scandals by his unrestrained lust and licence, in which the Empress—alone in Russia—simply refused to believe. If she had not added so many of her own improvisations, she might not have made such a pitiful exhibition of her complete political ineptitude.

It is not necessary to follow this high tragedy of tender devotion and political absurdity, in which all her best qualities were turned against her, through the successive phases

[1] Beletsky in *Padenie Monarchii,* IV, p. 521.

of her rule, except to show its absolute futility. In her first period she entrusted everything to two rogues who tried to please her by securing the life of Rasputin against the many attempts on his life, and meanwhile to soothe the Duma with the idea that they were out to ruin him. Rasputin completely outplayed them; and in the end one of them, the Home Minister, himself tried to plan his assassination. After that came a scoundrel of the lowest order, a sneak, pilferer and bully, named Stürmer, a mere puppet of Rasputin and immensely afraid of him, who at different times combined the premiership with the Home Office and the Foreign Office. Under him the whole administrative machine went out of action. Last came the tragicomic Protopopov, a sick man and former "patient" of Rasputin, who scribbled fantastic graphs showing his incoherent suggestions for a new regime to replace the Duma, of which he had at one time been one of the Vice-Presidents.

The rear was foul, but the front again recovered and, while the State was going to pieces behind it, the army shone forth in one more glorious exploit. General Brusilov, too original to condemn himself to a hopeless imitation of German efficiency and accuracy, devised surprise attacks by which he broke through the Austrian line at several places, and he won back miles and miles of lost territory and brought the war again to the Carpathians. He took hundreds of thousands of prisoners, but he had to break the enemy line not by metal but by storming attacks, which cost him immense sacrifices of human life.

In November, 1916, the Duma had at last to be summoned, and Stürmer, Protopopov and Rasputin were denounced in stinging speeches from all sides of a united House. The Emperor was induced by his mother and others to dismiss Stürmer, but the Empress saved her favourite, Protopopov. At this point Rasputin, who had survived all sorts of attempts on his life, was at last successfully assassinated by members of the imperial family and the strongest conservative in the Duma, Purishkévich, who believed they were thus saving the throne. Deprived of her political mainstay and the guardian of her son's life, the Empress no longer hoped, and Nicholas sank into complete apathy. Her will still prevailed; and though he was warned by pretty well everyone who had any opportunity to warn him, he remained obstinately inert and waited for the storm to burst.

Protopopov's idea of forestalling it, in the details of which he was guided by astrology, was to arrest just those workers who were doing most to munition the army, and to train the police to machine-gun the people. Nicholas at last went back to Headquarters, and the same day the storm began. Great crowds paraded the streets, for two days only asking for food. There was food enough in the capital, but its distribution was hopelessly muddled, and on Rodzyanko's suggestion the town council was allowed to take it over. The frightened rear-general in command of the troops telephoned Headquarters and was ordered to stop all disorders next day as "inadmissable in time of war." By this order Nicholas signed his own deposition. After a vain warning, General Habálov fired on the crowds, and in a single day the rotten edifice of the monarchy toppled over. The Volynsky Regiment of the Guard after taking a very half-hearted part in the shooting, went back to barracks, killed one of its officers and next morning came out on the side of the people. By midday most of the garrison—something like 170,000, mostly recruits still in training—had joined it. Only one officer, Kutépov, later assassinated in Paris, did anything to oppose it. The town was flooded with mutinous soldiers in lorries, and went over *en masse* to the Revolution.

Kerensky, the young labour leader, who alone showed any initiative at the Duma, had directed the mutineers to come to it and claim its control. The Cabinet, which itself asked the Tsar to dismiss it, willingly enough dispersed in panic. Rodzyanko was at last persuaded to appoint a Duma committee to take control, and this was followed by a Provisional Government of nearly all parties. The revolution spread at once to the Tsar's home at Tsarkoe Selo, and the Palace Guard came likewise to the Duma.

Nicholas sent a train-load of picked soldiers, who got stranded on the way. He set himself for the capital, but was unable to get through. Turning aside to Pskov, he sought the protection of General Ruzsky, a Liberal in command of the Northern Front. Both Ruzsky and Rodzyanko telephoned the various army commanders, and all except one insisted on the Emperor's abdication. This was demanded also by the Duma, which sent two of its leading members to Pskov to obtain it. Nicholas had already agreed before they arrived, but he now quite illegally, out of family affection, substituted his brother for his invalid son in the succession. The brother, the Grand Duke Michael, next day, after taking advice, made his acceptance conditional on the request of a Constituent Assembly, to be elected by universal franchise. That was actually the end of the Romanov dynasty (March 16th, 1917).

No one made the Russian Revolution, unless it was the autocracy itself; certainly no one on the other side, if one excepts the last-minute change round of the Volynsky regiment. Till then there was no organised opposition to the police and troops, and, indeed, that very evening, at a meeting of revolutionary leaders in Kerensky's quarters, it was precisely the Bolsheviks present who said that the moment had not yet come and that success was not to be hoped for. The moment came in the Volynsky barracks a few hours later. Lenin and all the principal Bolshevik leaders were not in Russia; Lenin and his nearest colleagues were in Switzerland. Their influence on Russia at this time was only now beginning to be of serious significance, and their pledged supporters probably did not number more than fifteen thousand. Neither did the Duma do anything to make the Revolution; when it came, nearly everyone there except Kerensky was scared of it. It was elemental, and for that reason all the more conclusive. It was a direct result of the utter bankruptcy of the autocracy, and for that reason it was irrevocable.

In the light of what has followed, the next eight months must be regarded as a fag-end of the preceding period. After the bankruptcy of "His Majesty's Government," came the bankruptcy of "His Majesty's Opposition"—to use the term which Milyukov had given for his Party in a speech at the Mansion House in London in 1909—and precisely for the reason that it had been His Majesty's Opposition. As leader of the Progressive Bloc, which was the great majority of the Duma in its last days, Milyukov had tried his hardest to avert a revolution by persuading the sovereign to accept the position of a constitutional sovereign without it, and he had failed.

The change was at the outset wholly destructive, but it was too great to be limited, and now that passions were kindled it made the whole of the past obsolete in a day. Though no one seemed to notice it, the substance of what happened every day was that more and more of the relics of the past were swept away. The police were abolished because they had fired on the people; the army broke up because its allegiance, and very soon its discipline, were gone. The local authorities were all swept away in the rush. What was there left to govern with? Guchkov, who had himself planned an abortive plot against the sovereign, had said that the power would go after the revolution to those who made it. The power, then, was now with the mob, and who could curb the mob? Not a Provisional Government, to call it by the modest name which it took. Every day it became more out of date, and from the first day of its agitated existence there was a Soviet representing the revolted armed force of the capital sitting in the Duma's own debating hall.

We shall have far more sympathy with the bankruptcy of His Majesty's belated Opposition than with that of His Majesty's Government, and indeed we showed it at the time. And well we might, for it proved loyal to the past commitments of Russia to us. But more than that, it was trying to do in Russia what had been done in long centuries of political struggle in England, and that in the last throes of an unsuccessful war. The Provisional Government faced three enormous tasks. First, it had to restore the whole administrative apparatus. Second, in doing this it had to satisfy the demands of the fundamental change which had taken place. Third, it set itself to keep Russia in the war and this of itself made all the rest utterly impossible. It was a cruel thing that Russia's first attempt at constitutional rule should have had to be made at such a moment. Yet it must be remembered that after ages of longing for liberty, the Revolution was to Russians a far bigger thing than the war itself; and immediately after the fall of Tsardom no government could have stood which did not satisfy that longing. So the war-weary army, which now felt its weakness far more than before, was to be kept at the front by persuasion alone. And yet there seemed no choice. One must take note that the World War had still a year and a half to run, and if Imperial Germany won it the Russian Revolution was as good as finished.

The Provisional Government wore away of itself. It soon —by May— shed the principal challengers of Tsardom, Guchkov and Milyukov. Kerensky, who was throughout its central figure, was always trying to create a national nucleus between the two extremes of Bolshevism and reaction; but the Commander-in-Chief, General Kornilov, marched on the capital to suppress the Soviet, the troops fraternised, and the game was up. As Brusilov saw earlier than others, the future was to fall to Bolshevism. Now that the Tsar's authority was gone, the officer, who had received his authority from him, was for the soldier "the squire in uniform" who was still insisting on going on fighting.[1] The better the officer, the worse it was for him; and the troops, whenever relieved from the front line, went off *en masse* to help their kindred at home to sieze this wonderful chance of at last becoming masters of all the land. That was the great elemental event of the rest of 1917. There were no police and there was no possibility of resistance. Sometimes, for good ex-masters, remarkable consideration was

[1] Brusilov, *Reminiscences:* Russian edition, pp. 209-10.

shown, but all that was required was to take and squat. This
vast process went on of itself through one of the most beautiful
autumns ever remembered in Russia. The land was just taken;
the livestock, too. The peasants came with their carts, and, if
they did not set fire to the manor, rifled its contents in a rough
and ready division, in which the strongest fared best. By the
end of the year the change was practically complete. What
was still wanted was a government which would legalise it.
Lenin, who reached Russia a month after the fall of Tsardom,
had been preaching this ever since. He had only to wait his
time, and in November the Provisional Government, with little
more resistance, faded out in the same inconspicuous way as
its predecessor.

V

LENIN AND THE BOLSHEVIKS

(1903-18)

I HAVE TOLD THE STORY IN THE PERSPECTIVE OF THE TIME
when it happened, and it was then the true perspective. But to
understand what followed the fall of Tsardom, we must go
back and go deeper.

I have written about a certain black streak which, as Dostoyevsky has written, "is peculiar to the Russian people at
moments when the head is in a whirl." When I first read
Dostoyevsky, I thought he must be quite unbalanced; later,
I understood that he was giving a wonderfully true picture of
others who were unbalanced.

The black streak came from generations of living underground. In England most people have their heads above water;
in Russia most people had not. That was why a movement
for liberty could so easily take the character of a slaves'
revolt. The savagery was the repayment of the age-long debt.
It does not in the slightest mean that the Russians are an
unkindly people; on the contrary, it is kindness that is their
most distinguishing feature; but the mind of the Russian
is typically anarchical—that is what makes him unintelligible
to the steady and docile German. He has not what Milyukov
has so brilliantly called "the cement of hypocrisy"—we sometimes call it "the team spirit" or "playing the game," a game
with which, perhaps, you don't agree. Add the great variety
of moods, natural to a primitive and unschooled people, and
you get what may be called the "all-outer."

In writing all this, my mind has been circling round the great looseness of the use of the word "Bolshevik." It is now identified in Russia with "Communist," and is marked with a small "b" in brackets after the official title of the Party —thus: "The Party of Communists (b)"; but it has meanwhile gone through many phases. Its first meaning was purely formal. In 1903, in Brussels, and later in London, was held a meeting of the exiled leaders of Russian Marxism, and there the Bolshevik was a member of the majority (*bolshinstvo*), whose view prevailed at that meeting. But "bolshe," in Russian means "more," so that Bolshevik could naturally be taken to mean the "all-outer," especially as his was the view that prevailed at that meeting. He was a "whole-hogger"—"maximalist"— and at the outset of the Revolution he easily foregathered with other "maximalists" who were not Marxists at all but were the hotheads of a rival and hostile Party, the so-called S.R.'s, or Social Revolutionaries. In fact, the first Cabinet after the Communist Revolution was a coalition of these two groups.

Then "Bolshevism" came to have an even more extended meaning. There were read into it all the savageries which can be associated with a successful revolution, especially if it has been too long delayed, whether committed by the Party, as they often and systematically were, or without it, or even against its wishes, but left unpunished. "Bolshevism" came to be used as discriminating something distinctively Russian from Marxism as it might be preached and practiced in other countries. "Bolshevik" even came to be used in families of the opposite camp, not unkindly, for a restless or wilful child: "He's our little Bolshevik." Now it is used in Russia for the man who does what Stalin directs with all his soul and strength. A Bolshevik greeting is a hearty greeting, a Bolshevik cheer is a hearty cheer. A Bolshevik Socialist is a man who carries Socialism to all its logical consequences, one who is not afraid how many eggs he smashes to make the desired omelette. One can see how this type would appeal under serfdom, under an unintelligent autocracy, in a time of world war, or in time of revolution.

Nearly every Russian has a big dose of socialism: the big distances, the remote work in the forest taught it. The deep Russian humanity taught it. Autocratic Russia was in many ways a socialist regime; whatever else, it was not individualist. The Tsar was father of his people, and all alike looked to the State for any initiative: in fact "nachalnik," or "initiator," was the ordinary word for any official chief. A Minister of the Tsar could sign away large sums of public money for some purely theoretical purpose with as much complacency as any Socialist bureaucracy.

There were two main Socialist Parties. They began with the "movement to the people" in the 'seventies, when young men and girls went down to the peasants to live their life and to stir them up to revolution. Some of these were propagandists, settling among the peasantry and serving them as doctors, nurses, teachers, booksellers, or maybe blacksmiths; some were conspirators plotting against the lives of peculiarly odious officials. Whenever the Government was crudely tyrannical, the propagandist tended to become a conspirator. These "men of the people" (*narodniki*) split into two groups. One, calling itself "The Will of the People," was responsible for the assassination of Alexander II, which was the work of not more than a hundred persons.[1] The other, "The Black Partition," did not believe in political terrorism, which was, after all, a question of method; it was these who later became the first Marxists in Russia, and they were called the Social Democrats, or S.D.'s.

Later on, successors to "The Will of the People," which had been stamped out after the assassination of the sovereign, organised themselves into the non-Marxist Party of Social Revolutionaries, or S.R.'s. They worked on the old lines among the peasantry, often utilising the posts created by the *zemstva,* or local county council for sober, practical work, but they included a terrorist organisation for those who had an inclination in that direction which from time to time, especially in moments of internal crisis, struck down this or that hated official. The Marxists (S.D.'s), like the "Black Partition," were opposed to such methods as futile.

The S.R.'s worked among the mass of the peasantry; the S.D.'s concentrated on the relatively small but rapidly growing industrial population. By the nature of things the S.R.'s were much the more individualist; they took over much of the character of the peasantry among which, alone or in small groups, they carried on their work. They were sometimes religious, nearly always patriotic. They owed no outside allegiances; they were typically Russian. There was the typical Russian vagueness in their program; they were simply men of conviction and courage, like the ordinary first British Radicals.

The S.D.'s, on the other hand, were only the Russian branch of a European Party—the Marxists. They were far more interested in theory (practical work was for them more diffi-

---

[1] Told me by one of them.

cult and dangerous). Like Marxists elsewhere, they were sharply divided into groups, each of which claimed to have the true gospel. The principal division took place at the London conference which has just been mentioned. It was really not a question of objects—for all alike, the goal was the socialisation of all means of production—but rather of how this goal could be reached, of internal organisation, of method and tactics; but this question of method raised issues at least as sharp as the question of Marxism itself. Was the goal to be reached by persuasion and a democratic victory, or by compulsion and violence? The first required only propagandists, the second needed a closely-knit party discipline and implied totalitarianism of the State after the victory. This last was the lead given by Lenin, and those who followed him were the first Bolsheviks.

The story of the Bolsheviks from this point is bound up in the tremendous personality of Lenin, but in 1903 he seemed thousands of miles away from his ultimate destination. The S.R.'s were only organising themselves, so far as they ever did so, from 1896. The S.D.'s had only really founded their party in 1898 (no more than nine delegates attended the first Party "Congress"), and now it had split in two; the "out-and out" Bolsheviks and the more moderate and democratic followers of the original organiser of the Party, George Plekhanov, known as Mensheviks, or men of the minority. The leaders of the S.D.'s and S.R.'s alike had to live abroad. They were, of course, not manual workers but intellectuals, often with a high standard of scholarship. In spite of all sorts of ingenious artifices, which the conditions of their work made necessary, they were almost cut off from their public; any open organisation inside Russia was unthinkable. They were, therefore, less parties than aspirations: the S.R.'s for the peasant, the S.D.'s for the factory worker. Of the principal leaders the most outstanding—for instance, Lenin and Plekhanov—were Russians, but a very considerable proportion were internationally-minded Jews, which was intelligible enough in an international party.

Lenin, whose actual name was Vladimir Ulyanov, came of the minor Russian provincial gentry. His elder brother, Alexander, took part in a conspiracy to assassinate Alexander III, and paid the penalty with his life. Lenin's head schoolmaster, curiously enough, was the father of his future rival, Kerensky, and his reports indicate an intensely serious boy, orderly in mind and aloof from his fellows. Lenin was deeply affected by his brother's death and early engaged in revolutionary activity, though on different lines—his brother was a disciple of "The Will of the People." For no particular offence, as it seems, Lenin's university career at Kazan was interrupted by relegation to his grandmother's estate and, like Belinsky before him, he had to get his degree in law as an external student. He was now much more active in revolutionary work, writing against those who seemed to him to limit their objects to academic middle-class discussions or economic grievances; and for agitation in the British-owned Thornton factory he was exiled for five years to a remote part of Siberia (1895-1900), where he was soon joined by his future wife and fellow-worker, generally known by her maiden name of Krupskaya. On their release they went to Zurich, Munich and London, and now he met the exiled leader Plekhanov for the first time and took part in the historical S.D. Congress (the second) of 1903.

From now onward he lived what may be called an international life studying in the libraries of Switzerland, London and Paris; he was a most assiduous reader in the British Museum. Lenin was a wonderfully clear-headed and astonishingly independent thinker. He had a mind of extraordinary intellectual power and, wandering about among the slums and libraries of Western Europe, while not at all indifferent to the life around him and keeping in surprisingly close touch with Russian realities, he was capable of charting unexplored problems of the future, to build up the new world of which he dreamed. He followed two main lines: on the one hand the widest agitation in factories to draw the working class more and more into the political arena, and on the other the organisation of a compact body of professional politicians to give the lead, and over this nucleus he established an imperative authority. Perhaps nothing gave better testimony to the clearness of his conviction than the ease and pliability with which he was able to face changing situations and alter his tactics without in any way altering his purpose.

He returned for a short time to Russia during the abortive revolution of 1905, when it may be said that his tactics faltered more than was usual with him; he advocated boycott of the two freely-elected Dumas, but participation in the much more restricted elections to the Third. On the triumph of reaction in 1907 he returned disillusioned to Switzerland and Western Europe.

In World War I he stood throughout *contra mundum* against the great wave of nationalism which in all countries seemed for the time to swamp socialism. He was before all things internationally minded, and in his march to the new world Russia was for him an objective factor. He desired before all things the defeat of Imperialist Russia, as opening the road to any further advance on his chosen lines. This position he took up at two conferences with like-minded extremists from other countries at Zimmerwald (in Switzerland) in 1915, and at Kienthal in 1916. He sent certain theses to his comrades in Russia which carried little influence there. Defeatism of a serious kind dated in Russia only from the failure of the constitutional movement in the summer of 1915, and even after that the general discontent remained inarticulate. But the Beletsky's, Stürmers, and other scoundrelly puppets of Rasputin were doing Lenin's work for him in breaking up the whole apparatus of the State, and the period of Protopopov, which dates from September, 1916, marks the real beginning of anything like successful propaganda in the factories and barracks of the rear. Even then, the very informing police reports of the period testify to the absence of any real leadership; and, as we have seen, there was no actual leadership in the Revolution itself, and the triumph was that of the mob, that is, of disorder, only partially directed by the eloquence of Lenin's fellow-townsman, Kerensky.

As we know, no sooner had Petrograd gone over to the Revolution than a Soviet was hastily and irregularly elected and next day installed itself in the Duma. It was on the model of 1905, and all the leading revolutionaries were in it, but there was one substantial difference. The soldiers had made the revolution, and they now formed the backbone of the Soviet. It was in session on the day when the Provisional Government was constituted in the same building. There was a constant rivalry between it and the Soviet. The Soviet would not share the responsibility of government, but it insisted on a right of veto. In the actual rush of the revolution an agreement was hastily concluded: there was to be a Constituent Assembly to settle the form of government, and the existing garrison was not to be moved from the capital. But the Soviet also put forward an Army Order abolishing the salute and claiming to put the troops under its own control. The Government refused to adopt it, but it was circulated by the Soviet and rapidly broke up all discipline on the front.

The Bolsheviks were at first quite in a minority in the Soviet. Lenin, by agreement with the German Government, which recognised his destructive value, was brought through Germany in a sealed van and reached Petrograd on April 16th, 1917, a month after the Tsar's abdication. Trotsky, a Menshevik who only now joined the Bolsheviks, arrived from

America a little later. Lenin's reception at the Soviet was at first rather mixed. Disregarding the advice of some of his own comrades, he fearlessly preached fraternisation at the front and the seizure of estates in the rear and, as we know, the peasants did what he suggested. On May 3rd-4th the Bolsheviks made an armed attempt to secure Petrograd, but failed, the Soviet itself ultimately coming out with its armed forces against them. They made another and more serious attempt on July 17th, when Kerensky was at the front stimulating the army to a last offensive. This too failed, but the Government made no use of its victory, arresting persons who had been active on both sides. In August, as we have seen, the new commander-in-chief Kornilov started an advance on Petrograd. This broke down in hopeless fiasco, the troops on both sides fraternised, and in the recriminations that followed, both Kornilov and Kerensky were hopelessly discredited.

The Bolsheviks knew their own minds better than anyone else. They set themselves to vigorous spade-work of organisation; they captured both the Soviet and the committees which had been set up in the army. Kerensky's various experiments came to nothing; and in November, when the Bolsheviks moved again, they met with very little resistance. It was almost as if they were walking into an empty place. They had already captured the soldiers' committees; they brought a warship, the *Aurora*, from Kronstadt to the capital, and it commanded the Admiralty and the Winter Palace. The last defenders of the falling Government were the cadets of the Officers' Training Schools and a battalion of women. The autocracy had always paralysed all local life in Russia, and the example of the capital was followed in Moscow, where there were a few days of fighting in the Kremlin, and easily enough everywhere else (November 7th-14th).

Lenin was now in a position to start his entire reconstruction of the Russian community. The conquerors appointed a government of "people's commissaries"; the word "commissaries" was taken over from the Provisional Government, which had used the term for its local officials while retaining the term "Ministers" for the higher; "people" (*narod*) had long come to be used for the masses and especially for the peasantry, while *obshchestvo* (public) was the word used for the educated classes. In principle, these commissaries were nominated by the national Soviet, but in practice they were appointed by the Communist Party, and for a long time remained almost unchanged. At the start, the Bolsheviks co-operated with the extreme left wing of the S.R.'s and accorded them a place in the Government.

One of the first things to be dealt with was the Constituent Assembly, which had at last been elected by universal franchise for man and woman to settle the new constitution of Russia. Only about one-fifth of its members were Bolshevik; the predominance and the presidency went to the S.R.'s, and it at once called in question the Bolshevik land policy. It was dispersed by force after a continuous sitting of a day and a half (January 18th, 1918).

Straight off, the Government confirmed the wholesale confiscation of squires' land by the peasants and authorised their village committees to divide up the estates. The peasants' settlement was of their own making; they had never supported state ownership and a general redistribution: their traditional view, which had a good foundation in history, was that the squires, originally put over them as officials, should be driven out and that each estate should revert to the neighbouring village community. This they had proceeded to carry out, sometimes setting fire to the manor to remove any inducement to the squire to return. This was the "Black Partition" of which they had always dreamed. Having taken the land, the peasants squatted on it, and this was sure to complicate any later government plan of universal distribution.

At the rate at which events had moved since the last Tsar fell, no one, not even the Bolsheviks themselves, felt any security in the permanence of the new Government. Their most notable precedent in the past was the Commune of Paris of 1871, which like themselves owed its chance to an unsuccessful war, and their gospel was the *Kapital* of Karl Marx. Being a wing of an international Party, their prime interest was in a world revolution, and their appeal was to the proletarian masses in all countries, all of which had suffered like themselves from the imperialist war. For these reasons propaganda was more important to them than legislation on Russia, and they boldly challenged all opposition by putting their program into action even without regard to the question whether the existing conditions allowed it to be workable. The administration of factories was handed over to general assemblies consisting of all concerned. House property was confiscated and living space disposed of by rough and ready allotment. All banks were abolished except the Co-operative Bank, which later went the way of the rest: the officials of the State Bank held up the change for a short time by their refusal to co-operate. All private trade was declared illegal. As no adequate working substitute, in the form of state stores, had as yet been set up to replace it, this spelt ruin and hunger all around. The privations produced by the war had become very much worse under the Provisional Government and now they became past all bearing, though somehow they had to be borne. The inflation of the currency had long since passed all rational limits, and now money was left more or less to extinguish its own value, to be replaced by barter.

There was still the question of the war to be settled somehow. By now the army had broken down completely. Kerensky's unwise offensive of the autumn, as soon as Hindenburg had been allowed by his Government to strike back, had ended in panic, flight and looting, and the Bolshevist triumph in November had finished off any discipline that was left. The Commander-in-Chief, Dukhonin, was notified at once by long phone from Petrograd that he was to treat for an armistice; in loyalty to Russia's engagements to her Allies, he refused to do this; he was dismissed at once, and when his successor, Ensign Krylenko, arrived at the front, Dukhonin was lynched by the war-worn and infuriated soldiers.

Negotiations were begun at Brest-Litovsk. The Germans had Russia at their mercy and left the Russians in no doubt of this. They were in a hurry to finish off the war on one front and to get desperately needed food supplies from the granary of Ukraine. Trotsky, who took over the negotiations, was waiting for the effect of the Communist Revolution on the other peoples and armies of Europe and spun them out in every way he could. He demanded self-determination for the conquered Russian territory, but in vain. In the end he broke off the discussions with the ingenious but futile formula: "no war and no peace." It was not long before the Germans, violating the armistice, went forward again to their objectives, especially in the German Baltics and in Ukraine. They treated separately with a delegation from an Ukrainian national assembly which had demanded independence. In this way they were able to impose the separation on Russia, and later they established their own puppet Government in Ukraine, whose rich resources they had so long coveted. They also sent help to the movement for independence in Finland, and advanced through the Baltic provinces: Poland of course was long since lost to Russia. The terms which they now (March 3, 1918) dictated to Russia meant the loss of nearly all European territory acquired by Russia since Peter the Great.

Even Lenin, with his enormous personal prestige in his Party, found it a hard job to get it to accept such conditions, and the mortification was far greater in the rest of the population. But, again, Lenin was thinking not of Russian territory but of world revolution, and of his chance of carrying through his transformation of what was left to him. He found a breathing space indispensable. After all, Germany had still to beat England and France and now America, and, in the end, ironically enough, it was we who upset the treaties of Brest-Litovsk. For us it was invaluable that these terms were ever put on record as types of a German peace settlement. Their conditions were immeasurably harder than those to be imposed on Germany at Versailles; they were completed by economic provisions which practically reduced the conquered countries, Russia, Ukraine and Rumania, to German colonies.

VI

MILITANT COMMUNISM AND CIVIL WAR
(1918-21)

THERE COULD HARDLY BE ANY COUNTRY IN WHICH ALL THIS would pass without opposition and civil war; in our own the opposition would certainly have been far more vigorous. Everyone was uprooted from his most intimate habits, and to this was added a great national humiliation; it is a wonder that the prestige of the Bolsheviks could outlive it.

To carry through their changes at all, the Bolsheviks used the starkest methods of all-round repression. The Tsar's police had been disbanded, but the most unlovely part of it, the political police, continued in their memories as an inescapable precedent: there had always been a strange common frontier between it and the revolutionaries, with adventurous intermixers from both sides, and it was easy enough to have the old methods repeated and improved on, sometimes by the same persons in the new employ. Following a war habit, the Bolshevist political police has been called by different portmanteau words consisting of first initials: at first it was Cheka (Extraordinary Commission), later it became GPU or Ogpu, (State Police Administration), and later still it went by the name of the Home Commissariat. In the contest between a fading old world and a thrusting new one, all old laws were disregarded: in fact, the study of law was discontinued in the universities. The only test prescribed or admitted for judges was revolutionary expediency. Bolshevist rule had grown out of the war, and opposition to it was punished with death.

The general scarcity of food, which resulted not from any lack of potential resources but from the breakdown of the whole system of production, seriously striken by the war and now swept away in ruin, was ingeniuosly utilised as a weapon against opposition. The government, possessing all that remained of the central apparatus of administration, had what there was at its disposal, and it allotted it according to categories. Manual workers had the first claim, next officials and workers of other kinds, and little enough was left for anyone else. The Party, being the real controlling force, practically stood outside all categories. With this went a system of hostages; the family of anyone who fought the new regime could be left without any food.

In a country such as Russia, where conspiracy had been endemic, there were sure to be plots in these conditions. The co-operation of the extremist S.R.'s, who claimed to have an equal voice in policy, lasted a very short time; the rival parties, S.R.'s and Mensheviks, who had never believed in such tight centralisation, complained bitterly that they were under a worse tyranny than ever before. The S.R.'s had a daring and clever conspirator, Boris Savinkov, who had been partly responsible for some assassinations of the Tsar's officials in the old days and had been much in the limelight in the Provisional Government. Uritsky, the head of the Cheka, was assassinated; and a young S.R., Dora Kaplan, succeeded in lodging a bullet in the spine of Lenin himself. The vengeance was terrible; the prisons were already simply crammed with representatives of the old way of life, including for instance as many of the Tsar's Ministers as had not been able to escape; a huge prison *battue* was ordered by Uritsky's successor, Dzerzhinsky, on the principle that many should pay for one, if that one was on the government side.

All this time Europe was still at war. Large numbers of Russian officers, in their shame at the surrender of Brest-Litovsk, offered their swords to the Allies—for instance, Admiral Kolchak—or organised centres for the continuation of the war. As to whether the Allies should have accepted the defection of Russia or welcomed such offers of help, the present-day reader can best judge by quite modern example —the seizure or destruction of the French Fleet and the support gladly given to General de Gaulle. The Bolsheviks, with definite German help, had come in by a *coup d'état*, and had dissolved the Constituent Assembly by force. Brest-Litovsk had knocked out the eastern wall of the blockade, and the Allies welcomed every effort to reconstitute an Eastern Front. It was thus that civil war and intervention went hand in hand, and it would be hard to judge them by post-war psychology.

The war had produced a very intimate co-operation between the Allies, and Archangel and Murmansk were already almost in our hands. We had also numerous friends among the officers of the old army.

Centres of resistance began to grow up at many points on the vast map of Russia, but always on the circumference, leaving the vast advantage of the interior lines to the other side. First there was a rising of officers, ably organised by Savinkov in numerous daring ventures into and out of Moscow. It was staged at Yaroslavl, the main town on the direct railway from Moscow to Archangel where it crosses the great water-way of the Volga. It lasted several days, and at one time it was touch and go; but it was suppressed by equal daring and energy on the part of Trotsky (July 6th-21st, 1918). If the Allies had made up their minds to do now what they did later, namely to occupy Archangel in force, it might well have succeeded. Slowly a great number of officers gathered in the south, where the Bolshevist control was weak, around two distinguished generals, both of them former Commanders-in-Chief, Alexeyev and Kornilov. This was called the Volunteer Army, and numerous officers served in the ranks. It made a difficult campaign in the Kuban district, where Kornilov was killed by a stray shell behind the lines, and Alexeyev died not long afterwards. They were succeeded by another general who had greatly distinguished himself in World War I and served as Chief of Staff of the Army, Denikin.

Another centre was formed on the lower Volga by members of the dispersed Constituent Assembly—mostly S.R.'s, with their leader, the ex-President V. Chernov. They were able to lean on something more substantial in their rear in the shape of Siberia. This was chiefly due to one of the most amazing episodes in the whole of this story. Many Czechs and Slovaks living in Russia had in 1914 formed the first Czech Legion on the Allied side. They received constant accessions from the enemy lines—so many that an instruction was given to the Russian staff, that in questioning these volunteers we should ask not "Where did you surrender?" but "Where did you come across?" In three cases whole regiments came over together, one under fire with its band playing; they came not as prisoners of war, but to take another turn on our side, because they regarded it as their own. In Kerensky's offensive of 1917 they did better work than anyone else, and he allowed them to organise regular units under their own flag. It was impossible for them to make peace; they would all be shot as deserters. They were ready to go on fighting by the side of the Bolsheviks, or anyone else who would go on with them. After Brest-Litovsk they asked leave to go by the Trans-Siberian and the Pacific to join up again in France. Trotsky agreed, but gave private orders for their arrest as soon as they had surrendered their arms. The Czechs, who were always in the know everywhere—their language is very like Russian—found this out and successfully resisted arrest. At this time they were in *echelon* eastwards at various points on the railway; and as the Trans-Siberian was the nerve of that country, their resistance practically amounted to a conquest of Siberia. The Bolsheviks were suppressed there, though there were partisan bands in the forests which often made raids on the railway, and a government, mostly of S.R.'s, was set up in Omsk. Farther east, along the line, a military adventurer named Semenov (pronounced Seminov), cleared that part of the line from Bolsheviks and, with Japanese support, set up a little piratical kingdom of his own at Chita; and in Vladivostok there were other competing "governments."

Through Vladivostok the Allies poured troops of all nations into Siberia, or formed units of their nationals there. English, French, Italian, American, Japanese, Poles, Serbs and Czechs; none of them took any active part in the fighting, they were there to help with munitions, and railway transport was their principal service. These Allied Missions, by their interference and also by their jealousies and quarrels, made their name odious among the population.

Omsk was the most important of all these centres, for in the main it had the Siberian population behind it. There was hardly any industry in Siberia, and the practical Siberian farmer, almost like an American farmer of the Middle West, had little taste for Bolshevism; on the other hand, a movement of co-operative farming, on lines similar to the British or Irish, spread all over the country. Omsk made an attempt to maintain through a Directorate some unity between all the scattered anti-Bolshevik forces; but this was a failure, and after a military *coup d'état* there, the Siberian government asked Admiral Kolchak to act as dictator. When he offered his sword to us, we had asked him to go to Siberia to set up an Eastern Front; he accepted therefore, but he had the greatest distaste for all the demoralised and self-seeking elements which surrounded him.

All these movements, though they had some initial successes, in the end failed lamentably, and the causes of the failure were everywhere the same. The leaders chosen were honest soldiers—Alexeyev, Kornilov, Kolchak, Denikin and Wrangel

—but, except the last-named, no statesmen at all. Behind them were wrangling politicians of the second or third order, representing every variety of opinion except Bolshevism, with no agreement at all as to what they would do if they won; but in practice policy was usually shaped for them by sheer adventurers, the leavings from the gallantry of World War I.

The Bolsheviks, on the other hand, owing to Lenin's iron party discipline, were determined fighters with precise methods ruthlessly applied. There were atrocities on both sides; but with the Whites they were sporadic and shamefaced, with the Reds purposeful, and in part at least controlled. When Trotsky took the Red Army in hand, he summoned all officers to register: if they did not, their families were left out of the food categories. For sheltering a defaulting officer the penalty was death. Commanders from the old army were used (Brusilov was one of these), but political commissaries were set to watch over them; in the rear the Terror was omnipresent and uniform, and an extensive use was made of a system of hostages.

But we must seek elsewhere for the chief causes of the Bolsheviks' success. The peasants were not Bolshevik, as they were soon to show; but in spite of all pronouncements of the Whites, who fought not in the name of the Tsar but of the dissolved Constituent Assembly, they felt morally certain that a "White" victory, led by the "squire in uniform," would mean the restitution of the land which they had seized. They varied in their sympathies between the two sides, and some of them even organised "Green" armies in Russia and Siberia, which joined neither. The town workers practically all sided with the Reds, and it was they who formed the mass of the Red Army. But probably the greatest of all forces on the Bolshevik side was the enthusiasm of the young, to whom the Revolution had opened an altogether new life. All the old ideals had crashed: the autocracy with the futility of Nicholas II, the official Church with the corrupt domination of the foul Rasputin, and this time there was no real chance of any recovery. The civil war gave the young every opportunity for courage, initiative, even for leadership, and they grasped with joy all the chances which it gave them. As in revolutionary France in 1793, fresh ability in plenty was raised to the surface: the military instinct of Frunze, the cavalry genius of Budenny, the courage and initiative of Chapayev, which is now commemorated by a striking monument on the Lower Volga. The Bolsheviks were like the garrison of a besieged city, fighting with their backs to the wall under a chief who had their whole-hearted devotion and, never thrown out of his stride even by the most desperate situation, seemed always to see his way past every difficulty. There was, as there had always been in Russia, a patriotism of the under-dog class, and the defence of the revolution blended with the defence of the country against the dispossessed bourgeoisie and its foreign helpers.

The real turn of the tide came with our armistice on November 11, 1918. It knocked all the heart out of the Allied intervention, for there was now no need of an Eastern Front, and our people wanted to go home. We faltered more and more in our support of the Whites, and our lukewarmness was one of the main causes of their failure. Kolchak at the beginning of 1919 captured Perm, this side of the Urals, and threatened the Lower Volga. Our seizure of Archangel was too late and too early—it was too late to help the rising in Yaroslavl, and it might have been more decisive if it had come later, at the moment of Kolchak's greatest successes; also we were by no means happy in our intervention in the local politics there. Dissensions in Kolchak's army had their effect on the operations. Denikin's furthest advance came when Kolchak was already retreating fast. He was rolling back—more by outflanking than by direct fighting—beyond the Urals. His army then broke up. At Irkutsk a "pink" government had been set up on his line of retreat. The retreating Czechs handed him over to it as the price of their passage, and he was shot. He died with signal courage. When Kolchak went back, we evacuated Archangel. Denikin got almost within striking distance of Moscow, but he was countered with effective measures by Stalin; his advance guard cracked up, and he was driven back into Crimea. A more spectacular blow was struck by Yudenich, who, starting from the new Estonian frontier close by, actually fought his way into the environs of Petrograd; there is still a bullet-hole from his advance in a window of the palace of Tsarkoe Selo; but he was stopped by a vigorous concentration of troops organised by Trotsky.

Meanwhile Wrangel, who had taken over from Denikin, restored the morale of his men and even made another strong sally northward from his nest in Crimea. The new Poland of Pilsudski was also on the move for the recovery of as much as possible of the debated provinces between Poland and Great Russia. Besides the "Green Army" of the peasant leader Makhno, the Ukrainians were also in the field under Petlyura. Kiev changed hands time after time. There was no kind of co-ordination against the Bolsheviks. They dealt vigorously with Wrangel and, crossing the ice that surrounds the isthmus of Perekop, pushed him back into Crimea and eventually to the sea; he had to withdraw to the Bosphorus.

The Reds now found it possible to concentrate against the Poles. And, wih rapid action under their cavalry leader Budenny, drove them from Kiev, and Tukhachevsky pursued them to the gates of Warsaw. It seemed touch and go whether they would make contact with revolutionary Germany; but with the help of General Weygand, who came post-haste from Paris, Pilsudski turned the tide and in turn drove the Reds back into Russia; the debated provinces fell to him as the prize of this victorious advance, and the Treaty of Riga on March 18, 1921, reversed the results of centuries of earlier conflict by making the Poles masters of a huge extent of White Russian and Ukrainian territory. Lenin paid this price for peace: within his own reduced borders he had won the Civil War and had deserved to win it.

Lenin had expelled not only the foreigners, but most of the personnel of his internal enemies. They passed away into lasting exile. The *diaspora,* as they called it, the scatterings of the old Russia, spread all over the world, living as best they could off the leavings of the lawful inhabitants. The more reactionary churchmen found a welcome in the newly-created Yugoslavia, which was Orthodox. The scholars were warmly welcomed in the new Czechoslovakia, which made a generous provision for them. The politicians mostly gathered in Germany or in France, according to the changes in the currency and in living conditions; a few, probably more favoured, settled in England. The luckiest were those, especially among the young, who sought a new life in the New World. America is well used to immigration, and the Russian is a white man. Much more terrible was the lot of those who drifted away into Manchuria and China.

Those who remained in Russia paid dearly for the rest. The Tsar with his whole family had been murdered on July 16, 1918, in a cellar at Ekaterinburg, near the Urals, and a number of their nearest kinsfolk were thrust down a deserted mine-shaft near by. Ministers and generals were killed off in reprisals for the actions of others. The possessing class had been dispossessed wholesale. There is no complete record of their various fates: shootings, hairbreadth escapes, humiliations, starvation.

And what was now the state of this poor country, devastated by foreign and civil war? The Bolsheviks had won where they deserved to win—as the better fighters, and the fighting had drawn off attention from the cause for which they were fighting, from the ready-made application of undigested theory to a country to which it was peculiarly ill-suited. Marxism was an industrial theory, and Russia was predominantly agricultural; and it was only because agriculture for a time evaded the application of the theory that Russia survived at all; in Germany, England or the United States it would have been far less likely. Money as a means of exchange of goods had ceased to function: it had been killed by unlimited inflation. Private trade had been destroyed, and there was so far nothing else to take its place. Markets were deserted even by the dogs and pigeons; Petrograd, now to be renamed Leningrad, had sunk to a third of its population; many of its wooden houses had been destroyed for fuel; many of its inhabitants were living in cellars.

The peasant farmed for himsef, not for the towns: he had no use for the worthless paper money. Where the townsman could not provide for himself by illegal sale of trinkets or other belongings on the black market, he had to go to the peasant, as the peasant would not come to him. This was the period of the "bagmen": they went immense distances carrying anything they could sell and returned to the towns with any food they could get, which was, of course, liable to confiscation if they happened to meet a rigorous or bullying Red soldier on the way back. The factories, depleted by the Civil War, were ruined by the application of the theory that pay was independent of work, by the leveling of skilled with unskilled labour, and most of all by administration by public assembly and entirely inexpert managers. According to Rykov, Commissar for Industry, factory output had fallen by 85 per cent, and what was produced was looted by the workers, and the plant to boot: he reckoned that the number of factory workers left in employment was not more than a million— and this was the boasted proletariat, who were to profit most by the change. There had been a wholesale exodus to the country for food, and country artisans were now, where they could, supplying to the townsmen articles which the peasants had formerly looked to the towns to provide.

This brought all questions back to the peasantry. The situation of the towns was becoming catastrophic, and they were the seat of the Government's power. Since the Black Partition which had most favoured the well-to-do, the peasants were only under a loose control. The Bolsheviks, being the extreme left wing of an international party based on industrialism, could hardly have contemplated the irony of being called on to administrate an agricultural country, and they had not really prepared a program for such an eventuality. They tried to apply a simple code of their industrial program. The peasant, they said, was now a citizen of a Communist State. The land was under his occupation; but what he grew on it, after deducting that proportion which they allowed him as his wage, was to go to the State. "And now," said one peasant, "I suppose we are to chew the land." The peasantry replied by growing only what they were allowed to keep, as they would have done in any agricultural community, and this countermove was checkmate. There was war between country and town: "We can do without kerosene," said the peasants. "Let's see if he (the townsman) can do without grain." At one time Moscow was surrounded by a whole ring of peasant risings.

Punitive columns, as under the Tsar in 1905, were sent down to the country, but this time to get grain; they sometimes confiscated even the seed grain which the peasant in his traditional providence had reserved for the next crop. The direct result was a colossal famine. As transport had broken down, famine was already at the door, and this year there was added to the war and the Terror a very severe drought; but foreign famine experts have estimated that in this case the dimensions of the evil were in the main to be attributed to the new legislation. In the wake of the famine followed—as usual, but much more widely spread than usual—terrible epidemics. Like the Tsar's government in 1891-3, the Bolsheviks were afraid to allow any scope to organised unofficial relief. The foreigner had to be admitted for this purpose, and splendid work was done both by the Quakers, often to the fore in good work in Russia, and by a much bigger new organisation, that of American relief. The Government itself had gone bankrupt.

Nature had called a halt; and Lenin, with the promptitude of a clear and courageous thinker, decided to make the halt official. It was only to be a halt; there was no abandonment of the ultimate purpose; and it was natural enough that the vast work of transformation should be attempted stage by stage. Anyhow, Lenin admitted his defeat and ordered a partial retreat. The peasant was to get back his free market, while paying a large tax in kind; shops were again allowed to open in Moscow; money was restored to its old place—and—most striking of all the admissions of defeat—attempts were made to reopen communications with capitalistic countries to get loans to carry on. This started a new period known as the NEP, or new economic policy—really a partial restoration of the old.

VII

COMPROMISE AND IRONY

(1921-28)

BUT WHAT A SITUATION FOR A FANATIC! FANATICISM AT HALF-cock! When shops opened again and trams ran again for payment, there were actually young people in Moscow who committed suicide at the thought of it. What! We were told that we were so right and they so wrong that killing was no murder. And now you tell us to put back what we have swept away. It was only the enormous prestige of Lenin that could have forced the retreat on the Party, and it was his last great achievement. He had never really recovered from the bullet of Dora Kaplan. In May, 1922, he developed sclerosis of the brain and had a stroke. He could still sometimes attend to work, but in December came a second stroke, with paralysis of arm and leg, and in March, 1923, a third. On January 21, 1924, came a fourth, which proved fatal. He received a tremendous national funeral.

And, indeed, this long pause of seven years (1921-9), a long night following a too strenuous day, was full of irony of every kind. The capitalist governments had been threatened with destruction, and now they were asked to help finance the halting experiment of their challengers. And the capitalist who gave such help, himself had his tongue in his cheek, for by giving it he hoped to lead this erring member of the European community back to the good old ways of Capital. At the congress of Genoa in the autumn of 1922, respectable Bolshevik delegates in the approved bourgeois costume mildly approached foreign governments for loans. A series of trade treaties followed, which at the time were indispensable. England had been the first to treat (March, 1921), and Mr. Lloyd George, who had earlier "refused to shake hands with murderers," was now depicted in a witty *Punch* cartoon as directing his hairy and primitive visitors to the tradesmen's entrance of No. 10, Downing Street. Ambassadors were not sent, but trade missions; everything was still ambiguous. Very soon our example was followed by nearly all other countries. Occasion quickly arose to show up the ambiguity. In making his "economic retreat" Lenin was withdrawing from his main line of attack. It was, as suggested above, a half-withdrawal. To use his own expression, Lenin retained those dominating heights which still towered above the inflow of old ways. The Communist Party, which was throughout the real ruler of Russia, retained a complete monopoly of political power; it also retained an equally complete and inviolable monopoly of the Press; lastly, it maintained a monopoly of foreign trade, which could only flow through the channels of the Soviet Government. With these safeguards for the future, the Bolsheviks turned with ardour to the task of educating a generation which some day should be able to advance again.

Public instruction, or the enlightening of the mind, had always been one of the highest aspirations of the Russian public, including the peasantry. It was comparatively few that got to the universities, but the standard of scholarship there was certainly more rigorous than with us, and there, through the most servile days of Tsardom, there had always lived a free and independent spirit of objective study. Moscow University, for instance, was like a light showing in a very dark place. When Gorky's election to the Academy was cancelled by the Tsar, other academicians of very different political views sent in their resignations.

During the first years after the revolution there could be but little peaceful study, and the revolutionary spirit had played havoc with the excellent old curriculum. Already propaganda had practically superseded instruction. A very large proportion of the Arts Faculty of Russia had fled the country. There was precious little freedom for such a subject as literary criticism when prescribed views on everything were dictated in advance. A systematic attempt was now made to staff the universities with students who professed communism; the party view practically took the place of the matriculation examination. Far the greater part of the leading scholars stuck valiantly to their sacred standard of objectivity, and a number of them were expelled from the country. If the Arts Faculty could be dispensed with, others such as Science and Medicine, in a vast country like Russia with so many problems for technicians, could not be spared unless the public service was to break down. Doctors must know anatomy; chemists must not dispense poisons; engineers must not build bridges that fall down. If the communist student remained chiefly a propagandist, he would probably fail in his examination; if he devoted himself to his studies, he might possibly forget his communism.

With the secondary schools it was a different story; they had never had the same independence. Here the chief mistake of the innovators was that they tried in succession a whole series of foreign theories—half baked and less than half digested.

With primary instruction it was again quite different. Here, if only economic conditions enabled schools to be maintained and warmed, the zeal of the Bolsheviks in founding them was beyond praise. In European Russia before the revolution the proportion of illiterates was over 75 per cent and in Siberia 85 per cent. It was a glorious chance to teach the alphabet simultaneously with the principles of the new world to be, and the Soviet record has no page more to its honour than the steady and surprisingly rapid extermination of illiteracy.

Formation of the mind is one thing and formation of the character is quite another, and with a true instinct the Bolsheviks saw from the start that the second is far the more imporant. They were also correct in regarding as the main sources in the training of character the family and religion. The mass of the parents still belonged to the old world, and the Bolsheviks attacked their authority in every way, teaching the children to distrust them and to spy on them. Marriage was attacked and could be dispensed with altogether, divorce was made as easy as possible, but the Bolsheviks were always most conscientious in imposing alimony and provision for children. The greatest opposition came from the peasants, on economic rather than on moral grounds, for divorce involved complicating divisions of the principal article of peasant property, namely land. In the attempt to separate children from parents, the State was not able to carry out the responsibility which it assumed. Families had already been thrown out of gear by war and famine, and for a considerable period marauding bands of youngsters wandered about, numbering in all even hundreds of thousands, addicted to every crime of violence and infected with disease. This was one of the greatest sores of the community. At last it was firmly handled. Institutions of the Borstal type but on typically human Russian lines were set up, which did indeed become real schools of character. I cannot remember anything more impressive that I have seen in Russia.

I have mentioned the devoted and energetic part played by the young in the winning of the Civil War. The Communist Party was seldom allowed to reach the figure of two millions. All power was entrusted to it, and the tests of membership were most exacting. As a supplement to this new ruling class, had been created a League of Communist Youth (*Komsomol*), which was there to back up and ultimately to reinforce the Party. It was the very best school of communism, for it had as high a standard of discipline as the Party and was called upon to supplement other agencies in any task which claimed devoted and spirited work. But the period of the NEP gradually played havoc with the Komsomol, for it took advantage of the general retreat from principle and was tending more and more to become simply a privileged class.

The Bolsheviks saw their most dangerous enemy in religion of any kind. Marx had declared it to be "dope for the masses," and these words had been inscribed above the most famous icon in Moscow. That is a German, not a Russian view: for instance, the great Russian prose writers of Marx's own time, which was the finest period of Russian prose literature—Turgenev, Tolstoy, Dostoyevsky—were full of the religious instinct, if only for the reason that they were the best representatives of Russia. It was also the view of a given time and place, in the light of a given purpose, the rising of the proletariat. While it was an attack on the history of the churches, it found ample fuel. The instinct of religion could be purged and purified by it, but could only be strengthened by the attack.

A strong movement for the purification of the Church and its separation from Imperial politics had begun in the last years of Tsardom. During the parallel movement of political liberation which led to the establishment of the Duma, a growing volume of church opinion called for the summoning of a Church Council and the restoration of the Patriarchate, which would be the outward symbol of church independence. The wavering Tsar nearly consented, but Rasputin was of course utterly opposed to anything of the kind. Religion gained greatly during World War I. The moment that Tsardom was gone, the movement was resumed and was now irresistible. The Provisional Government stood for it, and in its legislation offered complete tolerance and even state support for all forms of religion, Orthodoxy remaining the religion of the State. The Council was called and elected a Patriarch in Moscow at the very time when the Bolsheviks were making themselves masters of the city. The choice was an admirable one. The first act of the new Patriarch, Tikhon, was to try to stop the slaughter in the Kremlin. Later he issued an encyclical headed: "They that take the sword shall perish by the sword." Dissociating the Church from politics, and declaring that it recognised any form of government sent by God, he refused this sanction to the Bolsheviks on the sole ground of their professed atheism.

In the first stage of the revolution numbers of priests suffered violent deaths, but that was partly to be explained by the fact that the sympathies of the clergy were clearly on the side of the Whites, if only for the reason just given above. Church land was confiscated at the outset of the Communist revolution, but so was all other land. Religion was excluded from the state schools, but that was so in other countries: the difference was that there were no private schools, and that Bolshevist law forbade the teaching of any form of religion to persons under eighteen in groups of more than four. This law was now taken more seriously, and at Easter of 1923 two great trials were staged. That year the Latin Easter preceded the Orthodox by one week, and it was more convenient to deal with foreigners first—especially with Poles, who were Catholics. In the Latin Holy Week the Catholic Archbishop Cieplak and a number of other priests were put on trial, firstly for reserving the sacred vessels from their offerings for the relief of the famine and secondly for continuing to teach religion generally to the young. They behaved with splendid courage, refusing to obey a law which cut across their ordination vow. The Archbishop and his principal lieutenant, Monsignor Budkiewicz, were condemned to death; the Archbishop replied by giving the blessing, and several present in the court fell on their knees. Budkiewicz was actually martyred in prison; but when the news got outside Russia, there was such a storm of universal condemnation that it was decided not to proceed with the trial of the Patriarch Tikhon, which had been fixed for the Orthodox Holy Week. He was later released and was received everywhere by great crowds with devotion, but his health was broken and he died in April, 1925. When advised to rest, he always replied, "There will be time enough to rest; the night will be long, the night will be dark." The Catholic Archbishop was also released but died soon afterwards.

It is supposed that the Government was afraid of losing its slender link with foreign credit. In any case the frontal attack was not renewed. The fight went on, but with other weapons— chiefly propaganda, with persecution of priests on pleas only indirectly connected with their faith. If divine worship was to continue, the confiscated churches had to be leased back to the parish communities, and any excuse was found for closing them.

It must be clearly understood that the Bolshevist attack was not aimed directly at the profession of faith, which was indeed immune under the constitution, but against the teaching of it to others: that is, against the ministers of religion as distinguished from their flocks. The object was to cut religion at its source. The attack was directed against every form of religious belief.

The Soviet Government's foreign relations, based on the uncertain foundations which have been described, continued to give constant anxiety. Propaganda for a world revolution, which was always thought to be much nearer than it was in fact, was not discontinued; indeed the Soviet trade delegations were used actively for this purpose. This, after several notes of protest, led ultimately to the very ineffective rifling of the safe of Arcos, the Soviet Trade Mission in London, by the British police (May 2, 1927). The result was constant complaints and constant promises which were not kept. The double game really deceived neither side. It was useless to plead that the Soviet Government and the Third International were quite independent of each other when it was quite clear that the Russian Communist Party dictated every action to both.

Another significant change was made in the title of the new Russian State. Before the Revolution the Liberal motto "The United States of Russia" had found wide acceptance, and certainly it was only a federal system that could really cope with all Russia's national problems, whether within her boundaries or on her borders. The Bolsheviks, being internationalists, sincerely hated all forms of racial hatred. The State was now re-named "The Union of Soviet Socialist Republics" (USSR). Far the largest unit was naturally Russia proper; its title (RSFSR) actually included the word "Federative," as recognising the rights of the many small non-Russian units contained in the Great Russian mass. The second largest was the Ukrainian SSR, and there were a whole number others, each obtaining a status corresponding to its numbers and importance. The Bolsheviks—or to give them their new name, the Communists—in every matter except religion fostered the language, literature and traditions of each of the smaller units; in doing so they took their stand on justice, in sharp opposition to the rabid nationalism of Tsardom. All differentiation disappeared as if by magic, which was in consonance with the spirit of the mass of people. There was a separate State organ for the lesser nationalities, entrusted to the direction of the Georgian, Stalin. But here the principle stopped. Any republic was supposed to have the right of secession, but the Government had shown how it regarded that claim in the instance of recalcitrant Georgia, which was forcibly retained. As the Communist Party ruled the whole State, so branches of it ruled each of the minor republics, and the economic wealth of the whole country was kept entirely at the disposal of Moscow.

But there was also a special and ominous implication in the new title of the State. As the basis of the State was international, it was prepared to absorb any other State, quite apart from its nationality, which by propaganda, revolution or conquest might be brought into the Soviet fold; so that the title USSR at this time involved the aspiration of becoming the United States of the world.

One thing was unquestionable. The country rapidly recovered: this was natural enough in an agricultural country, in which agriculture, with the added experience of the last years, was allowed to take its accustomed way. But this for the Communists was the most disheartening symptom of all. During the period of militant communism, state farms, where the workers were servants with wages, had been set up on some of the biggest estates. These had proved a complete failure. Under inexpert communist management they had been drowned in an ocean of the surrounding hostile peasantry. Now that state compulsion was in the main withdrawn, private initiative resumed the advance which had already been so striking before the war. It was the most curious of contests. The government, which still used the Terror sporadically, had all the power; the country had nothing to articulate its wishes, but it was getting its own way. One typical symptom was this: co-operative farming—that is free co-operation, directed by the peasants themselves—had sprung up all over the country when Tsardom fell; then everyone became officially a co-operator under orders sent down by the State, which meant that there was no free co-operative movement at all; now the peasant co-operators saw their chance of going on as they had done before.

We may use this lull to take stock of the new Russia. The town workers had always had the central place in all Lenin's thoughts in exile. Though they were only a small fraction of the population, they were the nucleus of the so-called dictatorship of the proletariat." Of course it was not the proletariat that was to dictate—which would only have resulted in Babel—but the Communist Party of "professional politicians" in its name. But the town workers could and did now feel that the country was managed in their own name and in the interests of all; they were proud of this, and had a sense of independence which they could not have had before. In the matter of wages they received more (it had taken ten years to reach the pre-war level), but it brought

less; for the output was still very low and the distribution of
it quite out of order. They got the best of what there was,
but the best was so much less than before. The original idea
of separating pay from output ("to each according to his
needs") had been thrown over. There were great inequali-
ties—according to Tomsky, President of the Trade Unions,
varying between the figures of one and six, or even one and
nine. Hours of work were in principle seven, but according
to the Soviet Press, overtime was almost habitual. There
were two million unemployed, of whom about a quarter received state aid.

The Soviet Press, which allowed no criticism of the State
gospel, even when it changed, in every way encouraged criticism as to how it was being carried out, and it contained
hair-raising accounts of the living conditions of workers, even
comparing their accommodations to catacombs. Large houses
taken over from the previous regime were absolutely
packed and practically remained without repair. The floor
space allotted to the individual was in practice cut down from
8 square meters to 6.8, 6.0, or even 5.6, and was in the end
satirically described as "the coffin" standard. The Press reckoned that workers changed their employment as often as twice
a year, and the chief reason for this was the wretchedness of
conditions of housing. As to accidents, which had been regarded
as a bane of the capitalist system, they were more numerous
than ever.

On the other hand, there could be no question at all of
the care of the State for all, in the form of all sorts of social
services and benefits; above all, education and medical assistance, which were absolutely cost-free for everyone in the
country and every visitor to it. There was a complete system
of State Insurance. There was the utmost care and thought
for women and children. Women, politically and economically,
had complete equality with men.

For the greater part, the old bourgeoisie—still suffering
from heavy disadvantages, and at times pursued by the sporadic
Terror—had come out of their holes and taken up their place
like others in the ranks of skilled labour. In some cases, a
former proprietor was actually set to manage his old estate
as a state farm. But above all, there was now a new class of
technical experts, who were encouraged by the State's manifest need of their services; among them were numbers of
former German war prisoners who, as recovery was the word
of the day, were especially valued for their proved efficiency.
This new class of technicians, allured by their wide oppor-

tunities of service, had no love for those who fled from Russia
and no sympathy with their constant plotting; if only their
latitude lasted, they believed that the main work of administration would fall into their hands, for the reason that they alone
were capable of dealing with it. They were very unlike the old
intelligentsia; the long night discussions of every question in
earth and heaven were at a discount: talking could be very
dangerous, and in a train it would stop of itself when the train
stopped. Nor was there any place for the man with no backbone, and a general hardening of purpose was one of the
chief results of Communist rule.

But as of old, far the most important factor was the peasantry, and this was their high time. No one thought of any
renewal of the punitive expeditions: with the immense re-
buke of the famine so recent, it seemed that they had gone
for ever. The peasants felt, in a much more real sense than
the town workers, that they were the winners, and they went
forward on each main issue to remind the government of
their importance. Their first victory had been won before the
Communist Revolution when instead of waiting for a national
land settlement by the Constituent Assembly, on the insistence of the the Bolsheviks themselves they had seized the land
in their own way—that is, village by village—and had settled
on it. The Communists had explained to them that though they
occupied all the land they were to give the crops to the State,
and on this issue they had fought Lenin himself and won.
Next they raised the question whether the prices which they
got for their crops was a fair exchange for that which they
had to pay for the scanty supply of goods which they could
get from the towns. This problem—called by Trotsky "the
scissors"—engaged the very respectful attention of the Government. At one time it prepared a great scheme for the export of grain, which was in return to pay for manufactured
goods for the peasants, but they had no faith in its working out
to their profit and put difficulities in the way of the collection
of the grain required. Of all the ironies and contradictions of
this time the most striking was as follows. Under the Tsars,
the peasants of Great Russia had lived for centuries under
communal tenure. At last, following the example of Western
Europe, they had wakened to its many deficiencies—such
as the division of the village holdings into innumerable separate strips—and following the lead given by the legislation
of Stolypin they had been dividing up the holding into compact individual farms. Now they were doing this again in
place after place of themselves, and all that they asked of the

government was to confirm what they had done: a Communist Government was asked for a title deed. And in 1922 the Communist Government, in shaping its new land law, did indeed base it in the main on individual farming!

But the peasant went further than this. He had had a tremendous political education which had come home to every household. Past master of evasion, as he was, he avoided any individual challenge of the Government. Village Hampdens would be easy to deal with, especially with machine guns. But he would elect to the village Soviet men who would take their turn in keeping the Government quiet and help their fellows to go their own way as far as possible. More than this, as the peasants were listened to in this period, they had an actual opportunity of putting forward their own program, and it was in every way the reverse of Communism: a free market, no tax on thrift, restoration of the ballot, abolition of the practice of sending down from the Communist Party a list of persons to be elected, and lastly the equalisation of the individual peasant's vote with that of the town worker: at present, in the government of the State, it only counted for one-fifth.

For centuries the communal land tenure had kept the peasants at least artificially equal. As Lenin had always seen, there was now growing up a peasant bourgeoisie and a peasant proletariat—farmers and rural labourers. It was the prosperous peasants who profited most in the expropriation of the squires, if only for the reason that they had had more horses and carts to carry the plunder away. If the peasants now managed their own affairs, it meant that they were managed by the more prosperous among them. The town newspapers kept correspondents in the village to watch for any signs of exploitation, and these correspondents had a very poor time of it; quite often they were assassinated. What was more important was that the peasants had the power of holding up the food supply of the towns: this was their best weapon, and they were using it to enforce their own claims.

It was this that brought this long period (1921-8) to an end. One can imagine the effect of all this compromise on such ardent doctrinaires. What a position for a government—to hold the power on condition that you let the greater part of the population do the opposite to what you wished! Meanwhile the compromise was having an enervating influence on the governing Party itself. Over and over again, there were purges to get rid of the lukewarm, and yet the rot gained ground: it was particularly felt where it was most dangerous, in the Komsomol. One is bound to feel the most respect for those who stood firmest for consistency. The Party itself, and there-fore the Government, was soon split endwise. There were several groups; but the main distinction was between a right wing which said, give the country what it evidently wants and a left wing which said, practise what you preach. The original purpose of the Party had been world revolution, without any distinction between different countries. By a strange chance, the revolution had only brought the Communists into power in this particularly unsuitable agricultural country. Yet to make the world revolution, they would have to hold on to the one great foothold that they possessed. Should this be done at the price of the whole original purpose? In this issue, the one thing cer-tain was that there would come a demand for a new march forward.

VIII

STALIN *versus* TROTSKY

(1924-28)

IT WAS THE COMMUNIST PARTY THAT GOVERNED RUSSIA—not the Soviet Government. The Communist Party had two purposes, and for each purpose it had a different arm. Its primary purpose, up to the split, was world revolution; for this its arm was the Comintern or Third International. It sat ordinarily in Moscow; it fought the Labour International cen-tered in Amsterdam; it controlled communist parties in other countries, and used all of them for the purposes of Moscow; but it was only the left arm of the Russian Communist Party. The right arm of the Party was the Soviet Government; it was there to govern Russia, but every political question went first to the head office of the Communist Party, which dictated all its actions. For a long time there was still some mystery about this, which deluded many foreign admirers, and that was how the Communists could keep up the pretence that the Soviet Government was not responsible for the acts of the Third International. Its responsibility, to be exact, was really that of the right arm for the acts of the left. Later legislation was frankly published as coming "from the Party and the Gov-ernment."

Soviet, in Russian, has the double meaning of "counsel" and "council." Under the Tsars the institution which most closely corresponded to the House of Lords in England was entitled "the State Soviet." But the word came to have a special meaning, associated with the Petersburg Soviet of Workers' Deputies of 1905; when re-created during the March Revolution of 1917, this became "the Soviet of Workers', Peasants' and *Soldiers'* Deputies," and its power lay in the last-named words. Soviets were then set up in all other parts of Russia: their special significance was that, in principle, their franchise was restricted to the ranks of labour: "Soviet" meant the exclusion of all others. Soviets need not only be representatives of localities, but also of vocations; in peasant villages this did not involve any distinction.

Soviets were very irregularly elected—not by ballot, as were the Duma, *zemstva,* Town Councils and peasant assemblies before the Revolution, but by show of hands; in principle, deputies could be "recalled" by their constituents, but this was a dead letter. The persons elected were those designated in advance by the Communist Party, which sent down its list to the meeting. To hold up one's hand against anyone on that list was an act of challenge which would be paid for dearly, and consequently all Soviet elections are "unanimous." The Party has, at times, even decided in advance what shall be the proportion of communists and non-communists on a given body; it has also not scrupled, where necessary, to cancel elections.

Russia, being a mainly illiterate country when the Bolsheviks took it over, had always had the practice of indirect election; this, in the circumstances, was common sense, and this practice was with good reason retained. It would be absurd to ask illiterate peasants to choose this public man or that, of whom they could only have the foggiest ideas; they chose "electors"—that is, those among their own people whose judgment they most trusted.

The notable statesman who had modelled public elections in Russia was Michael Speransky, the Liberal Minister appointed by Alexander I (1801-1825) to draft a constitution. His scheme had four rungs: the district, the county, the province, and the State. Each rung chose out of its own body an executive for its own local affairs and also members to serve in the body just above it. Nothing was done at the time, for Speransky fell on the eve of the invasion of Napoleon in 1812. Alexander II set up the two middle rungs in his county and provincial *zemstva* (1864). Nicholas II at last conceded the top rung—the Duma (1905)—which at first was practically elected by universal franchise. The bottom rung, the district or cantonal council, was a constant claim of Russian Liberals.

In the Duma elections there were various stages. The peasants met first to choose their representatives; these met other qualified voters at the county town, and together chose those who were to go on to the provincial capital, and there the actual members of the Duma were elected. Similarly, the post-revolution system of Soviets is a pyramid. There are local, urban, regional, and provincial Soviets, crowned by a national Soviet. This last chose an executive committee. This committee elected as Commissaries (or Ministers) those persons nominated to it by the central organ of the Communist Party: in no case is there opposition—much less a disputed election.

The Communist Party is a very different story. "Few, but good," said Garibaldi, when he picked his "Thousand" to conquer Sicily and Naples, and Lenin said the same. This was the staff that was to win and the cast that was to hold. Even to reach the rank of "candidate" the severest tests are prescribed, and the Soviet Press again and again insisted on the most careful scrutiny of each individual claim. It is a handpicked party, and no other is allowed. We see in it now, in spite of its greatly increased dimensions, exactly what Lenin meant it to be from the outset—a picked body of professional political directors of all public activity, with an iron discipline. There had to be several sponsors for each person proposed and a period of testing, least severe for a town worker, more for a peasant, and most for an "intellectual." Parentage and past activities had to be examined. There will from time to time be statistical surveys to ascretain whether the different categories of the population are being covered in the proportion considered suitable at the time; for the peasants, and even the intellectuals, are now admitted to closer partnership. There are constant purges, with expulsion of large numbers as unsatisfactory. The Party was seldom allowed to exceed the number of two millions in a population of, say, one hundred and sixty millions. The Communist Party is the leaven in the mass. It must take the initiative in all public activities. It has its privileges; one of them, a noble one, was a fixed restriction of pay (now abolished) to a very modest level (two hundred and twenty-five roubles a month), applying to the chiefs as to anyone else, though, of course, in a State which controlled all food and housing, they were not likely to lack. An austere standard of conduct is set, and a Communist suffers more severely than others for any breach of the law.

The Komsomol, or reserve of young folk, is perhaps an even more severe school of character. In 1936 I had a long and fascinating talk with a picked man from among its leaders.

There is an age scheme in four rungs: Party Members from eighteen; Komsomol, nineteen to twenty-three; Pioneers, ten to sixteen; and Little Octobrists—in memory of the "October," or Communist, Revolution—from eight to ten. The ages will be seen to overlap; and the leaders of each group are taken from the one above it. My Komsomol leader was in the early thirties and had already had a surprisingly full experience of administration. This is sometimes gained in the backward "autonomous" republics of Central Asia, for there the Communist control had to be built up from the beginning; in some literacy was even below one per cent; and, on the other hand, each of these "republics" must have its own "Com-Party," which controls the local life and takes its orders from Moscow, especially on all major points of economic policy. On the other hand, the Party here definitely justifies the dictum of Bismarck on Russia's civilising mission eastwards, for a very great deal of its work consists of building up the elements of a civilised community—elementary habits of public health or education, even to the creation of new alphabets, which their languages sometimes lacked altogether.

I asked my young friend about the objects of the Komsomol, and he replied with the simplest honesty and accuracy that it was an educational society with a bias. Next I asked about the bias. "Well, to start with," he replied, "we teach them that religion is a myth." "If God had meant the same thing as slavery," I intervened, "I could have agreed with you." He accepted this as the expression of another opinion. "We teach them," he went on, "that drunkenness disgraces a human being; we are against casual ties (with girls)." All of which I knew to be true. "And how do you teach them?" "We warn them, and warn again, and then deprive them of membership"—a penalty which will be deeply felt as a social stigma.

The further one goes down in the communist scheme, the less one finds of politics and the more of education. Russians are at their best in the loving care which they put into their institutions for children—for the best of all reasons, that they are children themselves and feel no constraint in treating them as their own human equals. Much of the training of the Pioneers and the activities in which they are encouraged to engage is quite delightful.

The Party itself—and the State as well—is governed by a Political Bureau (*Politburo*) of nine or more persons. It will be manifest that this body is all-powerful. It is to it that goes first any question of legislation or policy: the Party and the Soviet Government do what they are told. It was in this body that were fought out the grave questions raised by the turn which the country had taken under Lenin's "New Economic Policy." All-important, then, was the personnel of the Polit-buro. The two outstanding figures in it, after the death of Lenin, were Trotsky and Stalin. Trotsky was a brilliant Jew who had played many parts. A Marxist, but originally a Men-shevik, he had been a Vice-President of the first Soviet of 1905. He had lived mostly in exile till after the March Revolution, and only became a Bolshevik on his return. He organised the regimental committees which carried out the Communist Revo-lution of November ("October" old style), 1917. He won great distinction as Foreign Minister, as negotiator at Brest-Litovsk, as organiser of the Red Army (where he even gained the sympathies of some ex-Tsarist officers). In 1918 he had suppressed the rising at Yaroslavl, and in 1919 driven Yuden-ich back out of Petrograd. He was a brilliant, witty and caustic speaker, essentially a platform man. But he made himself too prominent, and in the wrong way, and his acid tongue made him too many enemies. An acute critic who saw him at close quarters, has truly said that Trotsky by his nature and by his methods belonged to pre-revolutionary times. Demagogues were getting out of date. Stalin was a Georgian—the very antithesis to a Jew. He was of humble origin. He received his education in a religious college, from which he was expelled. He had been a Bolshevik from the outset, had carried out dar-ing acts of violence, had made daring escapes, but it was some time before he became conspicuous in the Party. His first official post was People's Commissar for Nationalities, as repre-sentative of the minor peoples of Russia in the original Soviet Government.

When Lenin died in 1924, Trotsky was kept out of the suc-cession, and it was shared by a triumvirate, of which it is true his brother-in-law Kamenev was a member and also Kemenev's friend Zinoviev, but the driving force was Stalin. The whole strength of Stalin's position was that he was General Secretary of the Party (it has no President), and that the Party governed Russia. He, more than anyone else, was the real distributor of posts—even in the Soviet Cabinet, to which he himself did not belong. He kept the books, he knew all the records—all the qualities, weaknesses and aspirations of his fellow-members. Stalin's methods in council were very differ-ent from Trotsky's, though he made long, clear, and detailed expositions of policy both in speeches and in writings. They were those of a business man. He did not harangue his col-leagues; when in council, he carefully followed all that was said, and by the time that he summed up, he was able to take his stand on ground where he knew he would be supported (at least, that is the record of Bazhanov, one of the secretaries of the Politburo). Trotsky might make the moves and the mistakes, and Stalin would wait for him and outplay him. Lenin has left his opinion of both men: Trotsky, a kind of mountebank, of whom you could never be certain; Stalin, one who might spoil everything by his roughness.

Their disagreement lay in their respective characters. The chief points of discord were two. Trotsky, like Lenin, had spent years of wandering in the countries of Western Europe; he was well known in the United States. Stalin had hardly ever gone outside Russia. Trotsky was for aligning Soviet Russia with Labour parties and governments outside and taking little thought of peasant claims and desires; he was, in fact, an international world-politician. Stalin was more inclined to agree with the new Soviet Prime Minister, Rykov, a Right Bolshevik, that account must be taken of those whom the government was there to govern. But, above all, Trotsky was for a more ardent pursuit of the long-awaited and long-delayed world revolution. Stalin, on the contrary, in view of its patent unlikelihood, was prepared to soft-pedal the world revolution, anyhow for the present, and called for an internal program of construction which would prove that so large and potentially rich a country as Russia could go her own way, in spite of her encirclement by capitalist hostility, and could give an objective example of Socialism by its success in a single country.

As early as 1924, at the thirteenth Congress of the Party, the dissensions were becoming evident. Kamenev announced that 64 per cent of home trade was practically in private hands, and of retail trade 80 per cent. Kalinin, the President of the Soviet Republic, himself a peasant, testified to the rapid differentiation into two classes—farmers and rural labourers—which was proceeding in the villages; there was growing up a vast rural class of unemployed. Beyond this, owing to the rapid setting up of new households, there were now twenty-seven millions of them instead of seventeen. Bukharin declared that the schools "were not yet conquered" for communism, and vacancies at the universities were again reserved for those of proletarian origin or communist tendencies, which clearly would do no good to the cause of learning. Rykov expressed horror at the idea of terminating the NEP policy when the class of workers still numbered no more than 40 per cent of pre-war, and the industrial output was only 45 per cent; in the villages, he said, there were practically no shops, or substitutes for shops; the peasants were getting only 30 per cent of the industrial output. The Rights in the Party were for banking on the more well-to-do peasants and extending their authority. On the other hand, to tighten up propaganda abroad, at the fifth Congress of the Comintern in July, the Russian Communist Party assumed the right of controlling and disciplining all communist parties in other countries. A large section of the Party, speaking in the interests of the workers, demanded "democracy within the Party." Kamenev scornfully suggested that very soon democracy for all would be demanded, and this challenge to the authority of the divided leaders was rigorously crushed.

In April, 1925, Trotsky was sent to the Caucasus for his "political health," but was allowed to come back in June. He was, however, removed from the key post of Commissary for War, which, together with his striking personality, had brought him great influence in the army. He was given a much less important post in another sphere—that of the national economy. In December there was a stand-up fight at the Party Congress, where Stalin defeated Kamenev and Zinoviev by five hundred and fifty-nine voes to sixty-five. Zinoviev had up till now been practically absolute dictator in Leningrad, where he had distinguished himself by ruthless and wholesale brutality to the beaten bourgeoisie. He was now detained in Moscow while his Leningrad organisation was systematically smashed.

In 1926 the challenge of the world revolution came to a head in England, which Marx had regarded as the vital test of success. When in September, 1925, the Trades Union Congress welcomed the Russian trade unionist leader Tomsky at Scarborough, it adopted from him the very program by which the Bolsheviks had come into power in Russia: the T.U.C. was to claim the obedience of all manual workers and practically take over the government of this country. The result was a most ironical failure. At the moment when the killing should have begun—"a heavy civil war," as Lenin put it—the British workers were far too respectable for anything of the kind. Moscow was furious—especially at the football match between strikers and police, in which the strikers won by two goals to one and the chief constable's wife kicked off. Radek, the witty writer in *Pravda,* described the result as a bombshell. Trotsky was for going on. Stalin might reasonably have asked his opponent whether all these abortive attempts at revolution in foreign countries had had any other result than the promotion of Fascism.

Trotsky was, of course, standing for Bolshevist orthodoxy

when he claimed priority for world revolution, but he was a discredited advocate as a former Menshevik or Moderate, and, generally, as an opportunist. Zinoviev and Kamenev, like him, were internationally minded Jews and all for the world revolution, but there was a vast difference in their tactics. When rebuked, they cringed and apologised, only to start again. Trotsky, whom no one could accuse of lack of courage, showed fight all through. For a long time the Party was most unwilling to display its dirty linen outside its own ranks; the Bolsheviks were few enough, anyhow, in a hostile world, and could ill afford to quarrel; consequently, the beginnings of the fight remained concealed. Trotsky formed a coalition with Kamenev and Zinoviev against Stalin; the joint attack was to be made at a meeting in the Throne Room of the Kremlin. Trotsky led off with a violent denunciation, and when he ended made a demonstrative exit, which he tried to make more impressive by slamming the door; unfortunately, this was one of those heavy and palatial doors which would only close slowly. This little detail is related by one who was present, and is perhaps typical of the struggle between the two men.

There were sharp hostilities at the party meetings of April and July, 1926. The Rights, such as the shadow Premier, Rykov, were all for Stalin. The Opposition was branded as "a gang of European adventurers." In the heat of the debate, Dzerzhinsky, the head of Ogpu, delivered a most passionate speech on the threat to the Party, and died directly afterwards. Zinoviev was suspended from functioning as President of the Third International. In October, Trotsky, at meetings of workers, openly poured his invective on the Government and was forbidden to speak in public. Zinoviev tried to recover his hold over Leningrad, but failed. The Opposition now half recanted to save the unity of the Party, but Trotsky was struck out of the Politburo and Zinoviev out of the Third International. In July, 1927, Trotsky returned to the attack with a violent denunciation of Stalin on the Central Committee of the Party. He was now actively engaged in intensive underground work of the kind which he had conducted against the Tsar. He organised groups of "fives," with a secret code and local branches. He and Zinoviev were now expelled from the Central Committee. He was allowed to put his case at a plenary meeting, but was boo'ed. In November, at the celebrations of the tenth anniversary of the Communist Revolution, he got up demonstrations in the streets. He was now formally expelled from the Party, and sent into exile on the Asiatic frontier at Alma Ata, probably in the hope that he would take this, the easiest, way out of Russia, and thus finally discredit himself as having joined the emigration. This he had no intention of doing. Kamenev and Zinoviev recanted humbly again and were exiled to various places. The Opposition carried the war outside Russia, publishing its case in the German *Flag of Communism* (Die Fahne des Kommunismus), and appealed to the Third International (the Comintern) for readmission. The Communist leaders still hesitated to go to all lengths, and finally, as Trotsky did not go and was still active, he was taken to the western frontier and pushed over it, still demanding that it should be recorded that he went against his will.

He continued the fight with energy and acrimony from abroad, whether in Turkey, Sweden or Mexico. He knew all the ruses of conspiracy. It was only like a resumption of the old fight against the Tsar from outside. There is no need to doubt that widespread roots of his organisation remained in Russia. After all, he had had an outstanding prestige among the elder Bolsheviks. Kamenev and Zinoviev followed a different course; they apologised, lay low, crawled back into the Party and began again.

Stalin's career at this point reminds me of Robespierre's arrival at absolute power, though in Stalin's case it was much more permanent. Robespierre, when threatened by the breakup of "the Mountain" into various factions, produced by the new responsibilities of government and the various views taken of its problems, carried out a remarkable double stroke, in which he eliminated first the Right Opposition of Danton and then the Left Opposition of Hébert and Chaumette; in each case he did this by killing them off; that kind of "liquidation" is final. Stalin moved no less ruthlessly but much more guardedly. He had dealt first with the Left, but later he showed the Rights—Rykov, Tomsky and Bukharin—that he was in no sense their man. He even turned round and appropriated Trotsky's own program of indifference to peasant claims and, as will be seen later, while Trotsky had done no more than talk, Stalin challenged, fought and won, where Lenin himself had failed. Among the leaders, Stalin seemed to stand alone, but he had behind him the rank and file of the Party and, above all, the Komsomol. At the beginning of 1929, Bukharin, the clever author of the A B C of Communism, and Tomsky, head of the Trade Unions, demanded his resignation, but the quarrel was patched up. In November, Bukharin was expelled by the Party Committee from the Politburo and Rykov and Tomsky were given a warning. In the summer of 1930, after further recriminations, Rykov was sent for a holiday in the south. He was replaced in the Premiership by one of the most devoted and able of Stalin's supporters, Molotov.

Stalin did obtain absolute power, such as Lenin never claimed, and has retained it ever since. After that, Stalin might say first one thing and then another; but whatever he might say, you had to agree with him because he was Stalin. Why did Stalin win out so thoroughly? Not by any momentary flash in the pan, not by any brilliant political improvisation, but by spadework. It was because he had built up a great instrument, a corps of fellow workers who—especially the younger of them—all looked to "Comrade Stalin" for the lead. They were dependent on him, they relied on him, and they went where they were told.

Stalin's outright victory opened a new period. Foreign relations became easier, the capitalist neighbours were less alarmed. "Socialism in one country" meant anyhow, it seemed, the postponement of the world revolution, which the course of history had already itself decreed. It meant, instead of incitement to sedition everywhere, the argument of example: "We will show how well our ideas work out with us here." I see in the conflict between Trotsky and Stalin an expression, in an entirely new and original form, of the old Russian conflict between the Westerniser and the Slavophil. The Westerniser said: Be European, copy in everything from Europe —in the given case from the latest word in Europe, from Karl Marx; Stalin, while in no way challenging the authority of Marx, took the sensible view that Marx's gospel, being a living one, must take account of changing conditions and adapt its interpretations to them. The Slavophil was before all things a Russian and sought in his own country the ways of his own further development. Stalin would seek the ways in which Marxism could best be adapted to Russia. Not only Trotsky but most of the earlier members of the Politburo had spent the best years of their lives abroad; as time went on, the new Politburo came to contain hardly anyone who had ever been abroad at all. The earlier men had made their way to office by agitation and conspiracy, the new men were to make theirs by administrative experience. Stalin was of course always under fire from Trotsky and, as head of the Communist Party of Russia, he was naturally jealous of his orthodoxy, but it seemed as if for a time he even turned his back on Europe. As a Georgian, Stalin stood half-way between Europe and Asia, and the main effort of the Third International was now directed on to China, where there were at first most encouraging successes but later another failure. It was in this period that Japan was also traversed by the propaganda of Communism, which won the sympathies of many of the educated young, and the alarm which this aroused in their seniors expressed itself in the sharpest repression. The reaction gave a new turn to Japanese policy and eventually launched the country on a program of military and imperialist aggression in China.

Once firmly seated in the saddle as the national leader, Stalin issued the bugle call for which so many of the Party and especially the Komsomol had been waiting. It was for a new march forward to the triumph of Communism, which is never officially considered to have been realised in Russia, but on new lines, very much more constructive than in the first great attempt. Trotsky clamoured that no victory could be won in Russia unless it was a world victory too. Stalin would show that, even encircled by hostility, Russia could utilise her inexhaustible resources to build up a Socialist State, in which all these resources would go to the service not of any individual capitalists and their parasites but of the community as a whole. This was a great and commanding idea, calling for arduous and self-sacrificing work from all; and just as when Lenin, like a new Moses, came down from his mountain with the new tables of his law, now the call rallied the Communist Party and awoke a new spirit of public service in the young. This was the genesis of the five-year plans.

IX

INDUSTRIAL PLANNING

(1928-33)

PETER THE GREAT HAD PLANNED EXTENSIVELY—IN FACT, HE had even made a five-year plan for industry, thoughtlessly condemned by the Bolshevik historian Pokrovsky before he knew what his friend Stalin was going to do. Within the conditions of his times, Peter was exhaustive in his industrial survey— he even took minute thought for the utilisation of by-products, for instance, peat. No doubt that is one of the many good reasons why he is sometimes regarded as the first Bolshevik.

State planning was set up by the Communists long before Stalin became the master, and the best minds were drawn into this work. It began with Lenin's attempt to achieve the quickest transition to the new State with the maximum of control by means of electrification (*Goelro*), which at the time was scoffed at by his critics as "electrifiction." Out of this arose a system of planning, which was constantly growing and extending and was incessantly amended and adapted to realities. In its extended form it works both through territorial and industrial units, that is, through local and through specialist institutions, and every rung of the state system of authority has been drawn into an active part in it. There are frequent, even daily reports. The Plan, so to speak, travels to and fro, upward and downward between the State Planning Commission at the top and the individual factory at the bottom. Every unit, down to the workers in a given factory, is required to discuss the practicability of the actual task set to it and to transmit its suggestions upward, and there is constant adaptation.

Planning is essential to any capitalist concern, but there can be no real comparison with the Russian system. It embraces not only production but every function of the life of the community: industry, agriculture, health and education—all come into the common reckoning. That is why it remains a single plan, though the issues are so vast and diverse that in this and the next two chapters we have to treat them separately. The planners have a bird's eye view of the whole.

Of course this would have been impossible where the State's control was not yet absolute and where it did not already possess a full and stratified system of organs for it to work through. The planners themselves are legion—thousands in Moscow alone. There are institutes and courses for their training, and the national Academy of Sciences has been active on this side of the work. There is a mass of research work, constantly subject to revision—for instance, the examination and comparison of family budgets. But throughout, the main drive, as in everything else in Russia, has to come from the Communist Party.

It must be borne in mind that the Plan had almost to start from scratch, if it was to turn Russia into a great industrial country, and that, too, so soon after the smashing up of nearly everything that had been achieved so far. The railway system, in spite of Witte's close attention to it, was still quite inadequate to the size of the country. In 1928, when, after a year's preliminary study, the first Five-Year Plan was put into operation, Russia's supply of motors was equivalent to 2 per cent of ours, or only equal to those of Greece, Egypt or China. The average income of the citizen was one-quarter of ours. To start from the beginning, the country had to be provided with the basic plant, which could not repay the State and its inhabitants until it could itself create those light industries which would be concerned in providing goods for consumers. This meant an enormous initial capital investment —as much as 30 per cent of the State budget, of which three-quarters was assigned to heavy industry. It was a colossal effort of "collective saving," for which every individual citizen would have to tighten his belt and, as the issue was clear, this was precisely the chief appeal in the Plan.

This effort had to be nation-wide; for all industrial production, which was the chief side of it, depended on food supplies for the greatly increased number of workers and on a surplus of grain for export, to provide the means of purchasing the necessary heavy machinery from abroad. This had to be done under the most disadvantageous conditions. The Soviet Union, after its wholesale confiscations, which included all foreign industrial capital in Russia, had the poorest credit possible, so that only short term loans were obtainable, whereas little can be done with short loans in Russia at any time, and least of all for such a gigantic enterprise as this. Just in the most critical year of the Plan came the European slump, which brought the prices of her goods so low abroad, that Russia had to pay dearly for everything that she bought there—an excess of 30 per cent, as has been calculated. And lastly the Plan involved a revolution in the supply and training of specialists, technicians, and mechanics, which at first was bound to emphasise Russia's long-standing dependence on foreign help.

Stalin's main part in the matter was the setting of various objectives with time-limits and providing the big drive both with compulsion and with stimulation exercised in turn; but that was, of course, the biggest contribution of all, and the Plan, in its essence, belongs to him. Just as foreign relations were eased by the new motto of "Socialism in one country," so foreign capitalists sat up and took note of the opportunities opened to them by the Five-Year Plan. Anything to do with Communist Russia was front-page news. The war, in alliance with the Western democracies, had brought all sorts of Allied missions to Russia. The Intervention had done much more to give numbers of intelligent foreigners of all nations a first-hand contact with the enormous possibilities of the country and particularly with its vastest and richest domain, Siberia. What a fascinating proposition—the utilisation at long last of all this natural wealth! It was something which might capture the imagination of any man with capital and enterprise.

It was the same for the foreign technician, with whose services Russia was less than ever in a position to dispense. In a country so poor in skilled knowledge as Russia, the immense casualties of the war, with the Civil War and the famine, in which it was especially the educated class that had been depleted, had to be reckoned not only in terms of officers or soldiers but also of technicians of all kinds, without whom even the existing rickety public services could not be carried on. The foreign technician saw a picture not only of a most novel and interesting experience but of scope for his vision and energy such as he could not hope to get in his own over-crowded country, and that in a land of the young, where seniority did not count.

The very shortage of Russian skill and experience opened a vast field for the Russian Komsomol. These young folk have regarded as their two most valuable schools the Civil War and the Five-Year Plan. But the second was far the more educative. The victories of peace are both more profitable and more satisfying than those of war. Russian labour, like the Russian technician, was in its present stage quite unequal to the huge task now prescribed to it. Generally, the Russian working man had proved physically incapable of the day's work of an ordinary American, and here he was ordered to get in front of America. A Russian engine-driver was physically incapable of constant and hurried traffic. Russian laziness—so far the most common feature of the Russian character—in the factories took the form of evasion of hard or prolonged work. From this came all sorts of so-called "breaches" in the prescribed plan; and into these breaches would be thrown a mass of enthusiastic Komsomols in a kind of economic picnic to clear up the mess—to cope with the stoppage of a coal mine, or to gather in a cotton crop that lay rotting in the fields. And this work was also a school of administrative problems; young persons found themselves in positions of high authority and responsibility, where quick decisions and quick action had to be taken. One of them told me with pride the ages and posts of his colleagues, mostly under thrity-five. In this great school, with its countless and far-reaching opportunities, was educated a whole new generation of vigorous young men.

The enthusiasm was inspired by the difficulties, and the difficulties were unending. Practically everything had to be created. The foreign technician was often at a loss in the lack of his most ordinary and primary instruments. Then there was the worker, who except under sheer compulsion, absolutely refused to be hurried. This led of itself to a simple and primitive sabotage, such as feigned illness or even putting machinery out of order. But there was more than this

There was active opposition. The leading Communists were former conspirators in a hide-and-seek war with the old police; they were fundamentally inoculated with suspicion, and were on the look out for any signs of ill-will. And had not they themselves made common use of sabotage to wreck the enterprises or services of the Tsar's Government?

And Trotsky had been one of them. On principle, he wanted the Five-Year Plan to fail, and was always saying it would; he wanted anything that would disprove Stalin's thesis that a Socialist Russia could be self-supporting and self-dependent. In the matter of Russian industry, all past history tended to prove his case. He had been much more prominent than Stalin in the early work of the revolution. He was able to use his countless connections with his old colleagues, of whom many agreed with him and many others, like most foreign observers, doubted of the success of the Plan. There is no doubt that before he was driven out of Russia he had organised extensive ramifications of opposition. The question became a personal feud between him and Stalin, on both sides regardless and ruthless.

In any case the Plan had to encounter deficiencies of all sorts. Its success, in all its earlier phases, depended on pitiless compulsion. Compulsion may produce quantity, but it cannot produce quality. Indeed, the Plan itself at first only reckoned by quantity. As mentioned already, the Soviet Press was always active enough in showing up deficiences of execution. To take two casual illustrations from it— twice the number of "rubbers" or galoshes might be produced as against the usual record, but they only lasted a quarter of the time; the requisite number of match-boxes was achieved, but some of them were found not to contain matches. It was calculated that about 40 per cent of the general output had to be discarded as scrap.

The issue was not merely economic but political, and even personal. Stalin was from primitive Georgia where, if they think necessary, they shoot at sight. His method in the suppression of opposition was extinction of the presumed opponent, and anything was done to prove the presumption. Russia had had a partial holiday from the Terror, but now it returned in full force. Plans are fallible; they do not allow for leakage or for accidents, but that was not to be taken into account. If the plan failed, someone must have tried to make it fail, someone was a "wrecker" and must be tried and punished as such. A Bolshevik imprisoned first by the Tsar and then by the Bolsheviks has made the following comparison.

The Tsar's police made every attempt to prove you guilty and you did all you could to defeat them, but you were punished only for what they succeeded in proving. The Bolshevist police had a simpler method. They wrote down what they intended you to say and badgered you days and nights on end until in sheer despair you would sign it. Take the published case of Vyacheslav Chernavin,[1] a distinguished Professor of Ichthyology, who was known to me before the Revolution. He was no politician—perhaps he may have been a Liberal. He was put in charge of the fishery service in the White Sea and told to bring about an enormous increase of the catch; he asked for the necessary trawlers, but never got them: he was asked to confess to deliberate "wrecking"; he refused; he was imprisoned, so was his wife; he was told that if he confessed, he would get a light sentence and she would be set free, if not, both would be kept prisoner. Both refused to give way, so he was sent as a convict to the Arctic, though still in charge of the fisheries; from there with his wife and their small boy, he escaped into Finland.

The technique of examination was as follows: You are waked in the small hours and are questioned for hours on end; there have been cases in which this went on for days and nights; your questioners relieve each other in relays; a fresh questioner may put the same question again in a different connection to see if you give a different answer; you are always asked to make a given prescribed admission of guilt: then the Plan will have been proved to be right, and you wrong. The prisoners, confined in common cells and therefore able to compare notes, also had their own technique. Stand up at all costs! If you are threatened with immediate execution, that is a good sign—they have not got the proof that they want. It is a grievous test of character, and hardly any two men will come out of it exactly alike. Some of our own people have had to go through it. The brave little Captain McCullagh for instance, author of several spirited books on Russia, had not unnaturally a hard time of it. So did Mr. H. V. Keeling, author of another book—skilled lithographer, trade unionist and athlete—but he knew how to deal with it. His cheerful and witty answers won the sympathy of one of his questioners, who suddenly asked him, "How do you manage to keep so fresh when we are asking you all these questions in the middle of the night?" "Oh, that's all right," said cheery Mr. Keeling. "I've been married for sixteen years." This quite exploded the examiners—but ordinarily it goes a grimmer way.

[1] *I Speak for the Silent.*

As time went on, those employed in the planning and even the higher chiefs began to find themselves charged with betraying the State interests. Owing to the unconvincing character of the methods of justice, this subject is still dark and mysterious. One of the best judgments on it is the book of Mr. John Littlepage, *In Search of Soviet Gold.* He was one of the higher foreign specialists employed, and sometimes accompanied the highest commissars abroad when they were making State contracts, and from his knowledge of the detail, it seemed to him several times that there was some large gap in the accounts which he could not explain. He says, too, that several of the "accidents" which he witnessed must have been planned deliberately. It was not a question of neglect but of the evident removal of essental parts of the machinery.

Charges of this kind began to be taken even more sceptically abroad when they were made against foreign technicians, as was done with German specialists employed in the Donets mines in the big Mines Case in 1928. On the other hand, Russians involved in cases of "wrecking" were very often charged with having made contact with agents of foreign powers in Russia, especially with those of Germany and Japan. The question came home to us here in the notable trial of employees of Metro-Vickers in 1933; no one here seriously believed that these British engineers had been monkeying with their own machinery. The origin of the case seems to have been this. At a time when the State was not contemplating further extensive purchases of foreign machinery, a circular was sent out to factories to examine carefully the efficiency of what they already had. This for OGPU and the judicial authorities suggested a "wreckers' trial," and Vickers' men were arrested and examined in the usual way. One of them, a vigorous fellow who could look after himself, when he had answered questions for several hours, insisted on a rest; next day he was told he would be released, but he refused to go till his watch and keys were returned to him. This, in the judgment of Russians who have had this experience, is exactly the right treatment. But another proved to be a weak link and was kept on till he had at last given in and signed everything that was asked of him. In court he retracted his confession; he was removed for a while and made it again when he came back. The British Ambassador protested strongly against the arrest, but it was impossible to claim special immunity for foreigners; if they came and worked in Russia, they were of course subject to Soviet law. Both sides were on uncertain ground; there was a compromise; the trial was completed, but the sentences were not enforced, and the "convicted" were expelled from Russia.

But Stalin did not by any means limit his methods to compulsion. Always the Bolsheviks held that compulsion and encouragement should be applied in turn, as might meet the case concerned. Equality has been denounced as a shibboleth, and piece-work with payment proportionate to value has been restored wholesale. A Donets miner, Stakhanov, devised his own system of rationalisation by which he could greatly exceed the task allotted to him. His immediate superiors regarded his feat with some perplexity, but Stalin at once made a national hero of him and set him up for universal imitation. There are now Stakhanovites—or record-breakers—everywhere, and their "records" are everywhere given the greatest publicity. The extra output is not paid at the same rate, but progressively higher. Some workers earn even more than their directors. Of course this enabled the government to raise the norms of work. The most common criticism is that the general strain, becoming almost obligatory for all, is not in the long run conducive to efficiency. But those who knew the old Russia will probably agree that the Russians could well afford to be hurried, and certainly the American or British levels of efficiency had not yet been reached. Another stimulant used is competition; this word is avoided, and it is called "social joint emulation." The achievements of rival factories or units of shock-workers are matched against each other. Even in the prison camps the same principle is applied: there are ways of earning money or, what is valued far more, the right to visits of one to five days from wife and family.

It was clear that the objectives set in the plan were much higher than the attainment. The results anounced were usually reduced in later estimates. It may have been good tactics to set the aim higher than could be achieved; but a great deal of the work put up in the first plan soon showed signs of crumbling. In the hurry to get each new enterprise to work, the housing of the workers was often, and for a long time, almost entirely neglected. But the first industrial plan did accomplish more than could have seemed at all possible; nearly a hundred big industrial towns came into being—some of them in parts where so far there had been no industry, for instance at the back of India. An excellently arranged Exhibition of Construction shows the chequered history of the Plan: the mistakes that were made and the lessons that were learned; for instance, the central site chosen for one big

new town proved to be a bog; a study of the local winds was
necessary before fixing on which side of the factory the workers'
quarters should be set up. The Plan certainly succeeded in
making the country feel that it had received a great push
towards industrialisation. Workers who had at first found
themselves hopelessly incompetent in handling expensive foreign machinery, in the detail of their work began to make quite
useful little homely inventions of their own. The Russian has
a ready resource: a machine is for him an interesting toy; it
was like when Peter the Great, in his visit to Holland and
England, used to take any instrument into his hands to see
if he could work it himself. And Peter certainly learned.

In the second five years (1933-8) very much more attention
was paid to quality. A great deal of taste was put into the newer
big buildings: one did not at all feel that the peculiar charm
of Moscow was spoilt by them, and the new architecture, often
very original and striking, seemed quite to fit in with the rest.
The planners felt that the one "proletarian" State in the world
ought to show the dignity of a great people in its work; the
Metro, for instance, is magnificent and even palatial.

In the second plan the asphalting of the main streets went
apace. By the end of 1935 it might be said that the corner had
been turned, and the city was plastered with some words of
Stalin. "Now, comrades, life is better, life is brighter." The
enormous assignment for fundamental construction in the
first plan, now largely gave way to the provision of goods of
consumption. This could only be done when the main plant had
been laid down; but once it was there, set going with all the
force and purpose of a socialist State, the actual goods came
out at a tremendous pace. In 1931 there were hardly any cars;
by 1935 I found the streets covered with them. Naturally and
of set purpose, as compared with the past, a levelling down
went with the levelling up. Good boots were rare, but the un-
shod now had mediocre footwear. So it seemed with other
clothing. The magazines and stores seemed full enough and
were crowded with customers. The general atmosphere was one
of lively satisfaction with the long-awaited and long-worked-
for holiday, and stimulation seemed for the general mass of
people to have taken the place of compulsion.

Then came another change, as the impending danger of
a new European war loomed larger. A far greater share of
the budget now went to national defence. This made a very
considerable dent in the growing prosperity: in some respects
it seemed to have reversed the motion. Also there was a new
atmosphere of militarisation. As industry itself came to be

more and more militarised, the State had less desire to use foreign expert help; and the young American or British technicians began to foresee an end to what had been a period of happy endeavour. The plans themselves had been a great school; Russia now had almost enough technicians of her own, and would ordinarily henceforward call in the foreigner only as a consultant for a special task with a time-limit.

Communist Russia, born in the throes of foreign intervention, has never got free of its obsession that the capitalist States all around her are planning her overthrow. National defence was one of the principal objects which Stalin had always had in view in the first Five-Year Plan. War cannot now be made without munitions. Russia could never supply herself adequately with them in World War I, and had to depend for the most part on the charity or avarice of her Allies. Perhaps it will be found that the most important of all the results of the Five Year industrial plans and the best justification for them will be that Russia will never again have to depend to the same extent on the outside world for instruments of defence.

But there is one other result of all this planning which should be noted here. Stalin, for the contentment of his people, could afford to give it a holiday when he was able at last to provide it with a moderate supply of articles of consumption. In the great trials which followed, Radek and others gave evidence of a convincing kind that the success of the plan, that is, Stalin's success in his great duel with Trotsky, meant that plotting was losing hope and purpose. But if all the old happy-go-lucky methods of production have been uprooted and replaced by a State apparatus which allows of no loopholes, the artificial new system is very delicate and is in need of the most careful nursing. Already I have said enough to indicate what have been the effects even of precautionary provisions for the defence of the country. That is why it had necessarily to be one of the first cares of Stalin to keep the country as long as possible out of war.

X

AGRICULTURE COLLECTIVISED
(1928-33)

IN REALITY THERE WERE THREE SIMULTANEOUS FIVE-YEAR plans, running concurrently from 1928 to 1933, and the second was a far more difficult challenge than the first. It was hard enough to industrialise agricultural Russia at this rate, but it was very much harder to socialise agriculture itself. Here Stalin was attempting what Lenin had failed to do and what Trotsky had only talked about. But he was quite logical, and ha had the courage of his logic. As he put it plainly, to socialise Russian industry and to leave Russian agriculture individualistic—actually more individualistic than before—was to fail to socialise Russia. But this task demanded the utmost daring and the utmost ruthlessness. If world revolution had to wait, as it evidently intended to do, that did not mean that Stalin was less enterprising than Trotsky: but his daring took a direction which was in line with his program, namely, of completing the socialisation of the country with which he had to deal. At the beginning of 1930 he announced that this was to be "the year of the great change."

It meant putting the clock violently back. Not that the old village commune was to be restored: quite the reverse. Nor that the utterly unworkable strip system was to remain; that was to go anyhow. But it meant cutting short the victory of the peasantry and making them take an opposite path, which they had clearly shown that they detested.

Lenin had seen how the village community was differentiating itself into farmers and rural labourers. According to him there were three classes in the peasantry: the "kulaks," the middle peasants and the impoverished. "There was a time, my dear," said an old peasant blacksmith of over seventy to the best writer on this subject, Maurice Hindus, "when we were just neighbours in the village. We quarrelled, we fooled, sometimes we cheated one another, but we were neighbours. Now we are poor, middle and kulaks. I am a 'middle.' Boris here is a 'poor,' and Nisko is a 'kulak,' and we are supposed to have a class war—pull each other's hair or tickle each other on the toes, eh? One against the other, you understand? What the devil?"[1] Lenin had set up committees of poverty in the villages, and had backed the impoverished against the rest just as Stolypin had backed the well-to-do, but he had had to beat a retreat in face of the famine. It was the well-to-do or "kulaks" who had won and were so far masters of the situation.

The word "kulak" means a fist. It was used before the Revolution for hard-fisted merchants or for peasants who got a hold over their fellows and were probably village usurers. They also gained power ovver others by hiring labour, or leasing out machinery or land. It was now used wholesale as a word of abuse for any who used machinery or em-

[1] *Red Bread*, p. 32.

ployed hired labour—in short, for the thrifty, who were the natural leaders of the village. "Actually," writes Hindus, "a kulak is a successful farmer as success is measured in Russia." Of one such he writes: "He was one of the so-called well-to-do, though by no stretch of the imagination could he have been called that in America, Germany, England or any other western land."

State farms, it has been mentioned, had been tried in the period of militant communism, and had proved a failure; either they had collapsed or they had fallen exactly into the hands of those for whom they were not intended, namely the more prosperous peasants, and state authority in the villages had itself fallen under peasant influence. They were to be tried again on a larger scale; but the Government did not hope to make so complete a change all at once, and for the present it put its hopes in in a milder form of its medicine, the collective farm, in which the peasants would have some measure of self-government. What the peasantry wanted was to go forward with its individual farming, while widely co-operating with each other in securing machinery and in marketing their goods. They were to be driven into collective farms, and this task, like other "forced marches" in the Communist program, was largely entrusted to the Komsomols. Force was used on the largest scale, and in the spring of 1930 the young enthusiasts reported that two-thirds of all the farms in the country were already collectivised. This was only on paper; the peasants might have been driven into collectivism but the farm work was being ruined. Stalin himself called them off in a famous article, entitled "Giddiness from success," and authorised the peasants to go forward with their spring sowing in their own way: otherwise there would have been no crops. As soon as the pressure was withdrawn, the new "collective farms" in most cases collapsed of themselves. But Stalin was not retreating. The task was resumed with a new soberness and with the necessary preliminary spade-work.

To start with, individual farmers were almost taxed out of existence and ringed round with restrictions of sales to Government monopolies. One, for instance, has to pay 150 roubles on his wool-carding machine and to bring in a huge amount of rye to the grain collection. Then, as the Government grimly put it, the peasants were "faced with the choice." This was followed by an individual attack on all who were labelled kulaks—and the labelling was often fixed by local rivals or enemies. Thousands of Communists and Red Army soldiers were sent down to the villages; the local paupers pointed out the victims. The condemned man and his wife were deprived of everything they had—house, stock, implements and everything else—put into carts in what they stood up in, and carried away to concentration camps, to work there as slaves of the Government. There were heartrending scenes.

Maurice Hindus, himself a native of a Russian village, had become a distinguished American man of letters. He returned to Russia to see the new experiment, with which he was and remained in sympathy. In his two very remarkable books *Broken Earth* and *Red Bread*, he gives us far the best pictures of what happened. In *Red Bread* he describes the collectivisation of his old village.

In his pages you can actually hear the peasant voices raised in indignation at this savage interruption of their old ways of life. "Barracks for life," says one. "Serfdom—that's what it is," says another. "You cannot put together a broken heart as you can a broken wagon," says a woman. A so-called "kulak" describes to him how he was deprived of everything, he and his wife, and sent off—"with my bare hands, so to speak"—to the north, packed close in luggage vans with numbers of others, and only brought back because his son is a Communist. "They have been dreadfully religious since they have been back," the son comments. "When we live long in one place and have a family, we are like an oak," says the old man, "we get rooted deep in the very soil on which we live, and when we are pulled up we just wilt and die."[1] "I could have got off and kissed every patch of this dear earth of ours," he says of his journey. "If we had known what was coming," says another, "we would never have bothered to work."

Hindus writes sympathetically of "the peasants with their burden of torture and bafflement," and he describes the whole class as "like grass torn out by the roots." For the mass it is a "forcible persuasion." He asks one if he is a member of the *kolhoz* (collective farm). "What else is there to be?" is the reply. "They don't let you live if you're not," says another.

In his pages you can see also the fanaticism of the Komsomols. Hindus tells us how some, but not all, of themselves felt the horror of what they were doing, which they carried through as a stern duty. Of one of these executants he writes: "She seemed no more concerned with the peasant's perplexity than is a surgeon with the pain of the patient over whose body he is wielding a scalpel. Her mind and heart were fixed on the

---

[1] *Red Bread*, pp. 243-5.

glories of tomorrow as she visualised them, not on the sorrows of today. The agony of the process was lost to her in the triumph of achievement." "But wasn't it a cruel procedure?" he asks another. "Of course it was," she says, "but do you suppose it was a joy for us to go through the villages throwing people out of their houses and confiscating their possessions? We are not entirely bereft of feelings." One of her comrades at the touching appeal of a little daughter of a "kulak" was so upset that he had to run out of the house to hide his tears. "And did he go back and continue the liquidation?" "Of course he did. He had to. The kulak is the bourgeois in the village and he has to go."

In many places there was the most stubborn joint resistance, culminating even in pitched battles and interspersed with isolated assassinations. The Government reckoned that there were as many as a million families on the list of the condemned which in Russia, with an average of two parents and three children, is taken to amount to five million persons. This does not mean that they were all destroyed; sometimes they were simply moved to other and worse land, perhaps outside the neighbourhood, and later moved on further, as the new collectivisation spread over the country; but as "kulaks" they were liquidated, that is, they ceased to exist as such.

The peasant was now "faced with the choice." The fight had been stubborn, but active opposition had been broken. Of course every "middle peasant" would want if possible to become well-to-do—that meant getting on in life, as he understood it—but by now he had a mortal fear of challenging the fate of the labelled "kulaks." There was no alternative but to do as he was told and enter the collective farm; but he determined, as far as possible, to go empty-handed.

Bolshevik officials have noted an extraordinary unanimity in the peasantry: "we don't know what they will do," one of them had said earlier, "but whatever it is, they will all do the same thing." This was not organisation: it was instinct; with their shrewd minds, in their old and new battles with their masters, the same ideas would present themselves to all. The Government's idea was that all stock should be pooled; this had even been done in the first of the new collective farms. The peasant thought that if the Government wanted him to go to the *kolhoz* it was for the Government to look after him there and, if the stock was to be pooled, he would prefer to go in with as little as possible. There followed all over the country a colossal slaughter of livestock. There was nothing that the peasant regarded as more specially "property"

than his cow; and indeed, whatever the advantages of brigades
in agriculture, they can hardly replace the individual care of
an owner for his cattle. The livestock of the country was reduced to one-third; half the horses, sheep and goats. The general supply of meat and wool sank to one-third. This was in
itself a public catastrophe.

In any case the Government scheme was a challenge to all
ordinary calculations. It was the well-to-do peasants who
had restored the prosperity of the country during the NEP;
it was they, too, who had supplied the national surplus for
export. The Government intended to fill the gap by mech-
anising agriculture as quickly as possible. There is no question that there was a great field for advance on this side.
Stolypin, in his land settlement, had put all the best technical advice and help at the disposal of the individual farmer,
and that had been one of the chief factors in his success.
Agriculture, it will be remembered, on the Stolypin lines,
had advanced by leaps and bounds before the Revolution;
and there were individual peasants now who said that if
both of the two conflicting principles received the same help
from the State, it would soon be possible to judge of the
practical merits of each.

The god of the new regime was the motor. Motor tractor
stations were set up everywhere at central points and took
the *kolhoz* under their leadership. But to replace the old
sources of supply, all this had to be done very quickly; it
was not quickly that the peasant would adapt himself to
the new machinery, and everywhere there was an immense
amount of wastage, quite possibly sometimes intentional, which
came under the same conception of "wrecking" as the Government was following in its industrial plan. The gap could
not so soon be made good. For the first year, it is true, the
Government had the very substantial advantage of its wholesale confiscations of all that had belonged to the "kulaks"—
worth 400 million roubles according to Hindus[1]—and it was
able to announce an adventitious success; but the sharp break
in the agricultural life of the country and all the social convulsions that accompanied it soon brought it to famine conditions not far less terrible than those which had induced Lenin
to retreat. There are no sure estimates on this subject, and
there was no Government admission and no organised foreign
help; but the loss of life is generally held to have been as much
as five millions. Russia disappeared from the world grain-
market and had to import large grain supplies from abroad.

[1] *Red Bread*, p. 74.

There was another adventitious advantage which the Government gained from its appropriation of the "kulaks." Pretty well any successful peasant might be labelled "kulak" through the jealousy of his neighbours, so that the word came to mean little more than a thrifty peasant, and this was the best labour in Russia, with not only mind but character behind it. The concentration camps which the Government had set up near the beginning of its regime were originally stocked with "social enemies"—priests or intelligentsia, many of them the most unsuitable persons to send to cut an appointed day's quota of timber in the forests of the extreme north. Where was the use of sending an aged priest with hernia? How much timber would he cut? He was only sent there to die off, as the prisoners were even told frankly on their arrival; they were given superhuman tasks and left in the forests without food if they could not complete them. The savageries of these camps were becoming known abroad through the few successful fugitives, just when the camps began to be recruited with the new and quite different labour supply. Now there was an enormous increase in their population, and these were healthy and sturdy fellows. With them were many of the best and most independent of Russian specialists, likewise impounded for the state service. The camps began to take on a new and useful character. OGPU, which controlled them and was almost like a State within the State, became a very important public enterprise. It has even been charged with cutting down prices on the ordinary and less privileged fficial producing agencies. In its search for foreign currency the Government was often ready to take almost any price for its timber or butter. This was not necessarily a deliberate policy of dumping; it arose simply out of the needs of the Soviet State, and if human lives were so cheap in Russia, this was a way of turning them to advantage.

But the Russian peasant is above all things tenacious. He has the vital quality of "lasting out," claimed for Russia by Pushkin. He lives in a world of his own dreams and aspirations: he believes the land to be of right his own, and so he had been told by the revolutionary Narodniks, and even in the first land decree of the Soviet Government, which claimed all the land for those who laboured on it. When the peasants began to join the *kolhozy* wholesale, the old ideas presented themselves in the form of new difficulties for the Government. It had been found earlier and was found now that those sent to manage the peasants, whether by fear or natural sympathy, tended to take the colour of their ideas. Specially competent individual farmers might take the lead inside the farms, and guide them in their own direction. There were cases where communities of Christians or even monks used the occasion to start their own collective farms. Anything of this last kind was stamped out at once.

The crisis of collectivisation came in 1931. There was a crop failure, and it synchronised with the world slump, which made it so difficult to obtain good prices abroad for Soviet grain, timber and oil, and therefore to buy the heavy plant required for the industrial plan. In 1932 the crop was again bad. Peasants who secreted some of the grain grown by them for their own use were decreed to be "grain thieves of socialised property" and punishable with death as "social enemies." Sometimes they consumed the seed supply, as was also done by Red Army soldiers sent to guard it. They would plant potatoes, as ordered, but at night would dig them up and eat them. Beggars were even coming from Ukraine to get crumbs of the grain grown there and taken to Moscow. In the Kuban area the Cossack population showed open resistance and was removed wholesale. Ukraine was put under specially rigorous control from the centre. Yet in spite of all difficulties the Plan went unrelentingly forward.

In strengthening its own control, the Government utilised the economic domination of the Motor Tractor Stations. It also set up a new unit of labour, the so-called "labour day." As there were many forms of employment on the farm—including for instance leadership, education, medical service, and accountancy—a common unit was required in the distribution of profits after the quota demanded had been supplied to the State, and this allowed of a differentiation in the rates of remuneration. A "labour day" did not necessarily correspond to a day's work; it was the amount reckoned by the Government to have been earned if the duties in question had been carried out efficiently.

Stalin, as before all things a practical man, had no room for inefficiency. He was beginning to encourage the skilled worker or the trained professional man to come out of his shell and do his best. The old formula that the State would provide everyone working for it "according to his needs," though retained for the utopia of the future, had long since in practice gone to limbo; the new formula read "according to his work." Stalin went so far as to denounce equality contemptuously as a shibboleth. As with industry, so with agriculture, compulsion began to be varied by encouragement. With these methods, introduced after the first hectic

mistakes, collectivisation went rapidly and steadily forward
till only an insignificant proportion of the agricultural production of the country still lay outside it.

The essence of the *kolhoz* lies in the system of brigades.
There was something of this in the old village commune,
though it was very vague and primitive. The work was to
a certain extent regimented, especially if in primitive conditions, as in Siberia. The elected village elder would send
a man round with a stick to summon all Heads of Houses
to a meeting—for instance, to decide when to go haymaking
in common. But that is only the feeblest precedent to the
stern regimentation of today. The *kolhoz* workers are divided
into brigades—each with a leader and an allotted task, and
in the *kolhozy,* as in the factories, there are shock-workers
to get a move on, who are regarded with special favour. Sir
John Russell saw, posted up in a farm, a diagram noting the
speed of work of each brigade in different categories, pic-
turesquely represented by tortoise, donkey, bicycle, train, auto-
bus and plane; six of the seven brigades were awarded "first
class."[1] The brigade system is at its best in the three main
events of the agricultural year—ploughing, sowing and reaping.
There is certainly a strong corporate spirit of loyalty in the
Russian peasant which makes him feel that he ought to be
ashamed of not doing his best for the common good. For
such work as the care of livestock the system is far less
fitted; but there are *kolhozy* devoted specially to stock-breed-
ing; and even in any *kolhoz* there are grooms and cattle-keepers
whose special job it is to look after the animals, and their
housing and tending is such as was not to be found in a pre-
revolution village.

The *kolhoz* has to contribute a fixed quota of its produce
to the government. In lean years it was a common complaint
that the planners failed to allow for variations in the yield
and that the government, in exacting what had been fixed
in advance, did not take account of how much was left over
for the actual producers. The Motor Tractor Stations take a
good share for their services, which every farm is obliged
under penalty to employ. A certain part of this total produce
is set aside for seed; another section of the "budget" is reserved
to pay for social services. When all dues have been discharged,
the remainder is distributed to the members according to the
number of labour days earned by each. This distribution is made
by the general meeting, which elects its own Chairman and
Audit Committee; the Chairman is apparently always a Com-

[1] Sir E. J. Russell in *Slavonic Review,* No. 47, pp. 320-340.

munist or on the list of candidates for the Party. The division was at first reckoned by "mouths" and not by working hands, but this way has been abandoned. Five per cent was also at first allowed on the value of property brought in, but this too appears to have been dropped. After three years of testing, former kulaks and their children may now be admitted to mem· bership; also the children of those who till lately were deprived of the franchise, after similar trial.

The *kolhoz* may only sell to the Government, which as maintaining and supporting it, pays only a very small proportion of the market value. Latterly, a very limited retail market is allowed at certain seasons of the year—at neighbouring towns or stations. For satisfactory sales to itself the Government allows priority in the obtaining of town manufactures. It is calculated by Sir John Maynard, expert in Indian agriculture, who made a very thorough study of the whole of this subject, that the Government took 18 per cent of the produce, the Motor Tractor Stations 18 per cent, and the contribution to seed grain is about 14 per cent. He reckoned (. 1936) that the peasant's earnings were still less than they were before the Revolution or in the six years following it, but that the cultivated area had increased by 25 per cent.[1]

Sir John Russell, then Director of our own Experimental Station of Agriculture at Rothamsted, who used to make periodical investigations in Russia, considered that in food supply the peasant was probably rather better off than before, but livestock was still much below the pre-war level. He found twice or even four times as many workers engaged in a given job as with us, and the work worse done. He hardly ever met illiterates. He found beds in the rooms (which he would not have found before) and "generally an icon" (or religious painting), usually by the side of portraits of the Communist leaders. The more recent houses were better built. In his visits of 1930 and 1934 the peasants were "extremely dissatisfied . . ." I have myself heard the same period described as "war" both by government officials and by peasants. He saw a great gap between town and country in Russia, with "no sight of any approach." "The peasant," he wrote in 1938, "is solely interested in how much he can get out of the kolhoz. I never in the villages met anything but a desire to earn as much as possible while there was a chance of doing it. His desire is to be secured in the holding of his land, to be left in peace to look after his animals and his crops."

[1] Sir J. Maynard in the *Slavonic Review*, No. 43, pp. 47-69.

There are other contrasts between the old village and the new in which the advantage is overwhelmingly on the side of the second. There is always a school. Any large village has a hospital, possibly with more than one doctor. In 1936 the amount and quality of goods, for instance of town food products which one could now find in the co-operative store, might have made a pre-revolution peasant open his eyes. Such children as used to go barefoot—for instance in the primitive Pinsk marshes—may now have stockings and some kind of shoes. There is sure to be a library, with local or general newspapers. There are also lectures—mainly political. Then there is the wireless, which is in itself a revolution in the village life. Old traditional amusements, such as music and dancing, are fostered and directed. Certainly all ways back to the old conditions have been decisively broken up.

XI

ANTI-RELIGION

(1928-33)

THERE WAS YET A THIRD SIDE TO THE FIRST FIVE-YEAR PLAN, and it concerned education. The Communist leaders felt seriously troubled by this question, as we left it in an earlier chapter. Very very few of the best professors were Communists; were their students likely to be so? The government had got as far as putting a number of the best professors over the frontier. Here too a new drive was undertaken, but with anything but happy results. The Academy of Sciences, founded just after the reign of Peter the Great, had a splendid record of faithful study and courageous independence which the Tsars themselves had seldom dared to challenge; for, as has been said, nothing in Russia was more courageous than learning. Now it was attacked wholesale. It was to teach everything according to the principles of Marxism as the Party from time to time understood them.

There was one outstanding figure whom it did not dare to touch, for he was one of the great glories of Russia in the world of scholarship. This was Professor Pavlov, the first of living physiologists. Science was always a side of learning which the Communists did their best to foster; it was always dear to the Russian and it was indispensable for the public services. Pavlov's studies were helped in every way. This could in no way affect his independence. When he came on any point in

his lectures which suggested plain speaking, he took the opportunity; no one present forgot the application which he gave
to the reflexes of animals when put under artificial inhibitions,
openly comparing them to the paralysis produced by the Communist domination. He was left immune. From the time of the
attack on the Academy he would never enter its doors again.

Others of the most eminent scholars, without the unique
European fame of Pavlov, were not so fortunate. This time
they were not expelled from the country, but sent to prison
and exile, and most of them died out there. When Professor
Chernavin came to England after his prison experience, he
was able to say something of the whereabouts (in prison)
of about a hundred prominent Russian scholars, whose names
and works were known to foreign colleagues in their various
subjects. In 1923 a Communist Academy got to work. Learning is a thing which dies under compulsion: totalitarian teaching can never be more that totalitarian rubbish, because it
does not come from the teacher himself, but from someone
who stands over him. But there was a poignant fascination in
watching how, under the successive dictates of the bosses of
the time, scholars, while paying the tribute to Karl Marx
which the times demanded, contrived—for instance, in such
a favourite subject as literary criticism—to interpret him in
their own individual ways. It was as if under the piecrust the
blackbirds were still managing to sing their own various tunes.

But, as earlier, the Communists were not nearly so afraid
of scholarship as of religion. They were constantly bearing
witness to its vitality and persistence. By now the organisation of all religious bodies had been entirely smashed. For a
time the Baptists and other "non-conformists" had comparatively escaped. Now they came in for the common lot. Believers were reduced to the conditions of the catacombs: it
was almost impossible for their highest authorities to visit
them: most of these had by now died out in Siberia or in
the prison camp of Solovetsk, where to the last a number of
Orthodox bishops, as a Guild of Fishers reminiscent of the
Lake of Galilee, joined in the Eucharist each morning. Training of new ministers was also practically impossible, though
curious attempts were made by a correspondence college working through a government press on government paper.

As to the Government's own propaganda, it was for the
most part beneath criticism and never found a way that led
to any solid success. The arguments usually put forward did
not deserve any—that the Holy Communion encouraged drunkenness and circulated infection: or even the evidence of two

airmen solemnly printed at a later date in the chief newspaper of the country, that they knew there were no gods
because they had been up in the skies and could not find
them. Great reliance was placed on the machine, as producing
better crops than any amount of time wasted in prayers. Karl
Marx might well have shivered at the utter unintelligence of
some of those who interpreted his materialism for him. The
favourite plea was that the achievements of science had left
no room for mystery or mysticism. In the Anti-Religious Museum of Moscow, where opposite walls were devoted respectively to the religious and the scientific explanations of phenomena,
the human soul was illustrated by a diagram of the nervous
system. The agents of the crusade misread their clever public
when they bored it with the eternal dinning of these superfi-
cialities.

As a matter of fact, the best medicine which the Russian
Church could have had after the terrible corruption of the
last years of Tsardom was a very strong dose of persecution;
in such matters the energy of the persecutor over-reaches
itself. The beautiful ritual with its heart-searching music was
historical and traditional and was somehow maintained with
loving care, for the Communists never attacked the celebration
of the rite as such. For the rest, all sorts of frippery that had
surrounded religion fell away in tatters of itself, like contro-
versial notes that might be pencilled on the margin of a Bible.
It was in fact to plain Bible Christianity that the Church was
brought back. That was what gave the Baptists their chance;
and the Soviet Press gave constant evidence of the vigour
with which they were using it. The fall of Tsardom had been
also the fall of Byzantium, with its pomp and formalities, and
the present sufferings of the Orthodox priests brought them
infinitely nearer to their flocks. In the compulsory public debates in which the priest might have to engage with professional propagandists of atheism he often found his best support in the shrewd intelligence of the peasant. Anti-religious
museums were set up, but the lessons which they taught were
negative and therefore empty. All that they could do—and
that was easy enough—was to point out the gross misinterpreta-
tions of the gospel which mar the histories of all churches, but
the original main content, as shown in the life of the proletarian
Jesus, remained unscathed. The formal State adherence of all
in Tsarist times was gone, and it was nothing that need be
greatly missed. The inner core of the spiritual life of Russian
Christianity was probably never stronger than now, when sufferings for the faith were common to all believers. The Com-

missar of Education, Lunacharsky, who as such had led the attack, made the damning admission, "Religion is like a nail, the harder you hit it the deeper it goes into the wood."

The crusade against all religious was led by a man of great intelligence and ability, Emelyan Yaroslavsky, now dead, who was also conspicuous on other sides of Russian public life. He was President of the Union of the Godless, at first a "volunteer" organisation. It could not have existed without the active partonage of the Government, of which Yaroslavsky was an important member. This society languished and made little mark: Yaroslavsky constantly complained of the luke-warmness of his followers. On the other hand, he was always pointing to the activity of the church organisations which set themselves to take an active part in the work of social services, one of the very best achievements of the government. The Komsomol and the Trade Unions, on the other hand, would pass formal votes requiring the extinction of religion, but not put a hand to the work. The Trade Unions, he wrote in 1937, so far from promoting anti-religious propoganda, have "liquidated it"; "they have ruined what had been done." Yaroslavsky directed that the attack should be aimed not at the congregations—the foolish closing of a church would alienate the very people whom they wished to convince—but against the ministers of religion as handing on the infection.

In 1929, simultaneously with the other Five-Year Plans—the Government itself instituted another great drive against religion. To start with, the Constitution itself was amended. So far it read: "Freedom of religious and anti-religious propaganda," representing the period when the "unofficial" Union of the Godless had failed so signally. Now the words "religious and" were struck out; only anti-religious propaganda was legal (April 14, 1929). Also a number of so far casual and sometimes local ordinances were bundled together into an omnibus law (April 8). In a word, the churches were debarred from all the social activities in which they had competed with the government, and were restricted entirely to the organisation and performance of worship. They might not organise any mutual or co-operative societies, no children's playgrounds, reading-rooms or medical help. They might not have any central fund, possess property, lease quarters "or conclude any kind of agreement or bargains whatsoever." Priests were forbidden to live within the towns, and had to come in from outside to do their work. They had often found homes among the peasantry, but such peasants as harboured them were more heavily taxed. Sometimes priests were arrested and imprisoned on charges of hoarding, because the parish funds were naturally passing through their hands. So far religious teaching had been excluded from the schools. Now anti-religious teaching was prescribed to all teachers. After a lecture to young children on Roman history which I heard admirably delivered, the teacher at the end stopped and, *à propos* of nothing, added, "And who was it who broke the yoke of religion? Charles Darwin, an Englishman." As it was accompanied by a bow to me, I took it that it was meant as a graceful compliment, but later she mentioned apologetically that it was the end of the term and the anti-religious idea had to be introduced somewhere.

I have always felt that this new rule was a great tactical mistake and a clear confession of failure. Russian children are infinitely more critical than German, and therefore far less suitable for spoon-feeding. To be constantly dinning in their ears the entirely negative idea that there is no God is just the way to stir up curiosity, and to suggest that even the teacher at heart half believes that there is one. If there is no God, why give Him all this constant attention? It reminds me of a Soviet book with a printed list of *errata*. "For God read god," and this was repeated with all the page references. It could hardly be excelled by the worst stupidities of the old censors of the Tsar: "God with a small g—official!"

Very much more effective were two other blows, aimed only indirectly at religion and connected with the other concurrent plans. The industrial plan introduced a five-day working week with no holiday; the workers took their holidays in shifts on the different working days. This was received with great dissatisfaction, for as members of a family would be working in different concerns, they could not take their rest-day together. The town workers were just that class which it was most inadvisable to displease, and the five-day week was altered to a six-day one: five for work and one for rest or holiday in common. Anyhow, this knocked out Sunday, and all the other days of the old week, and even visitors very soon came to forget which of them it was. Meanwhile, the Church stuck firmly to the old week, and even to the belated Orthodox calendar, thirteen days behind, a survival of Tsardom which the Soviet Government had early put in line with the rest of the world. As absence from work was an offense seriously punished and leave would certainly not be given for church attendance, the Sunday congregations were very much thinned down, except on the great feast days, which the Government did not dare to touch. Foreign visitors were not informed enough to take account of this, and thought the falling off was due to lack of interest, but they should have compared what they saw with week-day congregations here or those of a Sunday afternoon.

The other heavy blow came through collectivisation; this made it very easy to close the one village church by a vote—as usual by show of hands—of the majority. In fact the young pioneers of collectivisation from outside at first closed churches all round with such violence that Yaroslavsky himself found reason to protest. It was no longer a question whether some wanted to attend church, but whether the community as a whole would decide to convert the building to some other use—for instance a club or reading-room. This was found very much easier than forcible closing, which had often been met with fierce opposition and even with fighting. The priests, supported by the more prominent peasants, had of course resented this violent invasion of the village, with such tragical consequences, and they were now accused of preaching brotherly love—clearly an offence against the class war. Many churches which had lasted on bravely through all the early years now ceased to function.

The closing of town churches also went on rapidly with the new general offensive against religion; but this meant that the choirs of those which remained were greatly reinforced, and there was no more impressive experience in Soviet Russia than to join in the enormous crowds which attended on Christmas or Easter Eve. When I was there, the large church was packed as tight as the crowd at an English Cup Final, the deacons could hardly make their way through to collect the offertory, and in the surrounding oppression the deep reverence of the worshippers was something that one could not forget; young and old were mingled freely there, and an equally large crowd was collected outside and waited patiently for two hours, to come in for a relay service immediately after the first. Here is how a priest has described church services in present-day Russia:

"Now a man comes into church only to pray, and not to show any-one that he is Orthodox. Now he is not given credit by anyone, but rather loses by it. And he prays till the very end of the service. Also, the priest has no reason to hurry. At home he has only his family and poverty and thoughts of tomorrow, but in the church, at the time of the service, he has his 'family,' that is, his flock, and nothing to trouble him. He has even wealth and satisfaction, for he has come here for the riches of the soul and here he has enough, because he is here with the 'Giver of all good things,' even for the whole world."

The country, by the admission of all, is much more religious than the towns, but here the closing of so many churches meant great distances for the worshippers to travel. Hindus has given us a pathetic picture of the country priest—"the puzzled little Father." "The garden and our cow and the dozen odd hens we have, give us the things we need, and we get along," says his wife. "The most important thing is not to lose one's courage and not to give up one's faith. . . . If one has faith and courage, one can live and one has something to live for. Don't you agree? . . . "But think of it," says the priest, "the whole youth of our land is drenched in contempt for Him and His church, and all over the country He and faith in Him are impudently mocked and spat upon —and nothing happens. . . . Don't you suppose if He made Himself known, people would flock back to Him? Of course they would. . . . Yet here we are, His servants—waiting, waiting, and nothing happens! The heavens are silent, the earth is silent, the stars are silent, everything is silent. . . . Sometimes I say to myself, if He does not care, why should we? Isn't He expecting too much of us? . . . And for Him with His power it would have been easy to do something big and decisive. Or is He merely trying us out, to see how much we can endure?" And the Saviour's dying cry comes back to us: "My God, my God, why hast Thou forsaken me?"[1]

During the recent war with Finland a number of Red Army prisoners were carefully examined by an emigrant Russian churchman; and the very objective picture which he obtained certainly confirmed the judgment of Yaroslavsky that religion, if starved of teaching, is still a live instinct in the Russian peasant, and that, in any case, the anti-religious propaganda has had little effect on him.

Yaroslavsky himself has given us a striking and by no means unsympathetic picture of the work of the many travelling missionaries of religion, who are now brought back to working in the conditions of the first scattered communities of Christians in history.

"The 'travelling missionary' goes about with his simple equipment. It can be packed in a travelling case: censer, communion wafers, a bottle of church wine for communion, a stole—that is all that is wanted; and the servant of religion travels from village to village, wherever he is invited. If he has not been there for a year, then he at once christens all who have been born since, marries all who have mated, sings the mass for all who have died, and receives an agreed payment, and goes on somewhere else. When the church has been closed in a district where there is still a large number of believers, the priest does not cease to be wanted."[2]

It is not numbers, but quality that counts; and to show

[1] *Red Bread*, pp. 256-266.
[2] Yaroslavsky, *On Anti-Religious Propaganda*.

more clearly the moral forces which are opposed to each other in Russia today, let me place here the tribute which a sturdy Russian parish priest, who lasted out the hardest years of the struggle, has paid to the strength of the Communist education as seen in a typical child, trained as a "pioneer" of the Communist faith under the new regime.

"The Pioneer can be distinguished, whether at home or at school or in the street, from children who do not belong. He is as different from 'the rest' as before the Revolution a pupil of any privileged school or institution differed from the 'free' pupil. He has been trained and educated in godlessness. Himself, he not only will not go to church, but as he passes the house of God he will not even notice it. Perhaps, if he chances on the priest, he will meet him and follow him with a peculiar look. In his sensible clever eyes there will be either astonishment or curiosity. But if his parents are believers and take him to church, he may do everything that he is told by his father, his mother or the priest, though according to his rules he would not dare to do so; and if his superiors heard of such behaviour, he would bear the punishment assigned as part of his 'pioneer discipline.' Lord! what a good child of our Mother the Church might be made of him!"

The Russian mind is essentially religious, and anti-religion is itself a religion. The fierceness of the battle has sometimes thrown primitive minds into fantastic vagaries which have been duly illustrated in the Anti-Religious Museums—strange and mystic visions, the sect of the Red Dragon, who preach a baptism of fire of all who have been born since 1917. But the one thing that the Russian cannot do is to get away from idealism. Take this fascinating example.

Sergius Bulgakov was one of the earliest prophets of Marxism in Russia, and became Professor of Economics in the mother university of Moscow. Under singularly dramatic conditions he underwent a conversion which is strikingly reminiscent of that of St. Paul. Under the Bolsheviks he became a priest and was expelled from the country. He was later Professor of Dogmatic Theology in the Orthodox clergy-training college at Paris. In a most remarkable epilogue to a theological dissertation on Judas Iscariot he has tried to forecast the future of religion in Russia. Making no pretence to defend the purity of church history against its critics, he sees in the Communist faith a burning desire to create that which we should interpret as "the kingdom of heaven on earth." "And we may hope," he adds, "that this will for the future is not displeasing to God, and will not be turned to shame." But they can no more destroy Christ than He was destroyed at the Crucifixion. Without the Crucifixion there could have been no Resurrection. For that, Russian Christianity had to go into the grave and "taste" death to the full. Christ is being crucified over again in Russia now, and he is rising again there now.

Yaroslavsky in his report of the work of the Union of the Godless in April, 1937, reckoned up the results of all its attacks; one-third of the townspeople and two-thirds of the country people were still religious, which means more than half of the whole; calculating only by the quotas of parish churchmen who have to guarantee their organisations to the State (with 30,000 parishes still at work), there is an active nucleus of nearly a million leading churchmen. He warns his followers against the delusion that religion is now only a concern of the elders.

In a recent census, believers were to declare themselves such; there are known to be many who evade the question, but the number of those who declared themselves was a surprise to the Government, and a new census was held soon afterwards in which the qustion as to belief was not repeated. If this is all the result of twenty years of battering at religion, Russia has surely a greater right than other countries to regard herself as religious.

In the period of the first Five-Year Plan (1928-33), all the main objects—to industrialise Russia at this tremendous pace, to collectivise agriculture, to dominate education and suppress religion—were dead against the wishes of the majority of the population. They were possible only in a totalitarian state and with a pitiless use of its apparatus. Any attempt at organised opposition was impossible. The State possessed practically all the instruments of destruction, and it is the range of their present-day destructiveness that explains why in so many countries power has passed into the hand of the few. A heroic dash against machine-guns is not now practical politics. As usual, the population sought refuge in evasion. Especially during the famine phase in the period of collectivisation, great masses of people were on the move in search of any better conditions, and in such circumstances government control almost lapses of itself.

It was to counter evasion that serfdom had come into being in old Russia, and the Government now sought the same remedies. The legislation of the end of 1932 and the beginning of 1933 was a *crescendo* of harshness. The factory worker, for one day's absence without permission from his work, forfeited the government allowance of food and quarters, which there was no other source to replace (November 16th, 1932). Food supplies were moved from the stores to the factories. No work, no food! (December 4th, 1932). A most odious feature of the old serfdom was the internal passport system introduced by Peter the Great to fix the population. One could not travel any distance without being countersigned at point after point. This was brought back in a modernised form (December 27th, 1932). Incidentally, the great cities, as hives of work at high pressures, were purged of those whom the Government did not want there, and hundreds of thousands of persons, the least able to fend for themselves, were sent wandering. As the zones of prohibition continued to be widened, they had to wander on further, without any provision for their future. In the country, to uproot all remains of opposition to collectivisation, special political police were established, particularly around the dominating motor-tractor stations. This last measure was an act not of the Government as such, but came direct from the Communist Party (January 13th, 1933). On August 2nd this measure was also applied to the railways. All cattle were compulsorily socialised (March 27th, 1932). The Trade Union organisation was finally absorbed into the Commissiariat of Labour (June 23rd). On April 28th a severe purge of the Party was ordered. And suddenly, just when the repression was at its height, there came a sharp break in the clouds. But for this the explanation must be sought outside Russia.

XII

HITLER AND JAPAN

(1919-33)

GERMANY, LONG BEFORE SHE WAS HERSELF UNITED, HAD ALways been trying to push forward eastward. This urge goes back past the Middle Ages. When the Huns swooped down on Europe in the fourth century, they pushed the disunited German tribes over the frontiers of the Roman Empire, which was already crumbling. The Hunnish empire was a kind of snowball of various subject nationalities which broke up very quickly; and Slav tribes, which had been carried forward in the rush, were left occupying a great part of Central Europe and a good half of present-day Germany. All through the middles ages the Germans were pushing back eastward. This was the historic *Drang nach Osten* (the Push to the East).

When Germany, with the exception of German Austria, was in 1871 united into one powerful and military State, this push became a radical part of its foreign policy. One side of this policy concerned Austria. In 1866 Prussia drove Austria out of Germany: Austro-Hungary (to give it its full title) was a State of many nationalities, but dominated by a German dynasy, and a largely German bureaucracy and army. Bismarck, when he had expelled Austria from Germany, demanded no territory: it was his clever policy to go into alliance with her, nay more, to push her further south-eastward, so that she should bring into her fold as many Slav peoples as possible. Austria became the spearhead of Germany's southeastward advance. The Czechs and Slovaks were already Slav dominions of the Austro-Hungarian State: the Serbs of Bosnia were incorporated in it, and independent Serbia was constantly threatened. Bulgaria was brought into alliance. The Slav Poles had long since been divided up between Germany, Austria and Russia. But Germany always looked further eastward, and with specal covetousness at the great granary of Ukraine. We have seen that at Brest-Litovsk in their hour of triumph Germany and Austria were able for the moment to separate Ukraine from Russia and bring it under their own control.

In 1871, when Germany at long last arrived at national unity and power, she found the road to further advance blocked on all sides. It was the fault of her own national divisions. We ourselves, by methods which will not bear too close a scrutiny, had been before her in the world outside; and after the fall of Napoleon, when the continent of Europe was still mostly occupied with the quest of national or political liberties, we had also practically captured the trade of the world. France, full of resentment, was recovering within her reduced boundaries, curtailed by the German victory of 1870-1. In the east stood the colossus of the Russian Empire. The cause of the last war was Germany's urgent desire to get out and get to work in the outside world.

In the north, Scandinavia did not give the scope for a great world policy. Three other directions were possible. Much the easiest way was friendship with the Russian Empire, which was so rotten inside, with commercial penetration and ultimate domination. This did not involve any war, and Imperial Germany did enjoy very real success along this road before 1914. Her very capable and efficient traders, actively backed by the energetic support and help of the German State, were gradually expelling all commercial rivals from Russia. It was the greatest mistake for Germany to break off this valuable work by declaring war on Russia in 1914, but this came from her not making up her mind, and trying the different roads at once.

The second road ran south-eastward through the Balkans. Here Austria was already an invaluable advance post. In 1914 the advance post went forward on its own, by forcing a quarrel and declaring war on Serbia. Austria relied on her intimate friendship with Germany, and not in vain. It was to all intents an accepted axiom in Europe that the maintenance of peace in the Balkans depended on agreement or compromise between Austria and Russia. But this time Germany gave unqualified support to Austria and declared war on Russia.

The circle of Germany's enemies was completed by the march through Belgium, which brought England into the war. The third direction for Germany's challenge was a war with England. An outright win would give her the best way out of all —to the seas and beyond. Thus Germany found herself trying all the three roads at once; and she was defeated.

After the defeat, the chief thought of the military mind in Germany was that on all accounts she must not find herself having to fight again on two fronts at once. The natural way to avoid this would be an alliance with Russia. Even in the war, captured German officers or even men, on evident instructions, were always (sometimes in my presence) telling the Russians that they ought to be friends, as the common enemy was England; this view was extensively propagated in Germany.

But the cloven hoof came out very clearly in these suggestions. For instance, there was published towards the end of World War I a notable pamphlet by Werner Daya, entitled "The March Eastwards," with the significant sub-title "Russian Asia as the objective of German military and economic policy." It showed how muddle-headed the policy of Germany must have been, to arouse a whole world of enemies against her. Germany ought not to have bothered herself about the West at all. "The Atlantic Ocean got on our brains." She should have turned eastward, and got a firm hold on Russia. For a war of revenge, the alliance of the future should be "Germany and Japan *with* Russia." It appeared that Russia, while accepted as a kind of junior partner, was to be crushed in this double embrace. Japan's profit from the bargain was not made clear. There followed a very intelligent survey of the natural wealth of Siberia—which has far more to give than European Russia—with the perfectly true comment: "Siberia, in competent hands, would be a second North America," and the sub-title made it evident that the "competent hands" were to be German. A good deal of this pamphlet was an anticipation of the later program of Hitler.

The Treaties of Versailles left two outlawed countries in Europe—Germany and Russia. It was certain that the two would be drawn together; and this was the fear of all well-informed friends of Russia in England and of England in Russia, independently of their political views and preferences. In 1922 this development took shape in the Treaty of Rapallo, concluded between Russia and Germany at the time of the conference of Genoa as a kind of counter-insurance. This was a step obviously dictated by statesmanship. But it was not the German Socialists who inspired it. Like all supporters of the Labour International, they were scared by the hostility and threats of the Bolsheviks. The alliance was much more cynical: it was the special toy of the German Right Wing, and it recalled the agreement by which Ludendorff enabled Lenin to reach Russia after the March Revolution, and break up the Russian army.

I was well acquainted with one of the prime movers of this idea. His policy for the rebuilding of Russia, as he told me frankly, was "British capital and German technique": I replied that I expected our capital would go with our own technique.

Quite a good deal was done on these lines, by the exchange of visits, cultural and commercial. The writ of Versailles did not run in Russia, and German capital could escape its restrictions by transferring its activity over the Russian frontier. I think there is no doubt that the work of rearmament was begun in this way.

These were the short-lived days of the Weimar Republic. It seems to me that something on the lines of Hitlerism was definitely invited by us in the Versailles Treaty, only we could not have realised how formidable a shape the danger was to take. It was intelligible that this highly industrious and efficient people, teeming with compressed energy, should break out on all sides, even if it failed to find any outlet except by treading on every one else's toes at once. After the defeat all this energy was repressed within even narrower limits and was given the helot's task of slaving for the rest of the world.

It was a radical mistake to load it with "reparations" which it could not pay: either we should not get our money or by the time we did, Germany, working at a lower rate, would be able to undercut all competition. It was a mistake to rely on restrictions of armaments which could never be applied over a long period—least of all by Allies who were sure to separate after the victory. Territorially, though we failed to see it. Germany was united into one nation by the war itself as she had never been before. But probably the worst mistake of all was to give our victory the aspect of an Act of God, and when we had got our enemy on his knees, not to let him get up till he confessed himself the all-round criminal. After this, it was morally certain that whoever first called on the Germans to hold up their heads again and remember that they were a great nation, would sweep the country. The tragedy was that the man who did this was Adolf Hitler.

There is a good French proverb: "The hem is stronger than the cloth." An Ulsterman will be the most imperialist of Englishmen. The most violent Russian Anti-Semites were drawn from the province of Bessarabia, packed tight with Jews. An Austrian was to outdo the Prussians in the worst features of Prussianism.

It is even now too early to give final judgment on that extraordinary man. One does not pass final judgment on a man who once conquered nearly all the continent of Europe. We are only concerned with his reactions on Russia. Bolshevist Russia was his bogey, his frenzy—not only in his book *Mein Kampf*, from which none of his anti-Russian outbursts were ever removed, but in all his speeches up to that of April 11th, of 1939 at Wilhelmshaven, in which, in an almost raving passage, he describes Soviet Russia as "that Jewish sponge-fungus."

France was condemned in *Mein Kampf* with only less vehemence; Germany sought two Allies, Italy and England. England was offered a straight deal following in part the line laid down by Werner Daya. "Germany," wrote Dr. Alfred Rosenberg, philosopher of Nazism, in his text book *The Future of German Foreign Policy*, "honestly renounces her 'crusading' policy of the time of William II (that is, her naval competition with England): she demands in return unconditional English support—even against France—for acquisition of territory in Eastern Europe . . . for the support of at least 100 million Germans" (that is to say, a larger population than Germany herself possessed). In 100 years, according to *Mein Kampf,* there was to be room in Europe for 250 million Germans (Vol. II, 767). The Greater Germany was to be, not a country packed with industrial workers, but a vast expanse populated by factory workers and farmers, serving each other's needs.

The essential foundation of the whole vision was land-hunger. This was not a simple claim to recover all that was lost at Versailles: it was the old claim to world hegemony on a magnificent scale and in infinitely more precise terms.

And Russia was the primary objective. "When we are talking of more ground and room in Europe," wrote Hitler, "we can in the first place only think of Russia and the border states dependent on her. . . . The gigantic Empire in the East is ripe for collapse, and the end of the Jewish domination in Russia will also be the end of the Russian State itself."[1]

By the time when this scheme could become a practical proposition, the Jewish allusions had lost their meaning. Indeed in Moscow by that time there was in vogue a witty comparison between Moses and Stalin. "Moses led the people of Israel out of Egypt, and Stalin led them out of the central executive committee" (of the Communist Party): but Russia, as we have seen, even up to the eve of the recent war, continued to be regarded by Hitler as "that Jewish sponge-fungus!" Anyhow, Stalin's Russia was faced with as direct a challenge as one State can give to another, when the author of *Mein Kampf* became the absolute ruler of Germany.

The *Drang nach Osten*, the Push Eastwards, was very much older and more historical than the new fear of Bolshevism; and in the revival of this age-long German impulse one can see something much more real and practical than an ideological hatred of Communism. This was to be plainly shown later from another angle. Again following Daya, Japan was brought into the picture as the Ally of Germany in the Anti-Communist Pact of November 25th, 1936. They were later joined by Italy, lying on our main route to the Far East (November 6th, 1937), and now the tie between the three was drawn closer still.

It has been truly said that Japan became Nazi before Germany. Mention has been made of the time following the failure of the General Strike in England when Stalin triumphed over Trotsky and, in the main, switched the current of Communist propaganda from Europe to his almost-native Asia. It had a brief if brilliant success in China. The Russian agent Borodin won a commanding position in Canton and, with Russian advice and expert help, Chiang Kai-Shek was able to carry the authority of the Kuo-Min-Tang northward to the valley of the Yang-Tse. It was however he who put a check on the extension of communist influence and limited it to the north-east. It was also he who united China as never before.

But at that time Communist ideas, as elsewhere, proved a great fascination to many young intellectuals in Japan. In February, 1928, this movement had spread so widely that it

[1] *Mein Kampf*, Vol. II, pp. 742-3.

was officially described by the principal law officer "as a real attempt to destroy the foundations of the empire from inside . . . which is more serious than a threat of armed force from outside."[1] Mass arrests followed, at one time rising to a thousand, and state trials took place in several of the chief towns. It was from this point that really dates the sharp turn of the Japanese Government to a policy of militarist and imperialist adventure in China, which, obscuring the parliament, put the political power more and more in the hands of the army and navy.

This Japanese threat to China calls to mind the best political forecast ever made by Wilhelm II. In May, 1912, visiting the Tsar at Baltisch Port, he drew the Russian Foreign Minister, Sazonov, into a talk of over an hour. He spoke of the Yellow Danger. "How did the Powers regard my warning? They gave no response to it, thinking me mad. . . . England is responsible for this, and will not escape punishment. . . . The Yellow Danger has not only not ceased to exist, but has become more threatening than before, and most of all for Russia. . . . You have only one thing left to do—to take in hand the creation of a military force in China, to make of it a rampart against Japanese aggression. If Russia does not take this matter in hand, Japan will set about the reconstruction of China, and then Russia will lose once for all her Far Eastern dominions, and together with them her access to the Pacific."[2] China was then already in the throes of revolution and a prey to the pillaging of rival War Lords. His object was, of course, to turn Russia's eyes away from Europe and more particularly from her kinsfolk in the Balkans, but in this matter he has been proved right.

Japan, naturally, had not begun her imperial career by challenging her strongest potential rivals in the Pacific. On the contrary, she learned from them everything that she could —especially about war, but with a far wider program of reform, which covered all national life, including for instance, even religion. This wholesale reform embraced the very full life of her greatest statesman, the Marquis Ito, who began by working his way on the *Pegasus* to England, and later, after rendering the most distinguished services to his country as statesman, diplomatist, general and admiral, died by assassination in 1909, seeing his life-work fully completed. The first landmark of reform in Japan was the oath of the

[1] S. Vostrotin: "Russia's Crisis in the Far East," *Slavonic Review*, Vol. XIV, No. 20, p. 104.
[2] Sazonov: *Fateful Years*, pp. 43-5.

Mikado in 1868, which might have been written in England and reads as follows: "That a deliberative assembly shall be summoned and all measures shall be decided by public opinion; that high and low shall be of one mind in the conduct of the administration; that matters shall be so arranged that not only the government officials and Samurai (the aristocracy) but also common people may be able to obtain the objects of their desire, and the national mind may be completely satisfied; that the vicious and uncivilised customs of antiquity shall be broken through, and that the great principles of impartiality and justice . . . shall be the basis of action; that intellect and learning shall be sought out for the purpose of firmly establishing the foundations of the Empire." [1]

It is therefore from 1868 that we may date the "English" period in Japan; and to all appearances its end began in 1928 when the army first broke away and set about seizing the control. From that time onwards, Japanese policy might be described as Nazi.

Japan had taken her part in the international punitive expedition in China at the time of the Boxers' revolt in 1900. After she had finally established herself as a Great Power by her well-earned triumph over Russia in 1904-5, in which she was materially helped by her "preventive" alliance with England, she found herself taking part in the general crusade against German ambition in 1914-17. This was a purely utilitarian policy; for her sympathies were largely with Germany, and the Japanese have not unfairly been called the Prussians of the Far East. She again lined up with England, France and America in the intervention in Siberia in 1918-20. As Russia then seemed to be falling to pieces, this seemed Japan's best chance of getting a further footing on the continent. Southern Manchuria she had already won in the war of 1904-5; why not try to add Northern Manchuria and the Maritime Province with Vladivostok, which was indeed garrisoned by Japanese troops during the Intervention. But Japan faltered; she stayed on for a while after the other Great Powers departed, but she too in the end came out; and in 1922 she submitted to the somewhat humiliating bargaining on naval strength of the other victorious Powers in the Treaty of Washington, by which she was restricted to a lower limit than England or the United Sates.

All this altered in 1928. There is a document, called the Will of Tanaka attributed to the Prime Minister of that name and dated July 25th, 1927, when it is said to have been pre-

[1] *Cambridge Modern History*, XII, p. 539.

sented to the Japanese Emperor. It has been denounced as spurious; but one thing is certain:—that the policy of Japan has from that date developed entirely on the lines of this program.

It is a kind of Japanese *Mein Kampf,* with suggestions of Werner Daya. It contains a most careful analysis of the resources and the vast potentialities—not of Siberia, but of Manchuria. It recalls instructions dating back to the Emperor Meiji, which outlined a complete policy of aggression. First the island of Formosa (won from China in 1894), then Korea (won from Russian rivalry in 1904-5), and then Manchuria (only half won in the same war) and, to follow, China and, as the following passage will show, a very great deal else.

"For the defence of herself and others, Japan will not be able to remove obstacles in Eastern Asia, except by conducting a policy of 'blood and iron' (a quotation from Bismarck). . . . If in the future we want to seize control of China, we shall have to come into conflict with the United States of America . . . but to conquer China, we must first conquer Manchuria and Mongolia . . . to conquer the world, we must conquer China. If we are able to conquer China, all other countries of Asia and all the Southern Sea will capitulate to us. The world will then understand that Eastern Asia is ours, and will not dare to violate our rights. Such is the plan bequeathed to us by the Emperor Meiji. . . . If we have at our disposal all the resources of China, we shall pass on to the conquest of India, the Archipelago, Asia Minor, Central Asia and even Europe. . . . To take into our hands the control of Manchuria and Mongolia is the first step, if the race of Yamoto wishes to distinguish itself in continental Asia."[1]

The writer foresees, for the conquest of the Chinese Eastern Railway, "an inevitable conflict with the USSR." "Apparently it enters into our national program that we shall again have to cross swords with Russia on the fields of North Manchuria and Mongolia. . . . Till this hidden reef is blown up, our ship will not be able to go forward quickly."

In September, 1931, Japan created an incident that led to her occupation of Northern Manchuria, which was still legally Chinese territory. She scorned a European Commission and the adverse judgment of the League of Nations, to which she gave notice soon afterwards. Through Northern Manchuria ran a short cut of the main line of the Trans-Siberian railway, under the name of the Chinese Eastern Railway, connecting Siberia directly with Vladivostok. This was the work of Russian brains and capital, being the masterpiece of the Tsar's Finance Minister, Witte. To seize it was to cut an essential piece out of a world trunk line. Imperialist Russia would cer-

[1] Cited by S. Vostrotin, l.c. *S.R.* XIV, 40, p. 115; also in *Eastern Menace* (pamphlet of the Union of Democratic Control).

tainly have shown fight, but the Communists were absorbed in their vital task of transforming Russia; they did not take up the challenge and were content to sell the railway, now rendered comparatively valueless, for an old song. This was the first convincing sign that, while otherwise engaged, the Soviets sincerely desired world peace; but the blow rankled ever after, and an almost ceaseless succession of frontier incidents—the Japanese even demanded the demilitarisation of the frontiers of Russia along the Amur—has always kept the sore alive; in fact, the Soviets regarded Japan as typical of the frankest piracy of capitalist states.

In 1937, by another "incident" of a stray shot during Japanese manœuvres outside Pekin (July 7th), Japan launched a new aggression on the main body of China—an adventure in which for a time the Japanese apparently got stuck, unable either to advance or to withdraw. The way out of such an *impasse* which would be most convenient to the national pride would be to switch off to another adventure, at least in some apparent connexion with the first one. The Japanese had not really much more to gain from Russia; they could not settle in the Siberian climate; they were naturally drawn further south, where they were much more likely to come into conflict with ourselves, the French, as well as with America. But they now moved forward some thousands of miles along the southern frontiers of Siberia and reached the rear of North China. Japan held Inner Mongolia, and Russia held Outer Mongolia which was sovietised and was given a firm guarantee of Soviet protection. The Chinese Red Army, now aligned with Chiang Kai-Shek, was backed on Russia on this side. Russia took full control of the Chinese province of Sienkiang. She never wavered in her support of Chinese independence and sent material help to Chiang Kai-Shek.

This sketch will have made it possible to draw the full inferences from the Anti-Communist Pact concluded between Germany and Japan on November 25th, 1936, joined by Italy a year later, and later still drawn closer for all three. Potentially the world was now divided into a number of encirclements. France and Britain on the one side and Russia on the other, as in the last war, encircled Germany; Germany and Japan encircled Russia; Russia and America encircled Japan; and the foreign policies of all had no other significance than taking up positions for another inevitable and impending world conflict. The Anti-Communist Pact had little to do with Communism, for the three contracting Powers had all fiercely suppressed it within their own borders, but it had everything to do with territory. And a single glance at a globe will show that it was equally a threat against two Empires, the Russian and the British. Italy's role was here subsidiary. She barred the Mediterranean, the direct road from Europe to the East, and presented a most serious problem to the British Navy.

XIII

STALIN'S REPLY

(1934-37)

FOR STALIN THE ADVENT TO SUPREME POWER IN GERMANY of the author of *Mein Kampf* was warning eough, and he did not delay to take immediate steps to counter the challenge. There was first, of course, the direct danger of an attack on Russia. Hitler concluded in 1934 a ten years' pact with the Poland of Marshal Pilsudski; and it seemed that he was contemplating a joint assault upon Ukraine, where Pilsudski himself had tried to win as much territory as possible when Russia was torn by Civil War. It is true that such a deal would have been fatal to Poland: as with Austria after the joint aggression on Denmark in 1866, Berlin would have been sure to quarrel over the spoils and come out the winner; and the Poles were cautious enough to avoid the snare. There was also the danger to Stalin's delicate experiment which might follow from any state of war in Europe. Russian policy at this time was directed to preventing there being any war at all.

The countries which shared this interest in the *status quo* were of course those who had gained in the last European settlement. It was also discovered, in spite of the gibes of the Russian Press at "rotten Liberalism," that the Western democracies were just those which were not dangerous to Soviet Russia. Stalin's "Socialism in one country" led on to another declaration of his that "revolution was not for export." That would suit the democracies: Fascism and Nazism on the other hand were explosive forces, based on a bitter hostility to Bolshevism; in fact they affected to espy "Bolshevism" in the democracies also, or anyhow a super-influence of Jews.

The handling of Soviet foreign affairs had long been entrusted to Litvinov. Though an early Bolshevik, he was not one of the inner circle, not a member of the Politburo; and he used to be described as "Stalin's technician for foreign policy": one, who, if told what to do, could generally find a smooth way of doing it. He acted with vigour. First he visited the United States and was able for the first time to obtain from Franklin Roosevelt the long delayed recognition of the Soviet Government (November 16th, 1933). His attempt at a debt settlement was not a material success, as the Russian suggestion was always, "Lend me some more money and I'll pay you back some." Also to the general surprise, he brought Russia into the League of Nations, which had always been derided in Russia as a capitalist institution (September 15th, 1934). The League was not a government but a declaration of principles, and it was impossible to join it without paying some homage to those principles. But the versatile Litvinov found no difficulty in that, and in fact, was able to make himself perfectly at home in Geneva. He became an outstanding figure there, and several times came out with a bold view which appealed to many others besides Russians, for instance when he formally called for general disarmament. It was Litvinov who was more successful than anyone else in finding an agreed formula defining aggression.

Next he went forward from a Pact of Non-aggression (November 29th, 1932) to an Alliance with France (May 2nd, 1935), probably the most typically bourgeois country in the world and certainly not progressive. His course was beginning to recall the configuration of alliances that existed in 1914. Like the French Alliance of 1894, this Alliance— where there was certainly no more similarity of regime than between France and the reactionary Russia of Alexander III —had, so to speak, a face value as an insurance against attack; but it is significant that in its four years of existence there were never any consultations of the military staffs of both countries as to how it should be implemented. It is interesting to note in this connection that the French Minister, Laval, was able to pierce the pretence that the Soviet Government and the Third International had no connection with each other. He insisted on an interview with Stalin, who though not a member of the Soviet Government, as General Secretary of the Communist Party was in fact the master of both, and on the usual joint Press Communiqué, noting their agreement. There was also a markedly better tone in the Soviet relations with England. The new Ambassador, Maisky, sent to interpret them, who when a revolutionary emigrant had worked in London as a bookbinder, was certainly a friend of England, and was able to gauge acutely what was worth doing and what could be done to create a more friendly atmosphere between the two countries and, in particular, to create here a much wider circle of goodwill towards the Soviet Union.

But far more striking and far more convincing was the new direction taken in internal policy in Russia. In insisting, day in and day out, that a united attack of the capitalist world on "the one Socialist State" was imminent, Party and Government had perhaps over-reached themselves. In the hard years of famine there was even evidence that in some quarters such an attack would be welcome. Writing in our *Slavonic Review* on "New Trends in Eastern Policies," in April, 1935, I said: "It is more than possible that when this period is reviewed by history, the chief indictment of the present government of Russia may be the recklessness of conducting an internal warfare on the mass of the population between two foreign wars." I quote this because I am perfectly certain that I was stating the problem which was at that time the chief preoccupation of the rulers of Russia, for all their actions proved this.

Here is a personal word. It seemed to me obvious that I ought to take advantage of this. Not only because I had been following closely on developments in Russia most of my life. As Director of the only big School of Slavonic Studies, which we had built up in London University since the war, and responsible for the Russian department in it, I had got to restore connections with the greatest country in our field of studies. I had tried to do so in the poignant period of collectivisation and had been refused a visa. I had had throughout indirect sources of information of all sorts; but, particularly with Russia, that "jungle" of impressions, live contact is essential. But beyond all that, if Russia was coming our way, that was a great factor for world peace and for our national security, and we could not afford to miss the opportunity which it offered us. My suggestion at once had the whole-hearted support of the new Soviet Ambassador in London, and after a long delay the visa was given. I went, definitely not as an admirer of the existing regime, nor as parting company with my friends in the Russian emigration, as I made clear in the Foreign Office at Moscow, but as a serious student and friend of Russia. The impressions of my stay I published in a tiny book, *Moscow Admits a Critic,* and I have made several visits since.

On her side, Russia had every reason to take account of us. Now the often advertised danger of a foreign attack was actually there, though in much more restricted and precise proportions. It was a question not of propaganda, but of practical steps. Who was to be interested in defending the country—

only the two million communists with the Komsomol and the "pioneer" children, or was it also the 160 odd millions of the population, so far relegated to the rôle of second or third class citizens? It was always the peasantry that had formed the backbone of the army; and in the years of conflict the proportion of peasant recruits had been ridiculously cut down.

And for Stalin it was not only the country that was to be defended, but still more the regime. The Communist Government had never forgotten March, 1917, which first gave them the chance of power. The regular army had been mown down in a world war—in which the Russian casualties far exceeded in number the membership of the Communist Party—and then the extinguisher itself caught fire. It was imperative to come to terms with the peasantry. It was well for Stalin that against all odds he had just succeeded in making his great transformation both of industrial and agricultural Russia, and that he could afford to stretch out a hand to the population without any loss of prestige and as an act of grace. His policy has often enough been opportunist, but no one could say that it has been hesitant; and once the decision was taken, the thing was done handsomely.

One of the early signs of the new directions was that rationing was abolished (November 26th, 1934). This was decreed direct from the Communist Party, which could not have done it unless it had been in a position to do it. But the most material changes were mainly focused on the peasantry. It began with a remission of arrears of taxes (December 11th, 1933), significantly enough for districts closest to the Far East frontier, but this was soon extended to the whole country (February 27th, 1934).

By a most important decree of February 18th, 1935, the peasants of the collective farms got a considerably greater share in the management of their own affairs, which brought them closer to the popular ideal of free agricultural co-operation. Their houses and kitchen gardens, as in the times of the Tsars, together with all household articles, were declared to be individual property; but besides that they were given allotments—very small, it is true—on which they could labour for their own profit. This was immensely popular; the peasant naturally put in his best work on his allotment; ultimately the government cut down its dimensions and took measures to see that the collective work of the whole *kolhoz* did not suffer, but that was to come later.

Individual property had to be the result of one's own work, but it was now recognised as property, including all earnings, and was guaranteed by the State. Earnings could be invested in the national savings banks, which very soon were full, and could also be bequeathed. Horses were regarded as means of production and therefore remained nationalised, but in principle every family was to possess a cow, and a large household two, if possible (it was just in the immediately preceding period of harsh legislation that all cattle had been socialised). Pigs, poultry, bees could be personal property.

One specially popular decree was that which declared that the limits of the domain of each collective farm could not be reduced. This the peasants regarded as satisfying their claim that the given holding belonged to these and to no other peasants—the principle which they had always maintained, and on which they had acted when they seized the squires' land in 1917. They looked upon this as their charter, and in many villages showed it with genuine pride to Sir John Russell.

The peasants, in particular, were greatly pleased at the respect now again accorded to the family tie—heralded, it is said, by a rather demonstrative visit of Stalin to his mother. Divorce, so far, could be obtained with perfect ease; either of the parties had only to express a wish for it, or one could dispense with any ceremony at all, though alimony and provision for children were minutely considered in each case; but here too a vigorous change was made. Divorce was made subject to a progressive tax: this, with the other economic considerations, was quite enough to frighten the citizens off from a too frequent indulgence in it. Abortion, which had previously been winked at or even assisted, was now made a criminal offence with severe penalities (June 28th, 1936). Particularly interesting was the preface to this decree. It was always the custom, in Russian legislation, to begin with a kind of survey of the question and its antecedents, for the better understanding of the population. It was explained that abortion was really one of the evils of the capitalist system, but in the first rush of the revolution the Government had not been able to deal with it; *now* let everyone beware of doing such a thing. Population was now wanted for the defence of the country; and as time went on, high bonuses and other privileges were given for child-bearing.

The period of indiscipline was also well buried in the past. The waifs and strays had long since been cleared away from the streets and put into reformatories, and as these were real schools of character, some of these waifs, owing all that they knew of responsibility to the new creed, had become very valuable material for the Komsomol. Gone was the time when children had been encouraged to criticise or even impeach their teachers and to spy on their parents. Now in every school hung the legend that they were expected to show respect for their parents, their teachers and generally for their elders. While other legislation became milder, that which dealt with offences of youthful hooliganism was very much sharpened (April 8th, 1935), and parents were now invited by the school authorities to co-operate with them in maintaining discipline. I witnessed the discipline produced by these changes, and, as a former schoolmaster, I must say that I thought it had struck the golden mean. There was a vigorous initiative and a lively interest among the children which one could hardly have found before the revolution; on the other hand, the order was all that could be desired—an intelligent orderliness, as if the children understood very well the difference between work and play.

Perhaps the sharpest change of all was in the field of learning. The Communist Revolution had at first turned instruction wholesale into propaganda. The Chairs of History, famous for their holders before the Revolution, when I listened in Moscow University to Klyuchevsky and Vinogradov, had been abolished. Now they were restored; and the subject was divided up much as it might have been at Oxford or Cambridge: Ancient and Oriental History, Medieval, Modern, and native or Russian. Decrees of May 16th, 1934, demanded that the teaching of history and geography should be made interesting to the pupils; scorn was thrown on 'abstract definitions of social and economic forms" and "abstract sociological schemes": history teaching should be full of events and personalities. I was told that this was because Stalin had asked what a Soviet school child would know about Napoleon: "he might think it was a cream tart." Did this lend colour to Trotsky's charge of "Bonapartism"? Certainly from this time forward the portraits of Stalin in public places became more numerous than ever.

Still more striking was a decree of April 24th, 1934, "on the overburdening of school children and pioneers with civic and political training." The profession of communist views had been substituted for matriculation as the key to open the door of the university. A witticism of that period had pictured the examination as follows:

Q. What is God?—A. God is a prejudice of the middle classes.
Q. Well, you have passed.—A. Thank God!

Now circulars of the strictest wording (May 16th, 1934, and December 29th, 1935) warned all directors of educational institutions that the only road to the university went by the way of examination—that is, by merit. Independent research was now encouraged on the Arts side, as it had all along been in Science.

One also saw the encouragement of a growing tendency to take a patriotic interest in the old past of Russia. Of the plays, operas and ballets that I saw, most dated from before the Revolution, and the staging was not only as wonderful as it had always been—for this instinct lies in the Russian genius—but had even been bettered by many original improvements. Thrice I saw a Tsar of Russia presented on the stage and each time he was the centre of sympathetic interest. One opera turned on the affection of John the Terrible for a natural daughter whom he discovers in a provincial town. John the Terrible! One might almost have excused anything hostile which revolutionary Russia might have had to say of him. Another was about John's gentle and feeble son Fedor, whose futility ended the long line of the House of Rurik in the storm of the Time of Troubles (1598-1613). I saw the play before the Revolution, when it was withdrawn, as obviously a clever if sympathetic sketch of the futility of Nicholas II. Here it was again, but the sympathy was still all for the weak central character, who ends by saying in all sincerity, "Oh God, why did you ever make me Tsar of Russia?" The third instance was still more striking. In the *Queen of Spades* of Chaikovsky, based on Pushkin, the post-revolution version introduces a Court Ball of which the splendid pageant culminates in the entry on the stage of Tsar Nicholas I, who represents the very peak of the autocracy, and this was received by the audience as one of the splendours of the past.

Peter the Great is still a national hero, and no wonder, for Stalin has plenty of kinship with that enthroned revolutionary; and in the new film on the subject there is not a scene or a motive which is not true to history. Suvorov, the greatest of all Russian generals, who, though of noble birth, reached the very top by starting from the bottom, has also been specially honoured, and even St. Alexander Nevsky, the Prince who was "the Sun of Russia" in her period of greatest darkness, the first years of the Tartar yoke. Histories now admit that in early Russia, Christianity indeed represented a great advance in civilisation. Official criticism of the various manuscripts sent in for the prize for the best history of the USSR reproved "those who idealise pre-christian paganism and do not understand the simple fact that the introduction of Christianity was progress, in comparison with pagan barbarism." How different is all this from the teaching of the only recently deceased Communist historian, Michael Pokrovsky, who would not allow that individual character, not even that of a Peter the Great, competed in the shaping of history with the ponderous march of economic determination. Is it strange that when I came back from Russia, greatly enheartened, André Gide should have returned in the deepest depression?

In the first hectic years of Communism and civil war there had been no attempt at a balanced budget, and money had been left to extinguish its significance by extravagant inflation. From the start of the NEP when the Communists were compelled to go back to the wicked ways of capitalism and re-establish a currency, it was all uphill work. There had been set up special stores, trading in foreign currency—partly for the convenience of foreign visitors, but also to draw in whatever there might be of it in the country for the purpose of foreign trade. It was a sign of getting nearer to a balance when at the end of 1935 these special stores were abolished and by a stroke of the pen the rouble, which had meant 2s. 7d. in English with a purchasing power of twopence, became ninepence with a purchasing value of threepence.

It was announced that the tide of concessions to the public was to lead up to a Constitution. Stalin was known to be taking an active part in framing it, and it duly appeared on June 12th, 1936, under the name of "Stalin's Constitution." Its first appearance made a striking and even astonishing effect. To anyone who was familiar with the movement that led up to the creation of the Duma in 1905, it looked almost amazingly like the liberal program of the Zemstva which came to be adopted by practically the whole nation. Even the actual wording was sometimes the same. Here were to be found all the famous "freedoms" of conscience, speech, press, meeting and association, crowned by a new national assembly to be called "The Supreme Soviet" and to be elected by universal suffrage, for men or women, of the whole population over eighteen. No account whatever was to be taken of social origin or even of past activities of the elector; priests were enfranchised like everyone else. (Yaroslavsky himself defended this.) There was a Second Chamber, with the same rights as the first and sometimes sitting conjointly with it. It was to be chosen by nationalities to ensure that all the minor national fractions should get a hearing, such as they could never have dreamed of under the Tsars. One looked carefully to see what place was given under this constitution to the Communist Party, which was, of course, the ruling caste of the country. It would have been suspicious if there had been no mention of it. It was found in its natural place, as a special nucleus of activity, an organ of national leadership; but the right of putting up candidates was no longer confined to it, but allowed also to any legalised association of citizens, even cultural.

It has been suggested that the original intention of Stalin was to let his constitution work out as it appeared. In his terrific struggle with the remains of internal opposition he had everywhere been uprooting his former colleagues, "Old Bolsheviks," as they were called; not one of the original Politburo now remained. He was equally drastic with local officials who had been so long in power that they had come to regard it as permanent; and in this bitter struggle against bureaucratic tenacity he was often calling out for what he called "Non-Party Bolsheviks"—which in practice had come to mean new agents who would follow wholeheartedly his personal lead. It is more probable that from the first he knew what he meant to do. Anyhow, his intention became clear when it was announced that in each constituency there would only be one candidate, to vote for or against. This, to any western democratic reader, certainly seemed to stultify the whole plan; but now that we have been able to see it in its working, we must not satisfy ourselves too easily with this conclusion. Stalin wanted—especially with the threat of foreign assault—to give his power a broader base in the country, and in this sense his constitution was democratic. But when he set about this, he was copying what Lenin had done when, in exile, he first built up the Communist Party. In each case the process may be described as hand-picking. There was plenty of *triage,* plenty of selection before the one candidate was chosen, and in this work both party and non-party organisations were drawn into active collaboration. The actual slogan displayed everywhere during the election was "The Alliance of Party and Non-Party." Where were the men or women who in a "Stalin" or "Bolshevik" (that is, wholeheartedly) way would carry the lessons and instructions of their leader far and wide into the whole mass of the country? Where were the new fresh forces which could rise out of the mass to put more volume into the work of the Party? The Press was constantly urging the need of the most careful scrutiny of the whole past record of each prospective candidate. It was not unlike what we sometimes ourselves do with a less serious purpose: it was the good cricket coach who is constantly looking for budding talent in the lower games.

What made the grant of the Constitution look still less convincing was its coincidence with a savage spate of purges and trials, dating from the murder of Kirov, Stalin's deputy, in Leningrad on December 1st, 1934. Trotsky was now outside, ineffectively spitting brilliant venom in his book *The Revolution Betrayed*. But anyone who opposed Stalin and could be caught went down in these "grandes fournées," so suggestive of the mass trials before the end of the French Revolution. Eventually Rights and Lefts were mingled in the dock as conspiring together against Stalin. Nearly all of them admitted having done so, and on this point it is not necessary that we should doubt them, in whatever way their evidence was originally obtained. The bulky verbatim reports were in any case impressive. The most illuminating feature was the discrimination made by some of the more independent of the accused, as, for instance, the famous Bukharin, author of the *A.B.C. of Communism*: "I did this, but I would never have done that" (he admitted plotting against Stalin's life, which was after all the main point); or again Radek: "I did so at that time, but I did the opposite at this." This evidence certainly threw a great deal of light on the changing attitude of the country towards Stalin in his colossal and ruthless task—first mistrust and opposition, then conspiracy, and finally unwilling acceptance of his success. Some of these men, like those just named, were at their intellectual best in their "last words" at the trial; Zinoviev, who had escaped by the skin of his teeth in former trials, was now finally brought to book and died, still fawning, like the coward that he had always been (August 24th, 1936).

One celebrated trial, in June, 1937, was on a different footing to the rest—that of the most distinguished generals in the Red Army, headed by Marshal Tukhachevsky. As this was a court-martial we have no verbatim report, though the result here, too, was wholesale condemnation and a mass of executions. It seems that there was really a plot to eliminate, and of course kill, Stalin: after all, Stalin was killing his enemies. That the accused were "counter-revolutionaries" and wished to restore "landlordism" and "capitalism" was a charge which ordinarily had a place in any Communist political deed of accusation. But the circumstances are specially interesting as bearing on Russian foreign policy. In the period of Rapallo when Russia and Germany, both outlawed by the rest of Europe, were drawing closer together, it was natural that the General Staffs of the two countries should be instructed to confer together. On the advent of Hitler, with his menacing

program, the Russian generals were told to stop and did not
do so. For this Tukhachevsky and his comrades paid with their
lives. On the German side, about this time, Blomberg was
dropped in a less conspicuous way.

XIV

SOCIAL SERVICES

IT IS HERE THAT I WILL SPEAK OF ONE OF THE VERY BEST SIDES
of the Soviet regime, the social services of the State for the
community. One might go far and wide through Soviet Russia
and hear nothing of the quarrels of the leaders or even of
the sensational trials—not only because people would certainly avoid talking about them, but because they regarded
them as quarrels in the ruling set and were much more interested in their own lives, the new opportunities which were
given them, and the social benefits provided for them.

This side of the life of the community belongs alike to
Russia and to Communism: it is not, like the persecution of
religion, a matter of hunting down certain persons for their
opinions, which was always distasteful to Russians, but of
benefiting all. Foreign visitors who never saw Russia before
the preaching of Communism have taken all that peculiar
charm which Russia puts into its institutions as something
new; if they knew it, what attracts them very often belongs
rather to the ever old and new Russia than to the brand-new
Communism.

I have mentioned earlier that these admirable things now
being done under Communism had a very sound, if limited,
foundation in the work of the elected county and town councils which were in active operation for over fifty years before
the Revolution. They were Liberal rather than Socialist, but
surely in a matter like this the two can blend easily. The difference, in those times, was that the Tsar's Government
in its jealousy of the *zemstva* and its reactionary suspicion of
them, was always trying to cripple their work; but it was just
this that gave a strong spice of missionary spirit to the workers.
They knew that they were the positive as opposed to the negative in public life, and that therefore they held the key to
the future. The Tsar could come in and smash their organisation and drive them from their work, as he did in the universally
praised *zemstvo* of peasant Vyatka, manned almost entirely

by peasant farmers; but he could not put anything positive in their place. It became an altogether different story when the Government itself put all its own force behind this work and extended and deepened it beyond the dreams of the old *zemstvo* workers. But that was what the Soviet Government was there for, and that was what it tried to do from he very first.

I have said "tried to do," and the wish was wholehearted; but the first question was what it was possible to do, and I have placed this part of the record as late as this in the story because, with the best intentions, it was long before this work could attain such volume as to make its effects everywhere perceptible. Civil War, foreign intervention, famine, epidemics, the breakdown of currency made this for a long time impossible. How could you start schools everywhere in a Russian winter if you could not command fuel to warm them? How fill the country with doctors if medical training had been hopelessly interrupted? At such a time it was explainable why show-windows should be few and unlikely to sustain close examination; and as all this work was represented as entirely new and dating only from the communist revolution, the Government was not anxious to admit foreign visitors who could ask awkward questions in Russian and still less if they had seen the *zemstvo* beginnings earlier and could cast a balance between what had been destroyed and what was only just being created. The effects of the new construction were always becoming more visible, but perhaps a satisfactory picture of the whole could only be obtained when Stalin had broken the back of his great task and was able to call a general holiday.

The *zemstvo* budgets had been mainly devoted to public health and education, but in the most modest proportions as compared with what was now possible. According to Yaroslavsky, the number of doctors in Russia had increased from 1,380 in 1897 to 12,000 in 1935. Public health was a first consideration with the Soviet Government, and it watched over it with close and constant care from start to finish, and that without any kind of payment for medical service. An expectant mother is removed from work in due time—two months in advance in the case of manual workers, their jobs being reserved for them—and is put under medical care. A second doctor is attached as soon as the child is born. When after another two months the mother is allowed back to work, its conditions are fixed by her doctor. The child can be left in a crèche within reach of her, and can be fetched home and brought back on her way to and from work.

At the age of three or four it will be left in the same way

at a kindergarten, and there the simple and natural Russian artistic taste, and the special interest in and understanding of children will be seen in all the surroundings, for the Russian nature always itself remains child-like. There are flowers and sprays of pine, goldfish in a little glass tank, hanging toy balloons of various bright colours, everything to make a joyous atmosphere. Also plenty of clever toys which will at once amuse and instruct, coloured pencils for drawing, big building bricks to put together (the children can get inside the little houses which they build), simple tools for carpentry, picture-books and a nature corner. The windows are big, and outside there is a veranda for sleeping in the open. There are separate entrances for the different age groups. The child is given a bath on entering and put into other clean clothes—its own are put in a locker: all the cupboards are low. In everything the idea is that the children should "play at work"—as much as possible together, for the "collective" note runs through everything; but there are a couple of short lessons a day, from a quarter to half an hour, according to age, in drawing, painting, singing, dancing, reading, writing or arithmetic, also gymnastics. Even at this stage the children have little monitors of their own, and initiative is encouraged to teach responsibility.

A specially attractive institution is the so-called "Mother and Child." Really long continental journeys are often unavoidable in Russia, even for the poor. A mother coming to one of the greater towns in search of work will find at the terminus a suite of rooms specially provided with taste and charm for travelling mothers and children. Someone is playing a piano. There are toys and other amusements, especially singing and dancing, under the care of the attendants —almost any educated Russian woman seems a born governess—and here the child can be left while the mother makes her inquiries in the town. The suite seems a complete whole, with accessories such as provisions for travelling fathers in charge of a child, a reading-room and so on.

The child's visits to the crèche and kindergarten are at the option of its parents. The kindergarten is already educational and is under the Commissariat of Education, and from this it will pass to a preparatory school, often attached to the school which it will enter at eight. School attendance runs from eight to fifteen and is compulsory. The State is extending it to the age of eighteen years. At the foundation of the school curriculum are the nature studies, such as biology, always the favourite subjects of Russian children who have so much to interest them in their own country in such fields as geology, geography, zoology, ethnology and natural history of all kinds.

With book studies at one time ran parallel, throughout, a graded system of practical work with tools and instruments of increasing complexity. This was dropped in 1937—its object had been the speeding up of training for industrial work; but behind it was a far-reaching idea, which remains. It is one of the main objects of Soviet education that the worker should become an "all-rounder," with an undersanding not limited to one particular process. This is called "poly-technisation" or at a later stage "mixing of specialties." The Soviet citizen is to understand as a whole the functioning of the work of the community; of this a mere division of labour would leave him unintelligent. He is to understand the inter-relations between the work of town and of country, and not to regard them as separate compartments. He is to have an idea of the whole organisation and distribution of production. For that reason, even at play, he is to be extending his knowledge.

In earlier years it was the practice to give a large portion of the school hours to object lessons, such as visits to factories, villages, railway stations or other working enterprises. These were called "complexes," divided up into a number of "projects" or special studies of various functions of the factory or village work and life, but they proved such a nuisance to the institutions concerned that they were abolished wholesale in 1931.

From 1926 to 1932 schools were dominated by the psychological analysis and study of eccentric children, but this, too, has been in the main abolished. One specially good feature which has endured and prospered is the admirable use of museums for teaching; whole classes are brought there for lectures. One of the many experiments made in the secondary schools was the Dalton method, by which the pupil himself maps out his day's work; but with the stricter new discipline that is now out of vogue.

Both at schools and universities it was the pupils who were at first in charge; they were encouraged to report on their teachers and could even bring about their dismissals. They could even sometimes dictate the syllabus and the time-table. There were committees of pupils for every imaginable purpose. Work was done largely not as individuals, but in small groups, which gave no guarantee of individual progress. All that has now gone by the board. Ordinary classes and lectures have been restored; the teacher's authority has been fully re-established. In the last three years of study 30 per cent of the time is still given to practical work.

The Soviet school originally had two chiefs—one educational and one political. The second, not necessarily a man of higher education, was much more important. Now the contentious period seems more or less over, and the two posts are ordinarily combined. On the management there were now a method master, a psychologist and a cultural supervisor. The period of distrust of parents is also past: there is a Parents' Council, and it is also represented on the Committee of Assistants, which takes a special interest in school finance, school meals, pupils' clothing and summer camps.

The class work, on our last information, was four hours a day, rising to six. Special attention is given to art in all its forms. Voice production is taught, and is practised in choral singing, also the acting and even the writing and staging of plays. So is the telling of stories. Teaching is in general kept as close as possible to problems of real life. Economic geography is a special subject of study, and includes the capitalist States. Social science—that is, of course, the Marxist view of the world—is begun at thirteen, with particular emphasis on the capitalist encirclement of the "one Socialist State."

There are schools for factory apprentices, with a short course of up to a year, and so-called "Technicums" with a course of four years' technical study begun at fifteen, which includes politics and Marxism (dialectical materialism). Thirty to forty per cent of the work is practical. These technical colleges have always been popular with young Russians.

The drastic reform of 1935 made access to all institutions of higher education obtainable only by examination and on merit; and two of the biggest facts about Soviet Russia are that practically all education and all medical attendance are free to the individual at the expense of the State, which pays all teachers and doctors. Controlling the universities and technical colleges, the State is able to adapt the numbers of their students to the needs of the public service of the country. I have mentioned earlier the restoration of the teaching of history and geography, the comparative discounting of propaganda, the return to objective study, and the special encouragement of research.

Even before the Revolution, there was always a large number of sons of peasants in the universities; now the proportion of peasants and workers is from 75 to 90 per cent and 80 per cent of the whole number receive bursaries. The students' personal discipline is still in their own hands, but the lecturers have full authority to exact punctuality, good order, and respect. Students' meetings now take place ordinarily not more than once a month. On the other hand there are circles for every kind of study. The instruction is a mixture of the lecture with the tutorial, and there is a large proportion of practical work.

There are now numerous institutes for specialisation in given studies. Sometimes the Press, which is encouraged to criticise freely in such matters, has insisted on a closer connection being kept between the study-work of students and the practical experience for which the majority of them are presumably being trained, even if at some expense to purely theoretical research.

Then there is a very far-reaching organisation, both intensive and extensive, of extra-mural education for adults. This was bound to be of the first importance to the Soviet Union, for it had to capture what it could of the older generation; besides, how could a man work a machine if he could not read his instructions? It might be easy enough to teach literacy to the young; with their elders it was a very different matter, especially in the Central Asiatic provinces where it had practically to start from scratch and even in many cases with the creation of written alphabets. This was a veritable crusade, and almost the foremost part in it was taken by children organised in brigades. In the face of all obstacles they made their way into the poorest houses and drew up lists of the illiterate. They cut out alphabets, they gave lessons, they even deputed some of their number to look after the baby while they taught the mother. They captured any odd accommodation for their classes. The factories joined in. Names of those who would not learn were written up on blackboards, or the names of foremen whose gangs included a defaulter: they even held "trials" of the malingerers. By 1932, in the Russian and the White Russian Republics, nearly everyone under fifty-five had been roped in.

With literacy had to go the beginnings of further teaching. The semi-literate were attacked in the same way, but with even more organisation. The teachers themselves had to be further instructed: and at the top specialists in teaching were engaged, conferences were held, till the whole process became systematic. Nothing does more honour to the Soviet State than its now nearly complete triumph in this field of literacy. A scholar employed in the tasks necessary to success might well feel with enthusiasm that he is serving the cause of objective knowledge for the community as a whole. When I was in Kiev in 1936 and was entertained by scholars of the Academy and University, I was made to feel this. One of them had made the first dictionary of English and Ukrainian, and remember that in the days of Tsardom the idea of a dictionary of Ukrainian was itself anathema. They told me that they felt an altogether happier perspective for their work.

The instruction of peasants, and town workers too, in the use of machinery is another vast task in itself. The very modest efforts of the *zemstvo* in the supply of agronoms or agricultural advisers might well seem nothing at all in comparison with the present great state provision of help of this kind. Some *zemstva,* for instance that of Samara (now Kuibyshev), were able to set up bacteriological stations; but that was a drop in the ocean to what the State is doing now; and with the huge sanitary problems of Russia, its original almost universal backwardness, and specially the great waves of epidemics and cattle diseases, this work must long maintain its missionary character.

The Soviet Union has a complete system of insurance, not only against old age and against acidents, but also against other circumstances which have resulted in a reduction of working ability. There are also extensive arrangements for holidays without loss of pay, which are operated through the trade unions. These trade unions have, of course, long since ceased to have any independent existence and are nothing more than a branch of state activity, but they are not without value to the worker, as through them he has the right and opportunity to put his claims in such questions as dismissal. A demonstrative use has been made of imperial and other palaces for workmen's holidays, but this is not likely to have affected large numbers of persons. Tsarkoe Selo, the Russian Windsor, was called Detskoe Selo (the Children's Village), up to the Pushkin centenary in 1937; it was then renamed again after the great national poet, who was at school there. The favourite haunts of the revels of Rasputin and of the young aristocracy in the "white nights" of summer at Petersburg are now reconstructed as rest houses for workers. Crimea and the Caucasus, with their lovely scenery and luxurious houses, have been specially used as rest houses for workers and intellectuals.

Great care and attention is given in the organisation of pageants and other popular feasts, and of these a Russian crowd is particularly appreciative, throwing itself wholeheartedly into the enjoyment of every detail. The "crowd sense," which is just another expression of the corporate instinct, is peculiarly strong in Russia, and it is often curiously reminiscent of an English crowd, particularly in its broad and jolly sense of humour. But Russians of any class have a much stronger artistic sense than we have. This was so before the revolution, and it comes out in the organisation of these festivals. They are all out to enjoy themselves, and anything particularly clever or pretty gets them at once. In Kiev, still as always a beautiful city on its lovely site, in the late summer of 1936, I saw a march past of all the wards in turn. They swung past with splendid vigour, squads of men or of women—one squad of women had in the middle of it a fine old man with a long beard who looked very pleased with his company. There were flowers and dancing everywhere; each ward was preceded by a dancing band of girl skirmishers in the picturesque Ukrainian costume, sometimes singing the charming Ukrainian folk songs. At one point various forms of recreation and amusement were represented: the fishermen carrying long fishing rods with coloured paper fish hooked to them, the chess players[1] carrying enormous cardboard knights, bishops and castles. Interspersed between the detachments came curious and fanciful constructions, sometimes very ingenious; an effigy of Trotsky with long nose and black eyes and curls made an excellent Mephistopheles. It was a family feast of old and young, and we all exchanged our comments as each new surprise went past. With the usual courtesy to guests there was a chair set for me, and when I wanted to let a lady have it, I was genially told "that I had to submit to the will of the majority." At one time a torrent of rain came down, but the marchers swung past with all the more vigour and enjoyment. And so it was with the onlookers. After several hours of it, I asked a neighbouring policeman whether I couldn't go away: "No," he said very nicely, "you must stay and enjoy it." And enjoy it they certainly did, for in spite of more downpours of rain, from my room in my hotel I could hear them singing and dancing on the square outside till two in the morning. The one thing that fell below the level of all the rest was the exhausting reiteration of the portraits of Stalin and the other "big noises" of Communism. There must have been about forty of Stalin alone: one ten foot high, of the face alone. I noticed a sympathetic cheer when there came past a single portrait of Lenin.

This was for everyone, people of all sorts, but what has struck me most in the new Russia is the organisation of the young. In that same year, 1936, I travelled through a good part of Russia with a party of English public schoolmasters and boys, none of whom spoke Russian or had ever been

[1] Many account the Russian chess players the best in the world.

there before, so that, except for the lady guides put at our disposal, I was the only means of communication for them. As to the guides, in four successive visits with several guides in each, I only met two who seemed to me in any way unsatisfactory. They spoke perfect English, were highly educated, and knew their work thoroughly. We had a 'bus of our own in each place, just holding our party; the guide would sit in front and I in the rear, both of us explaining the same objects as we passed them. The outside of Leningrad, as apart from special sights, is shown extremely well and with wonderful dispatch in a single day. The lady guide was excellent on all the artistic and historical monuments. In the little palace of Nicholas II at Tsarkoe Selo not an unkind word was said of the last Tsar and his family: he was described exactly as he was—an admirable husband and father, a healthy out-of-door man, and really there is nothing more to say, for when I spoke with him, it was almost impossible to remember that one was talking to an Emperor. I hardly ever found it necessary to make any correction to our boys. Once, in the cottage of a Christian peasant, the icons were explained as only there for decoration, which was quite different from what their owner had said; so I had to put that right. It may be taken, then, that our party did really see all of Russia that could be got into the tour, and everywhere we were brought into close contact with the youth organisations. The result was that we all agreed we never had a more heartening holiday.

There is something peculiarly inspiring in these young folk of the new Russia. The young seem to count for more than anything else there. Childhood was always the most charming age for Russians, and their children had always a natural attraction for ours; but this was individual; there was very little discipline in the old Russia—except for a few *élite* families of the gentry, some families of priests, and some of the better and more self-respecting peasants. They had not an open door in front of them, and a way pointed out to them. Whatever else communism has done, it has re-created Russian childhood.

The innumerable children's organisations elect their own little monitors—girls and boys, and the girls looked to me the most self-possessed and efficient. One only had to notice with what simplicity and grace they would shepherd wandering members of our party; the Russian child is a born little host or hostess. These leaders did not seem at all conceited about their authority, but rather full of keenness to play up to their responsibilities.

There are now palaces for children, as for workers and for soviets, and the buildings are palatial as much in their art as in their dimensions. In the dethroned capital which has passed through so many names—St. Petersburg, Petrograd, Leningrad—I have never seen anything so absolutely and healthily joyous as a feast day of the little pioneers (ten to sixteen) in their palace close to the Anichkov Bridge. To start with, there were so many of them, and that in itself was a happiness—fresh and budding human life all round one. Then there was a perfect unconstraint, and they all seemed to feel like one enormous family. There were the theatres with troupes of child actors, generously applauded; of course there was folk singing. On the more serious side we learned that these children had constructed a little railway of their own, somewhere in the suburbs, and were responsible for the running of it. The feeling that they imparted to us was of a great zest in life and a great hope of the future.

When talking with older children, I got this same impression of the open door. Perhaps I had expected a parrot repetition of propaganda. What I found was very much more self-expression, more thinking, and more independent ideas of their own than before the revolution, and I ought to have anticipated that with a Russian child this was just the effect that propaganda would probably have.

We saw these young people in their work and their sports, and afterwards it all blended with us in a common memory of pleasure, usually bringing back to us the refrain of a certain song of hope and endeavour which they were always singing. We saw the final tie of the Volley Ball championship between the healthy-looking Muscovites and a swarthy young team from the Sea of Azov, boys and girls on both sides; also a very creditable imitation of a League match, except for the passing and goalkeeping, between the local Red Army and the Waterworks in Kiev; the two sides marched on to the field in pairs, a red and a blue together, in the most approved manner prescribed by Mr. Herbert Chapman, and the refereeing was above criticism.

In a school at Kiev a Russian boy and an English one (through me) exchanged a comparison of an ordinary day's work: our boy included prayers, which was accepted without a murmur. Finally, the local authority came to me with a charming proposition: "Do you mind?" he said. "We have picked the best of our children, and we have told them that as a reward for the best work of the year they might spend the evening with your boys." With flowers and singing and a beautiful banquet, no joint merry-making could have gone better: and most thoughtfully, as a professor, I was ensconced in a slightly raised alcove, surrounded with scholars and talk of dictionaries, and sipping the traditional beverage of English dons, an excellent and particularly fruity port wine. No wonder everyone enjoyed it.

It is a very charming experience to be admitted to the children's theatres—practically no grown-ups; a whole audience under, say, fourteen. The children come not in classes but in groups of friends. The plays are first class—no playing down—and are very well chosen. My neighbour, a small girl, said to me, "You'll enjoy this, it's very good." There was rapt attention and the most perfect discipline, and the moment the curtain was down the place became like a wood full of small birds all chattering at once. It is the young who give all the colouring to the public parks "of Culture and Rest," for the workers' families visit them *en masse,* the men and boys in their cloth caps, and everything is designed for the young—especially for the youngest; for these, there is a kind of special fortress-citadel to which adults are not admitted. I always have a vivid remembrance of Moscow in Battersea Park, the loveliest that I know, at whose gates I lived. This is not a park that belongs to no one in particular; it belongs to the people of Battersea, and they know it; there on a Sunday evening, listening to the band, with the little kiddies dancing on the asphalt or twirling in and out among their elders on their scooters, there is the same feeling of one big united family.

And the value of all these social services of the State is not to be measured against its equivalent in wages. To start with, England has "arrived" and Russia so far has not; out own community, both employers and workers, in well-being lives on a much higher level. But apart from that, there is a special value that attaches to thought and care; and the Russian workers—and everyone in Russia is a worker now—while they are profiting by the help and enjoying the pleasures provided for them, feel that they are all of one stock and are all alike the children of one great mother—Mother Russia (*Matushka Rus.*)

To return to a thought which I carry with me all along, one needs to have seen Russia before the Revolution to know what among all this was there before, for it is just that, that is surest to remain and grow. There was always this genius of the great family in Russia; in some ways it was cramped or suppressed, but it always succeeded in expressing itself and carrying everyone with it, especially in any great emergency of trial, such as war or famine. That is what always charmed us Englishmen.

And the old Russia, or what is best worth keeping of it, is still there, even its charming foibles and failures. You feel it, the minute you cross the frontier. There is always some "history," some "incident,"—to be frank, some incipient muddle, that makes the social life worth living.

As I first tread the snow outside the terminus at Moscow, I feel I have forgotten my snow-shoes: everyone seems to echo my cry of annoyance: there is the traditional Russian village chorus, and in a minute or two up rushes the conductor waving them triumphantly in his hand, fully as pleased as I am (and by the way, there are no tips now).

Or again, on coming in at the desolate frontier station, I find myself engaged in a typical village debate on social justice, in which each speaker enthusiastically backs the other side, because one of our party has taken a sleeping berth which does not belong to him; and it ends with the conductor, the doctor and myself joining hands and saying, "It's all settled."

Or once more, the schoolboy party is leavnig the wharf at Leningrad. In the wooden custom house, which has a charming array of Russian toys, I am enlisted to call out all the English names correctly, there is only the most superficial examination, and the obliging chief official says genially: "Now that is all, and you just go through on to the boat"— and there is no boat, no boat for half an hour! Never mind, there will be a boat—will be, will be—and in the end there really was a boat. It is still dear old Russia.

And from this generic "Russian-ness" the new government is not immune. In 1914, before the war was in sight, the Tsar, after long deliberations by his Ministers, gave judgment on a proposal of an Anglo-Russian Exhibition in London. "It is to be (*Byt po semu*), he decided, "but not this year." In 1937, after equally long deliberations on a proposed hostel for British and American students in Moscow, on the eve of my departure, the final arbiter of the question himself most kindly rang me up to say: "This is a very good idea, it is most promising. You shall have a decision quite soon," and, later, again came the usual last word, which has remained valid till to-day. "It must wait."

XV

FOR A "UNITED FRONT"

(1934-38)

WHY I WAS SO ANXIOUS TO GET A HOSTEL FOR BRITISH AND American students in Moscow, was because nearly all cultural ties between us and Russia have been cut off, and with that any real knowledge of Russia; and if we are to keep our world position we have got to have it. This is chiefly their fault. They have been so suspicious and so niggardly about entry to their country that it was almost impossible for any of our younger people to sit down there for years and get to know about it: the only way was by technical service, and that has now failed us. The American scholars feel the same as we do, and we act together; so, whenever we get the chance, we all ask for just the same thing—namely a hostel, with access to Soviet colleges and libraries, and at such an expense as a student's pocket can meet.

But there is another obstacle, and that is our own profound insularity, which at bottom remains triumphantly indifferent to our imperative need of thorough, not merely journalistic, study of the remoter countries. This indifference is quite out of keeping with the English mind: we are greatly interested in unkown peoples; we are more objective in our impressions of them than any other foreigners, and we are quite good linguists, whenever we have to be or will take the trouble. But in general we seem to be content with being carpet-baggers or with reading their reports. As a nation, we don't get down to spade work, as the Germans do, and make a thorough job of it, though in the case of Russia we are ever so much better qualified to understand what we see there and have far more in common with their thought and life.

I write all this because, at the point which we have reached in our story, Bolshevism, as an international danger, had withdrawn into its shell. If it came out again, and tried to force itself on our own country, then I should combat it here as I tried my best to do in 1920, when it was at its peak; but if it does so, it may be very largely because we missed our chance when we had it. Many of us, I am afraid, and very important people too, have thought throughout in terms of Bolshevism, and not of Russia, though Russia was obviously always far more permanent and important; and that is a mistake, which this book is another belated attempt to correct.

Without discussing who was to blame—it is a very mixed question, which I have dealt with earlier—it was the omission of Russia from the Treaty of Versailles that deprived it of the character of a world settlement. It threw Russia and Germany into each other's arms, and left the way open for important evasions of the Treaty by Germany, especially in the matter of rearmament. This added an ominous danger to the faults in the Treaty which, if frontiers in Central and Western Europe were to be fixed on the basis of national claims, was the most just that there ever has been. The war guilt clause, the reparations clauses, the restrictions on armament were all made more dangerous in the presence of a material force outside the Treaty, which the Soviet Government has never recognized. Russia's initial absence from the League of Nations was as important as America's.

We have, in fairness, to remember that then we were all thinking of something else, and for that the Bolsheviks themselves were responsible. While we interfered with them, they interfered with us. The Communist Revolution in Russia, with its active menace to our own internal peace, had stirred up all sorts of dangers for us at home. Kamenev was active in our Black Friday. Tomsky had a hand in our General Strike. Zinoviev's chief job, as Head of the Third International, was to work for revolution in England. So there was a constant exchange of futile moves and counter-moves from both sides: Joynson-Hick's discovery of a tobacco-pouch in the safe at Arcos may be matched with the decent failure which our good Labour leaders made of Tomsky's prescription. Mr. Baldwin was a Peace Minister—for peace at home, which was then gravely in question, and most of us at the time were very glad to have him. But, partly in consequence of our own divisions at home, foreign policy, in the fifteen years when we really had a chance with Germany, stumbled throughout.

Versailles was slowly and clumsily liquidated, being made thereby to confess its own partial failure. Dawes Plan (1924), Young Plan (1929), and then an end of reparations—leaving no one really satisfied, and a fitting preface to the great slump here and in America. No steps in common to all-round disarmament, to justify our restrictions on Germany; only inadequate proposals from ourselves and especially from France, leading up to the opposite of what we aimed at, rearmament in Germany without the equivalent in England. Perhaps nothing bore clearer witness to the continuance of the rule of material force than the fact that not one of the major questions which concerned the major powers was settled by the League of Nations—if we except Locarno and the temporary acceptance of the demilitarisation of the Rhineland, which was certainly achieved under its influence but in no way applied to Eastern Europe. It was only the minor States that had to obey the League—not even Poland in the matter of Vilna. But so far, the territorial provisions of the Treaty stood. It was only with the advent of Hitler that we had to face the question whether they were to go the way of the rest.

It was intelligible that Hitler, when he had got Germany to hold up her head again, should be out for the recovery of all lost territory: the loss was not really accepted in maps publicly displayed at stations and elsewhere; but he had himself already in his book made it abundantly clear that he was out for something very much bigger than that. There could not have been a clearer—or more extravagant—announcement of intentions than was contained in *Mein Kampf*. Even if the author refused to allow a full translation of any foreign language, it was up to foreign statesmen to acquaint themselves with it not a moment later than when the author became the ruler of Germany, for *Mein Kampf* was a major fact in foreign policy. The Russians did so at once, and not only drew the necessary conclusions but put them into practice. And this, too, was another major fact which there can be no excuse for ignoring.

It is proper here to make one qualification. Stalin reversed his peasant policy, his family policy, his foreign policy; he came out for the propaganda of Socialism by example, by showing what it could do in the country under his rule. But he could not be expected to renounce his faith in ultimate revolution. As head of the Russian Communist party—remember, that was then his only post in Russia—he was throughout under a cross fire from two sides—from the capitalist world in its objections to Communism, and from Trotsky for his alleged betrayal of it. Trotsky had even appealed in vain to the Comintern against him. Trotsky was still a big enough man to be heard everywhere; he remarked ironically that the Fifth and Seventh Commandments had been restored in Russia, though so far without reference to God. It was not strange, therefore, if there were still signs outside of the work of the Comintern established in Moscow. Meanwhile in Russia it was not allowed to meet for six years after Stalin's triumph; and when it appeared later (September, 1935), it was in a very purged and chastened form, as an instrument for propaganda behind the line of actual or prospective enemies, such as Germany's dealings with the Irish or ours with the Czechs in World War I. Its headquarters were moved away from the centre of Moscow. It had become a side line.

Already, in Japan's invasion of Manchuria in 1931, which ended in Russia's loss of a vital link in her Trans-Siberian trunk-line, the Soviet Government had witnessed the first conspicuous failure of the League of Nations in a question in which she herself had a lively interest. At the outset, the Soviet Government had renounced the imperialist claims of Tsardom on China, and the one direction in which its foreign policy was unvaried, was its consistent support of Chinese independence against Japan. The League did condemn Japan, and Japan left the League; America's attempt to check Japan received no active support.

Now that Hitler was in the saddle and was threatening the independence of Austria, there was a move towards joint opposition from England, France and Italy at the conference of Stresa in April, 1935; and there was no suggestion of inviting the co-operation of the Soviet Union, though Russia had then for more than six months been a member of the League. In 1925, at Locarno, a really substantial settlement had been reached of the differences between France and Germany; but nothing had been done to remove the dangers to peace in Eastern Europe, where Poland and Czechoslovakia, both of them new to the map, and other States which equally owed their position to the Allied victory, were left in the air. Litvinov at Geneva strongly urged that the peace of Europe, to be stable, must be indivisible, and stood for collective security of the *status quo*. This was another proof that the Soviet Union wanted to avoid war; and it was all the more striking because Russia, who did not acknowledge the Versailles settlement, had lost more territory in the last war than Germany or any other country. But he was never successful in getting any response. Anyhow, Russia had no sympathy with the Austrian Government after it had fired on the workers' quarters in Vienna.

When Mussolini scraped a quarrel with Abyssinia on the model of Japan's procedure in Manchuria, the Soviets were more interested. They have always regarded Italy as a typical capitalist State of the second order, deserving little respect whether for its power or for its changing policies—a kind of international jackal; and the Abyssinian conflict was a classical example of the worst kind of colonial adventure —the worst kind of attempt of a European people to exploit Africa, for which Lenin's vocabulary had long since found the appropriate terms. Russia had already been a year in the League, and represented her view with vigour. It was France this time that took all the life out of the League's counter-action. The French did not want to quarrel with Italy. They did not see that if they paralysed the League's action when Italy was in question, they might be faced by the same coldness on our side when it was Germany. The "sanctions" against Italy were never made effective; the Abyssinians got no help —for instance by the closing of the Suez Canal or the cutting off of petrol supply to their enemy—and Italy was able to complete her conquest. In the following March when Hitler boldly remilitarised the Rhineland, we were as lukewarm as France had been about Abyssinia and gave no encouragement to the idea of a "preventive war." Litvinov strongly criticised the weakness of the League.

France and Russia had been in defensive alliance, directed of course against German aggression, since May 2nd, 1935—that is, just after the conference of Stresa; and the declared policy of Soviet Russia was a united front with the democracies against the Fascist and Nazi Powers. This policy was prejudiced by the Communist attitude to Labour in the western democracies. In England, especially, Labour firmly resisted the too familiar infiltration of Communism into its own organisations. Stalin, of course, if he had wanted the support of British Labour, ought to have called it off. As early as January, 1934, before Russia joined the League, he had seen—what was becoming clear—that Europe was shaping towards "a second imperialist war" which "would inevitably unleash revolution" but, of course, the quarter from which he expected it was Nazified Germany. He followed out his principle of "working relations" with such States, capitalist or not, as were at the time friendly towards the Sovie Union. These, at this time, were the western democracies. All this was a part of the manœuvring to avert or postpone the expected joint attack of the capitalist world on Soviet Russia. Stalin definitely wanted peace, and wanted it ever since he had abstained from taking up the Japanese challenge on the Trans-Siberian—not for altruistic reasons, but because any interruption of peace, even outside the Russian borders was bound to prejudice the completion of the economic transformation of Russia in which he was so deeply absorbed.

The policy of "the united front" was to be subjected to a much more grueling test with the rising of General Franco in Spain (July 17, 1936), which was to lead to two and a half years of civil war. As is well known, the Spanish Parliament, which supplied the authority of the Spanish Government, contained numerous Syndicalists and still more numerous Anarchists (in general, simply upholders of the decentralisation traditional to the country), with only a small sprinkling of Communists; but, as the struggle hardened, and exactly as in Russia, the Communists, by virtue of the vastly greater compactness of their doctrine and discipline, gradually took a more and more central place on the government side.

It was impossible for Stalin, with his antecedents, to have taken any other side, and in one period the Russian bombers were very effective. The fighting, at this stage, was a kind of try-out between the rival ideologies of Communism and Fascism on someone else's ground, and in this military sense it was no doubt useful to both. But in Spain Stalin was fighting not only Franco but Trotsky, whose supporters were also very active there. Stalin's dog-fight with Trotsky was a personal vendetta sharper than any disputes which this shrewd politician had to wage with any capitalist State. Stalin was fighing on both fronts for the same reason, that in the interest of his own country it was now his policy to stand in with the western democracies; and in the perspective of that time it could well be hoped that, after the lesson of 1914-18, any common action by England, France and Russia would prove so effective in checking the disturbers of the peace that there might be no European war at all. Which is certainly what Stalin most of all desired.

But to this lead—and on the side of Russia it undoubtedly was a lead—the western democracies gave no response which could have any effect. The non intervention committee sat on and on in London. The Russians, for the most part, gradually withdrew from Spain to make it look really like a non-intervention committee. The Italians poured in regular troops more and more openly, and the Germans sent Franco very effective technical help. There is no real doubt that the wholesale obliteration of Guernica, the capital of the democratic Basques (April 27, 1937) was the work of German airmen. Maisky, who had charge of the Russian interests on the non-intervention committee, had an extraordinarily difficult task. A totalitarian government, such as Stalin's, looks for results. On the Committee it almost seemed as if Russia were only allowed to participate on sufferance. Appeasement—only of one side, Hitler and Mussolini—seemed the only thing that mattered. Let Russia above all things keep quiet. If she showed that there was another side, she was the restless boy in the school, she was prejudicing the success of the negotiations. Maisky showed a remarkably cool head; he never broke up the committee, and he made the Soviet Union count in a way that won the respect of many more of our public than had any sympathies with the principles of communist rule. In the end the committee broke up of itself ingloriously in face of a victory for Franco, which under the conditions had at last become inevitable, and a veritable triumph of the Nazi and Fascist Powers.

We were now on the main road of appeasement of these Powers even, if it had to be so, at the expense of others; and never did our indifference to a knowledge of the factors with which we were dealing come in with more damaging effect.

On March 10th, 1938, Hitler, anything but "appeased," brought off his first great international burglary in Austria; he marched in while his Ambassador here, Ribbentrop, was at lunch with our then Prime Minister and Foreign Secretary. Some of the details of the burglary were rather clumsily managed, but the Germans all the same attained the speed usually associated with their week-end enterprises. The murderers of Dollfuss now became heroes.

The most important effect of the seizure of Austria was that it really smashed up that rickety system of alliances with the smaller Eastern States, which France had first set up in order to recoup herself for the loss of the Russian alliance in 1918, and to create a "cordon sanitaire" against the then active menace of Bolshevism. France had allied herself with Czechoslovakia in 1923. Since then she had allied herself with Soviet Russia, and Russia took the Czechs into alliance on May 25th, 1935. Both France and Russia were now cut off from giving the Czechs direct aid. Czechoslovakia was practically encircled by Nazi Germany, except for two gaps where she was faced by hostile Hungary and doubtful Poland.

One cannot refuse one's respect to the Czechs. They are Slavs who were taught by Germany to counter German measures with German effect. But in this long struggle of the obstinate under-dog they built up a great school of character and acquired a wonderful discipline, which was nation-wide. In World War I their marvellous Anabasis in Siberia—that country was for the time really captured by Czech prisoners of war who had joined our side—they were the outstanding refutal of Bismarck's reliance on "the big battalions" and the most consoling proof that quality may count for more than quantity after all. In their well-won restoration of independence —it was not a gift of Versailles, for they had won it for themselves before the Treaty—they proved a model to all their neighbours. They had too much good sense to waste time and the future on reprisals: they actually contributed substantially to the financial stability of post-war Vienna, their recent master. In their treatment of their inevitable minorities—in language, schools, representation in parliament—they stood out above all other States on the Continent. Democracy for them was a faith for which their own generation had had to fight. It was not for nothing that their chief was also their teacher—that great philosopher Thomas Masaryk, and, curiously enough, it was they who, under bondage in the 17th century, had revived the educational tradition of Plato's Republic, before these principles were again to come to life as one of the European gains of the French Revolution.

No part of Czechoslovakia had ever been under the rule of Berlin. They had a natural frontier which had stood for one thousand years, in three linked ranges of mountains on the north, west and east. Bismarck had described Bohemia as a fortress made by God for Himself. The northern mountains and the adjacent plain country were peopled by Germans who, also under Austrian rule, had for centuries lived intermixed with the Czechs and without any claim to separation from them: it was only the focus of neighbouring Nazi rule and Nazi propaganda that ever raised the question. Some of those of us who knew least about history were actually at one time bluffed into admitting Hitler's claim that all Germans, wherever they lived, should belong to the Reich: they can't have done much thinking, for of course this would include large tracts of Pennsylvania and other parts of the United States.

The Czechs, as Slavs, have always relied on Russia: in fact, every Czech in their famous legions realised that, without a Russia that counted, Czechoslovak independence hung in the air. The Russian alliance with Czechoslovakia was contingent on the French: in the protocol it was definitely stated that, if France came to the assistance of Czechoslovakia, Russia would then do the same. The French had themselves helped to construct the Czech Maginot Line along the mountain frontier, which cost Czechoslovakia 100 millions: we are told that German officers when they visited it later said that it could have held out for two years.

The Sudeten Germans were systematically worked up by Nazi propaganda—"self-determination" conducted from outside. As is made clear in Dr. Hugh Dalton's admirable *Hitler's War*, Hitler had given the Czechs one assurance after another against attack. But now, while he reiterated his demands, he poured extravagant abuse on the Czech nation, which should have warned us of the measure of their justice. On May 20th, 1938, he had mobilised on the frontier; but the Czechs were equally prompt and the stroke was postponed. We sent Lord Runciman to investigate the question, and at his insistance one plan after another was proposed by the Czechs to meet the Nazi claims. By the last of these plans the Sudeten Germans would have been in a highly privileged position as compared with the rest of the population. The Sudeten leader, Henlein, had earlier been far more moderate in his claims, but he had visited Hitler and acted on his instructions, and his reply was to fly to Germany and invoke intervention.

For so small a country, the Czechs were extraordinarily well prepared, both materially and morally, for national defence. They had the Skoda munition works, one of the very best in Europe, without whose help hardly any Balkan country could go to war. They had a strong and highly trained army and large numbers of daring pilots, of whom many later showed their worth in our air-warfare. They had even done much to fortify their new Austrian frontier. That they would put up a fine fight was certain. On their side, the question offered nothing new; it was simply whether France could face a major war, and, if so, whether we, though unpledged, would come to their help.

No one should underrate the overwhelming responsibilities that lay on the British Prime Minister of that time. We should have to know much more about the attitude of the French Government to pass an adequate judgment on our own. We can appreciate to the full his spirit in brushing aside any question of personal or national dignity in an attempt by three arduous journeys to Germany to avert a European war. But foreign policy is a most difficult field to enter late in life; Grey had prepared himself by years of study before his time came to take office. Even sovereigns and dictators in their foreign visits take with them their responsible Foreign Minister and, if they do not know the language, they would take their own interpreter. The Czechs were not invited to take part in the discussion, nor did the British Premier go on from Berchtesgaden to Prague. Surely there were two sides to this dispute. We did, indeed, communicate with Prague. Dr. Benes, the able pupil and successor of Masaryk as President, at 2 a.m. on September 21st, was waked up to receive a surprise joint visit of the French and British Ministers, and was told that the French alliance could not be counted on unless, without parliamentary sanction, he agreed to the cession of the mountain frontier with its Maginot Line. Could it, then, be counted on for anything else? If the French, who were pledged, would give no support to Czechoslovakia, we, of course, could not. On September 23rd Litvinov, then at Geneva, renewed the Russian pledge to come to the help of Czechoslovakia if France carried out hers. At Godesberg the British Premier began to realise that Hitler's claims were unlimited and returned without agreement; it was a question of what local proportion of German population was to justify Czech cession. Hitler, on September 26th, still declared that "he did not want any Czechs." But at Munich, on September 29th, we accepted his terms. For the assurance of peace, whatever it was worth, we allowed Czechoslovakia to go under. We gave with France a joint "guarantee" of whatever might be left to Czechoslovakia without knowing how much would be taken; we never took any active part on the joint commission which was to settle this point; we even let pass the surrender to Germany of the considerable holding which Czech thrift had built up in the Bank of International Settlement at Basle.

It was a complete surrender of Czechoslovakia, as was to be made quite clear later without any further opposition on our part: and this settlement was arrived at without any invitation to Russia to take part in it—in a word, it was the acceptance of Hitler's principle that as "Bolshevism" was in disgrace, Russia should be left out of European agreements. Russia, it should be stated, even after the withdrawal of France and England, had still shown her willingness to aid the Czechs.

The Munich settlement, while it set no limit to the will of Hitler, put Russia in Coventry, as unworthy to take part in the common affairs of Europe. It was even explained that she was not invited to Munich because Hitler and Mussolini would not have accepted such a suggestion. In a word, Hitler got his way without argument on this major point, and at the outset of 1939 the British Premier declared that "no one would have dared to prophesy that the *four* great European nations would have advanced so far along the road to co-operation."

It would not have been surprising if Russia had turned away from us, though she could hardly at that time have turned towards Germany. This was a poor enough result of all Litvinov's overtures, but he himself was identified with the new policy of friendship, and he did succeed in persuading his master to wait—"six months or so," as I was told at the time—and see if we adhered to our Munich policy.

If so, Russia would retire into her isolation and look after her own defences.

But as far as Russia was concerned, Hitler played our game for us in a way that could hardly fail to help us. On March 14th came his next burglary, than which nothing could have been fouler in its details. The French and British Ambassadors in Berlin were assured that "Germany intended no drastic move"; but the same day the aged Hacha, the new President of Czechoslovakia and his Foreign Minister, Chvalkovsky, were summoned to Berlin. There, in a terrible all-night scene, they were ordered to sign away the independence of their diminished country, which of course they had no right to do, under threat of the destruction of Prague by bombing at 9 a.m. The bombers were to start at 6:00 a.m., and troops were already on the march. Hacha fainted several times and doctors attended to him; at 4:30 a.m., in a state of collapse, he signed. This course of events immobilised any organised Czech resistance. The Germans entered Prague in the morning and Hitler slept in the historic palace in the citadel that night.

The Czech provinces of Bohemia and Moravia were incorporated as a "protectorate" in the German Reich. Hitler described them as *Lebensraum* (living space) "torn by force and unreason" (not, of course, from Germany, but Austria) by the "dictate" of Versailles. Force and unreason! And what was this? This time the argument of self-determination could not be used, as the population in question was Czech—that is, Slavonic. So instead of being "self-determined" from outside, they were told that they must be "protected" against themselves.

Meanwhile, the foolish little Slovaks, who had been squabbling over petty points of details with the Czechs in the vain hope of entire independence and without any eyes for the major danger, had been traversed by German intrigues and through the mouths of puppets of Germany asked Hitler to take charge of their interests.

The Slovaks, like the Czechs, are Slavs, and their language is a first cousin of Czech. Before the Great War, in the Austro-Hungarian dual system, which divided the Slavs between Austria and Hungary, they had been under the Hungarians, who are not of European origin at all. Their practical annexation by Germany pushed out a great new claw of German aggression some two hundred miles eastward along the Carpathians, between Poland and Hungary. Hungary was now faced with a new double German frontier—on the west (in the former Austria) and in the north (Slovakia). Poland was

now encircled on three sides—by Slovakia on the south, by
Germany on the west, and by German East Prussia on the
north. Already the coming war with Poland was half won.

Slavonic Russia had always taken a close interest in Slavonic
Slovakia; but the new aggression included another stroke,
which implied an even more direct menace to Russia. At the
eastern tip of Slovakia, still in the Carpathian range, lay a
fragment of Ukraine called Carpathian Russia. The Carpathian mountains were an important part of the original home
of the Russian race. These "Carpathian Russians," who had
got left behind in the ancient migration eastward, belonged
to Ukraine. Pre-war Austria was a bundle containing all sorts
of various and discordant national fragments—German, Czech,
Polish, Ukrainian, Rumanian, Serbian and Italian; and it was
one of the chief merits of the Treaties of 1918 that they did
so much to restore each of these fragments to the national unit
to which it really belonged. The great mass of the Ukrainians,
extending over that rich granary nearly to the lower Volga,
were and always had been inside the Russian State, of which
they were the second most important racial element. A much
smaller proportion had been part of the old Poland, and had
been reconquered for Poland by Pilsudski in his war against
the Bolsheviks in 1920-21. But the "Carpathian Russians" were
a far smaller section which, in the confusion of treaty-making
at Versailles when the Russians were out of the picture, had
been entrusted on conditions to Czechoslovakia. In the complete break-up of the Czechoslovak State, Hitler was able to
set up here a sort of little "Piedmont" of Ukrainian "independence"—independence, of course, from Russia. It was a "show
window" under German management, and was bound to re-
vive in the liveliest way the old German menace to Russian
Ukraine which had so nearly become a reality in the peacemaking at Brest-Litovsk. It seemed, then, that, after indulg-
ing his land-hunger in Central Europe and at the expense of
Czechoslovakia, he was telling the world that the great "drive
eastward," the historic *Drang nach Osten*, which was the chief
plank in the program of *Mein Kampf*, was again in the very
forefront of his policy. Russia was not only to be shut off from
Europe, but dismembered. One can hardly imagine anything
which could have set a higher value to Russia on the co-
operation of her old allies of the last war—France and England.

Hitler's next move, which followed almost immediately,
carried just the same significance. Look on the map for Lithuania, and you will find that it lies immediately to the east of
East Prussia. With all their talk of being encircled, the Ger-

mans themselves followed an almost monotonous technique of encirclement. After the burglary of Czechoslovakia, which incidentally pushed forward a pincer along the Carpathians, came the seizure of Memel, port of Lithuania, and this was another pincer of 1915, further encircling Poland and menacing Russia.

With Lithuania Hitler followed the same python procedure as with Czechoslovakia. The Lithuanian Foreign Minister was called to Berlin and made to surrender Memel under a threat to bombard the new Lithuanian capital, Kaunas.

Again, the *Drang nach Osten*, and next Poland. This gave us a great chance of facing Hitler with two fronts, as was done in World War I. The Poles have had a cruel geographical position and a cruel history. Let me briefly recall it. They have no natural frontiers, except in the famous Pinsk marshes, always disputed between them and Russia; the very name of the country means "Plain." They adopted Latin Christianity about the time when the Russians adopted the Eastern or Orthodox, and by that, more than anything else, they split the Slavonic world—for the Bulgars, the Serbs and even the Rumanians are Orthodox, and the Czechs mostly Protestant. A religious and national feud was waged between them and Russia for centuries and became traditional. A foreign mediator, trying to make peace between them in 1617, said that it was like trying to reconcile fire and water; and a Russian Tsar (John III, 1462-1505) declared that every treaty between them could only be "a truce to draw breath." Each of them triumphed in turn. The Poles absorbed Lithuania —then a far greater State than now—and thus annexed a number of Ukrainians and White Russians (a small and backward nationality lying on the main road from Warsaw to Moscow); at one time they actually held the Kremlin. Russia recovered, Poland declined, and then came the Partitions— a peculiarly dirty deal between Russia, Germany and Austria, in which, it is true, the Russian gains were almost exclusively of White Russian and Ukrainian population. No one could have predicted that the three robber empires would all collapse almost within a year. But that was what happened in the World War (1917-18). In 1920 the restored Poland drove off a wave of Bolshevist attack which had reached the gates of Warsaw and recovered that White Russian and Lithuanian territory which it was so soon to lose again.

The Poles were never cast for the role of a conquered people: they are proud, high-spirited and, though they are stalwart fighters, they had a terribly perilous position as between Russia and Germany. I put this question to Marshal Pilsudski in 1922, and he talked for an hour on this vital theme. They were unpopular with both, though for quite different reasons, and when I think of their fate in their Partitions I always remember that grim proverb, "The offender never forgives." Any course which they took was sure to be a gamble—beyond sitting where they were, which was perhaps the biggest gamble of all. Hitler, who professed a great admiration for Pilsudski and a great hate for Communist Russia, three times proposed to them to come in with him in a partion of Russia—principally of Ukraine. He made the third offer just before he attacked them himself. In each case they wisely refused. In my view, there was only one gamble which would be worth the paper it was written on, and that was a joint guarantee from England, France and Russia, the three countries whose alliance in the previous World War had brought them out of their century and a quarter of bondage.

But everything depended on Russia sharing in the pledge. It was the signature of the other two powers that could make the Poles feel sure that the pledge would be honoured; but without Russia there was nothing effective that France and England alone could do to help Poland. Could our fleet help Poland, with her one port in the Baltic? In World War I, it was only with great daring that six British submarines got into the Baltic at all. We might have sent Poland some planes, but had we enough to defend London? And as it turned out, we did not even enter the second World War before the Polish aerodromes were smashed up. The French might have attacked from the Maginot Line, but they didn't. And what else? Thus it all depended on the Russians coming in, and a pledge that could not be implemented might be almost worse than no pledge at all, unless Hitler was induced by it to call off the war altogether. I think it must have been in reliance on that hope that our pledge was ever given.

The negotiations with Russia, which followed in Moscow, though they extended through the summer, did not lead to an agreement. The reason was, undoubtedly, the antecedent suspicions on both sides. There was no direct exchange between Prime Ministers or their Foreign Secretaries as in the case of Germany, and the specially sent representative of the British Foreign Office, a man of recognised ability, was not in a position to give a definite agreement. Any decision involved both the Poles and the small Baltic States, but there were no joint meetings of all those concerned. Consequently the proceedings required consultations of all those interested.

The Russians at one time offered the restoration of the old alliance of World War I between Britain, France and Russia with the addition of Poland; at another, a joint guarantee of the Baltic States to be secured by a joint military force. Rival propositions were put forward by both sides. The negotiations would have gone much more easily if it had been realised on our side that Russia had returned to a national outlook and was claiming, before all things, to be approached as a great nation. This was the point of the replacement, during the proceedings, of Litvinov, as Foreign Commissary, by Molotov, who was unacquainted with foreign languages. The Russians suspected an attempt of the British Government to switch the attack of Hitler onto their own country. They proposed a military consultation before the principle of alliance was fixed. It gave no results because of differences between the Poles and the Russians. When these were removed by us, Molotov brusquely informed our negotiators that he was expecting next day to receive Ribbentrop to conclude a treaty of non-aggression. As I had been warned, the Russians were going to lock their own doors, and see to their own defence. There is now no doubt that this treaty, concluded on August 23, was what it claimed to be, an insurance of Russia against immediate attack, but this Russo-German Pact made war inevitable for Britain and France. Germany was practically secure against the principal bogey of her generals, a prolonged war on two fronts.

After all, what had we to offer as compared with Ribbentrop? We asked alliance and championship of Poland. Ribbentrop only asked for non-aggression: but once war was the order of the day, the door was open for easy gains for Russia, and that not only at the expense of Poland.

XVI

THE ROAD TO ALLIANCE

(1939-41)

As we all know, Poland was easily crushed in a month. The Poles never stood a chance. Hitler attacked at dawn on September 1st without declaration of war. The Germans had absolute mastery of the air, and that meant everything. The aerodromes were smashed, and the German planes not only saw every movement in the rear but broke up all combination there, destroying telephones, bridges and railway junctions. The Poles had a kind of quadrilateral near Warsaw, which in Russian hands had made a pitifully feeble show in World War I, but they never had time to concentrate on it. Their only hope was to retire to the Pinsk marshes and emulate Hereward the Wake, but these marshes lay far back, embedded in a White Russian population, with a few Polish squires and some recent Polish settlers. It was at this moment that the Russians took the chance offered to them, justifying themselves by the plea that the Polish government were now seeking cover in Rumania and that therefore they had to look after their own interests and those of the White Russian and Ukranian populations in Poland. The Polish Ambassador in Moscow was curtly told that his government was no longer acknowledged there, and the Russians went straight in (September 17).

They had an easy task. It was the Germans who had broken the back of Poland, but that only favoured the Russian plea. There was hardly any resistance. Even the British Government, when on September 20, 1920, it had proposed the "Curzon Line," had recognised that this territory was not properly Polish, and if Germany had completed her conquest of Poland, she would have been annexing a population that belonged to Russia.

Stalin had long stood for a "Soviet patriotism," which recognised Russia as well as Communism. Here was an excellent chance of combining the two, and the Russian entry was given the character of a crusade—for brothers of blood who were also brothers of class. It worked quite simply. Political agents (who were later separately and publicly thanked and honoured) accompanied the army and, in the social chaos created by the invasion, were very likely sometimes in front of it. White Russian troops of Poland offered no resistance. Officers and squires alike could do nothing but fly into the woods, and many were followed up and killed. Telephonic communication with Moscow was put up as soon as possible. Under directions from there, meetings of the local proletariat were held, and the estates were then and there partitioned among the villagers, preference being given to the most impoverished. Local Soviet institutions were set up without delay, and for months afterwards the Russian Press was full of the rapid progress made in sovietising the whole area, including new big economic enterprises such as road and canal building, aligned with the Russian system of planning. Preparations were at once begun for typical soviet elections. The assembly thus elected asked unanimously for admission to the Soviet Union. This passed through the Russian Supreme Council, which joined the "Polish" half of White Russia to the already existing White Russian Soviet Republic on the other side of the old frontier. This frontier, which I lived on with the Russian Army in 1916 and passed through again on August 19 of 1939, never had any real basis either in territory or population. It was in fact more or less the same as the limit of the German offensive of 1915.

Exactly the same story was repeated in the Ukrainian population of Poland. This territory was simultaneously traversed by the Soviet army and the Soviet propaganda and was sovietised straight off, and then, by the same procedure, it was annexed to the Ukrainian partner in the Union of Soviet Socialist Republics. In both cases—White Russian and Ukrainian—there was one reservation: in neither territory was there an immediate attempt to introduce the last achievement of Stalin, the collectivisation of agriculture; and this, in Ukraine, was natural, for the Ukrainians were stronger individualists than the Great Russians to the north of them and had never under the Tsars had the full system of communal land-tenure.

To the march into Polish Ukraine there was an appendix which made close observers think. We had all been wondering whether behind the Russo-German Pact of non-aggression there lay a secret alliance. Soviet representatives insisted that there was no alliance, political, military or economic. They were borne out by what followed now. There developed a race between the German and Russian Armies to cover as much territory as possible. To everyone's surprise the Russians won, and pursued their way through southern Ukraine until they had cut off the Germans on this side both from the Rumanian and even the Hungarian border. Clearly Russia was not surrendering the way to the Black Sea and Russian Ukraine, and was taking up the most advantageous positions against the possibility of a breach between the two new friends. Hitler had made an enormous sacrifice of his convictions by concluding any pact with Russia, and this was already a big dose even for docile Germans to swallow, but it was much worse to ask them to accept this blocking of the main road of the traditional *Drang nach Osten*. Ukraine was now practically all united, as never before, under Russia, and the little show-window of Ukranian independence under German "protection" so recently lit up by Hitler in "Carpathian Russia" had to be closed down. The German Army had borne the sweat of the day, and Hitler was being made to pay a heavy price for Russian friendship.

The German and Russian armies met in the middle of Poland and fixed a military dividing line along the Vistula that actually ran through parts of Warsaw. The vital nerve of Poland, the Vistula, seemed to be the designed frontier between Russia and Germany. This was indeed a challenge to the rest of Europe; but soon it became clear that this was only a line of occupation, and in fixing the actual frontier—for Poland was anyhow to be partitioned—the Russians, apparently on their own initiative, withdrew the northern part of the line so that they only included a major fraction of purely Polish population—probably about four millions, though Molotov implied, in his speech on the subject, that it was not much more than one. Like Catherine the Great, the Soviets were apparently anxious to be able to say that the population which they annexed was nearly all Russian. Nor, in the German suggestions of peace that followed, to which the Russians gave their full support, was there any sign that the Soviets were committed to the defence of the German conquests.

Molotov had announced the Russo-German Pact to Russia with a great deal of abuse of England and France, cleverly based on the disagreement on "indirect aggression" in the Baltic States. These had been parts of the Russian Empire and were regarded as the gates of Leningrad. So with strained reasoning, he interpreted our disagreement as a direct attempt on our part to side-track the coming assault of Germany onto Russia by leaving open an easy road thither. This was later backed up by demonstrative commemorations of any incident of British or French armed intervention twenty years before. As a matter of fact, the Germans had intervened there as much as anyone else, but on this both they and the Russian Press observed complete silence.

Hitler, it will be remembered, after crushing Poland, made a speech, suggesting peace on the basis of the accomplished fact (October 6). This helped Molotov in his very artificial explanation of the sharp turn in Soviet policy which had resulted in the Russo-German Pact (October 31). He utilised our indifference to Hitler's vague "peace offer" to make us henceforth responsible for the war. He must have felt how strained his reasoning was, for he felt it necessary to say that the word "aggressor" had changed its meaning. He left out Hitler's unprovoked attack on Poland and started straight from the "peace offer." By refusing to accept this and continuing the war, he argued with studious care, England and France became the aggressors; they were the "war-mongers" who wanted to extend the war to the whole world. The Soviet Union, on the other hand, was keeping Russia, the one socialist State, out of the capitalist war, and was making every effort to pre-

vent it from spreading. Russia, in spite of her invasion of
Poland, reasserted her peace policy, and Germany got no
encouragement to think that she could turn the Pact into
an alliance.

The same argument came in very useful on another side.
It was Versailles that had revived Lithuania and for the first
time in history had put Estonia and Latvia on the map of
Europe. As a result, Russia was driven from the coast. If
between the two wars one sailed direct from London Bridge
to Leningrad, as I have twice done, one touched the Russian
frontier a whole day and a half later than in 1914—not at
Libau, in Latvia, but two-thirds of the way up the Gulf of
Finland. As a naval power, Russia was now absolutely bot-
tled up. Now England and France, the makers of the unrecog-
nised "Versailles," had their hands full and could not interfere;
and Germany, the natural objector to a restoration of Russian rule on the Baltic, was tied by her Russian "friendship."
Russia seized the opportunity to recover her road out. On the
claim of withdrawing them from the war danger by putting
them under Russian protection, the Soviets imposed on these
small States—Estonia, Latvia and Lithuania—agreement to the
concession of naval bases—practically, the old naval bases of
the Russian Empire (September 29-October 10); the agreement was "safeguarded" by the most precise pledge of non-
interference in internal affairs, which was constantly quoted not
only by the little statesmen of the Baltic but by the Soviet
Press. But, later, after the collapse of France, this pretence was
thrown aside. The little States were not only annexed, but
completely sovietised—again with the exception of compulsory collectivisation (June 15, 1940).

Thus, by a few strokes of the pen, and without any fighting, the left-hand side of the road out was completely recovered. Molotov, echoed by the Soviet Press, had constantly
been charging us with wanting Russia to "pick up the chestnuts" for us, by diverting on to herself the coming attack
of Germany. But this was "picking up the chestnuts" with a
vengeance, and at the expense of the new-found "friend."
This of itself is enough to explain the Russo-German Pact,
for without it all this could not have been done. Russia was
securing herself against aggression. Any aggression? Certainly, but, in spite of all their references to our intervention
of twenty years ago, of course the real danger would come from
the side of Germany.

And here comes the most extraordinary part of the story,
with the highest price that Germany had to pay. Hitler not

only accepted but claimed the repatriation to Germany of those German families which, for centuries established on the Baltic coast, had served as the spearhead of the famous "push eastwards." Seven hundred years of history were reversed—Riga, the chief German foothold on the eastern Baltic, was founded in A.D. 1200. These poor people were made to get rid of what they could, pack up what they could take with them, and settle themselves, as best they might, among the Polish population of the so-called corridor, now uniting East Prussia to the rest of Germany. They might be thought useful here, but what of their removal from where they had always been?

So much for the left-hand side of Russia's way out, but what about the right? This consisted of the solid block of Finland, a very different proposition to the small new Baltic States. Finland had always been semi-independent, whether under Sweden (till 1809) or under Russia. She had seized the opportunity of the Russian chaos of 1917-18 to make herself entirely independent. When she was doing this, she had the most substantial help from Germany, in training and in troops; in fact Germany had almost taken possession of Finland when she was driven to ask us for peace. The Finnish frontier was some twenty miles from Leningrad. The Tsar's Minister Stolypin, even when Finland was still associated with Russia, had said to me, "How would you like to have the frontier of another State at Gravesend?" One can therefore understand Stalin's action.

Stalin began by demanding naval bases, as he had done on the other side of the road out. Though still in this framework, his demands rose as the negotiations proceeded. In the end he broke off the negotiations and invaded (November 30, 1939).

He went straight forward with a disregard of treaties and rights. So confident was he, that he took it on himself to declare the Finnish Government deposed and set up in its stead a puppet affair under an emigrant Finnish Communist, Otto Kuusinen, whom the Russians produced out of their pocket, so to speak, as they marched into Finland and installed in the first small place that they captured. With this imaginary government Molotov signed a treaty according the desired Finnish naval bases to Russia and guaranteeing the rest of Finland, even with an extended frontier at the expense of Russia. But the Russians had made an enormous miscalculation. Not only was their propaganda quite ineffective but the Finns made a magnificent resistance, with a courage and resource which won the admiration of the world. The Finns protested to Geneva, and Russia was declared to be no longer a member of the League of Nations (December, 1939). But no effective help came from outside; Germany, who was in the best position to give it, did nothing, tied up by the Pact. The Finns, in the end, were overwhelmed by sheer weight of numbers. Before they were exhausted, they managed to secure a treaty which left them with a minimum of losses, though of course weakened as against any future attack. The Russians, on their side, put Kuusinen back into their pocket and treated with the government which they had refused to recognise (March 12, 1940).

This episode served to give a good indication of Russia's determination not to be entangled in Germany's war against France and England. The Russians, who had occupied the little port of Petsamo on the Arctic Ocean, had engaged to return it to Finland; and this they did, laying great emphasis on their loyalty to the peace treaty, just about the time when the western war was spreading to Scandinavia and was concerning itself specially with the near-by Norwegian port of Narvik. As our war came nearer, the Russians demonstratively retired.

It may be taken that up to the end of the Finnish War, Russia had followed a clearly marked policy on the following lines. In all her public expressions of opinion, she was entirely on the side of Germany as against France and England— especially against England, whom she rightly regarded as the senior partner in the Alliance. She indignantly resented any suggestion of a cleavage between her interests and those of Germany. All sorts of extensive economic co-operation between the two was always being planned but apparently producing no very great effect; anyhow, as a Soviet spokesman put it, it was in no way comparable to the increasing help which the Allied Powers were already receiving from America. The Russians were always slow, especially in transport, and any serious attempt by the Germans to take over the arrangements inside Russia itself would raise very serious internal problems. Nor was Germany in any sound position to carry out her side of the exchange. But there was no alliance; the actions of the two partners to the Pact were parallel and often rival.

With its close and astute touch on the march of events, the Soviet Government could not fail to see that the whole situation was revolutionised by the colossal changes of the earlier half of 1940. Denmark in a day was occupied and for all immediate purposes annexed by Germany. Norway was invaded, and the Allied Powers, with their belated and inadequate help, were driven out. Holland was hurled into the war and conquered from front and rear in a few days. Belgium was entered. French troops, called to the help of Belgium by its King, left a gap through which, like a boring file, passed the impact of the German mechanised advance, ultimately surrounding the northern Allied group and driving it into the sea; the only relieving feature for us was its apparently impossible escape by grace of the British navy and air force. Italy, like a jackal, came in for a share of the loot, just before the collapse of France was complete. France, humbled to the dust by her new rulers, seemed to have lost everything that she stood for, including her form of government, and became a simple field of action for Germany against the one outstanding enemy that was left—England. We were brought back to the times when Napoleon, with his Grand Army at Boulogne, was waiting day by day to pounce on us; and this time were added, not only the ingenuities of submarine warfare, but a numerically superior air force. Under these vastly less favourable conditions was renewed the old direct duel between sea and land; and the massed power of the conqueror with the added resources of the conquered territories was directed, in a straight fight, against the British Empire as a whole.

Soviet circles, no doubt, wished and till now had probably expected, a stale-mate. After the fall of Poland, they were in favour of a negotiated peace. An outright victory for either side would mean a vindictive settlement and probably another big war. It is true that a negotiated peace, with what they and everyone knew about Hitler, would only be an armed truce. To keep the rival forces in balance would be something, and their chief desire was to avoid war themselves. But the prospect of an outright victory for Hitler was the worst that they could have to face. They could not believe that he had really forgotten or renounced the program of *Mein Kampf*, which he could carry out far more easily, once all other opposition was over. The Germans would not forget the advantages which Russia had been able to extract from their somewhat equivocal friendship. The Finnish campaign had not increased their respect for the Red Army. However, there was no visible change in Soviet policy, only some significant modifications of practice. The Soviet Press, which had been full of abuse for the Allied Powers, suddenly passed over to a remarkable objectivity, clearly wanting its readers to have an accurate idea of what was taking place. This would be the natural preparation for any variation of the Russian attitude which might seem appropriate. Continuing to emphasize every weak spot in England's economic conditions and in her hold on her Empire, and not yet suggesting the existence of any corresponding difficulties on the German side, it now began to hint that both sides were "imperialist."

The naval blockade was become not only the main but almost the only offensive weapon at England's disposal, except her heroic Air Force. The Soviets had been directly opposed to it from the start, and in a plain note, in which they compared it to the bombing of civilian populations, they had refused to recognise it and reserved the right of reprisals (October 25, 1939).

It certainly seemed to many outsiders that England might quickly follow in the way of France. Mussolini, in particular, made the very worst of guesses. From various evidence it is clear that this opinion was not shared in Russia. The outstanding fact of the late summer and autumn was the glorious resistance of London and the rest of England to the menace of invasion, with the fine exploits of the R.A.F., duly recognised in the Soviet Press. This, with the intense admiration and growing sympathies of the American public and the renomination of Franklin Roosevelt (June 20), brought a new change in the perspective. There was a noticeable heartening of some of the smaller neutrals, earlier paralysed by the fate of Scandinavia and the Netherlands. Mussolini's precipitate attack on Greece (October 9) was met with splendid courage and success, in which British help played a large part. The British Fleet and Air Force had rapidly achieved decisive mastery in the Mediterranean. The Russians, generally contemptuous of Italy, were opposed to the Italian attack. It extended the War, and to a region in which Russian interests were peculiarly sensitive, the Balkans. Hitler felt that it was premature, and no doubt resented the jackal's feeble attempt to assume an equaltiy which it did not possess. But he, too, was forced in the same direction. Checked in his invasion of England, he found himself in the same position as Napoleon, thrown back on a less direct attack on England's position in Europe and outside; and this inevitably brought the struggle into a wider field, in which Russian and British interests had very much in common.

It was the glorious defence of our own homes that started a new period, which was to lead to a much clearer prospect of victory. History has offered convincing precedents; but in the little detail of a narrow perspective they were for the present forgotten. We were still hoping to piece together out of the fears, hopes and jealousies of the small neutrals some kind of bunch of faggots which would, under our direction, offer resistance to the great aggression. We should have looked back to Napoleon. His one persistent and invariable enemy was England, though there was a mutual effort at "appeasement" in the short-lived Peace of Amiens. When he failed in direct invasion, he turned by a natural reaction to an alternative plan, a *pis-aller,* an attempt at indirect triumph by conquering the rest of Europe, and that inevitably brought him face to face with Russia. Russia tried to compromise at Tilsit in 1807, but cracks in that friendship soon appeared, and then came invasion, which proved the beginning of the end. In the last war, in the face of another all-round aggression, this time from the side of Germany, we and Russia again perforce found ourselves together, fighting the same common enemy.

Let us follow Hitler on his fateful round route from the Channel to the doorstep of Russia.

In the Baltic, Germany was always a source of danger to Russia, and we could not be. Hitler's advance had already begun with the annexation of Memel before the war. The little States detached from Russia had no possibility of independent defence. Only the almost simultaneous collapse of the Russian and German empires in 1917-18 had given them the fictitious appearance of it. Once the war had begun, they had become a *glacis* for either Russia or Germany, and Russia retook them while Germany was preoccupied elsewhere. But in a war a *glacis* was all they could be.

Finland could be more. If our belated and insufficient help had reached the Finns, we should have been at war with Russia. Here, too, Russia, in 1940, was trying to recover a *glacis* against Germany out of her territory lost in 1918. If Germany moved against Russia, she would now have here a springboard far closer than before to Leningrad. If she chose to do so, she was now well assured of Finnish support, and the course of the recent Finnish struggle with Russia could only be an encouragement.

Let us now take a look at our position. Our hold over the Mediterranean had been seriously altered by Italy's entry into the war; that is, our ordinary direct route to India and Australia was cut, and our position in Egypt and Palestine threatened. We had already had to move our main base of defence from Malta to Egypt. We were now challenged at both ends: at Gibralta, where the Germans had a road through France and only needed the active co-operation of Franco; and at Suez, almost surrounded by possessions of Italy— Somaliland, Eritrea, Abyssinia and Lybia. If Italian personnel and enthusiasm had been in any way equal to Mussolini's ambition, the challenge would have been hard to meet. As it was, we drove his army in rout through Libya, and his fleet was ultimately rendered almost negligible by the twin blows of Taranto and Matapan. Hitler had to occupy Italy and make himself hateful to the Italians. But a far more serious inconvenience to him was Mussolini's precipitate and unauthorised attack on Greece. The sturdy resistance which he encountered there and the difficulties into which he got himself compelled Hitler to hasten his advance eastwards.

Hitler, in working out his cunning and elaborate combinations, must have been greatly annoyed at having to move at someone else's pace, that of so unequal and troublesome an ally. We are reminded of the time when in World War I, Ludendorff, after a visit to the Austrian headquarters, reported: "We are allied with a corpse." Hitler's method involved a preliminary sounding of the weaker elements at the head of those States which he meant to cajole and intimidate, and a penetration which in the end practically faced the peoples concerned with an accomplished fact. He now got to work on Rumania and Hungary, the first countries which lay on his through road to Greece. Hungary had been a vigorous ally of Germany in World War I. Rumania, after long temporising, had in the end joined in on the other side, and after initial catastrophic failure had profited in the final allied settlement by the annexation of Transylvania, with a predominantly Rumanian population. Hungary had never reconciled herself to this loss.

Russia, seeing the menace come nearer to her, decided to move first. She, too, had her dispute with Rumania. Bessarabia, with a mixed Ukrainian and Rumanian population, so awkwardly placed as to make division almost impracticable, had more than once changed hands between the two, and in the crash of the three East European empires in World War I, it had passed on an uncertain tenure to Rumania. Russia now reannexed it by ultimatum alone, and with it the northern or Ukrainian portion of Bukovina; this last was the first territory now annexed by her which she had not possessed before World War I (June 27, 1940).

This was a challenge to her dubious friendship with Germany; but Hitler had other fish to fry before he was ready for an open breach. With Mussolini as a kind of junior assessor, he now gave judgment between Hungary and Rumania. The major part of Transylvania was given back to Hungary, with a frontier which took no account either of nationality or geography, and extended a great claw towards the Black Sea (August 30). Hungary was now a through road for German advance in that direction. Russia gave her a sharp warning, but did nothing. Rumania deposed the unsuccessful King Carol, replacing him once more by the convenient boy prince, and threw herself at Hitler's feet in complete submission, no longer hoping for anything else but his support against Russia. By February, 1941, German heavy guns and dockyards had been established on the Black Sea, reviving the old threat to Ukraine.

This German success, achieved, like the Russian, without firing a shot, brought into the picture two countries where Russian influence was strong, Bulgaria and Yugoslavia, both of which lay on Hitler's through road to Greece. Yugoslavia lay farther off from the possibility of Russian help. She had been one of the winners and gainers in World War I, and therefore relied more directly on British support. The population, or at least the dominating Serbian part of it, was one hundred per cent pro-British and pro-Russian. But the Regent, Prince Paul, was closely connected with the fallen Romanov dynasty, and he was so strongly anti-Soviet that it was only now that his government renewed relations with the Soviet Government (June 23, 1940). Russia even went so far as to offer him a pact of mutual assistance.

Bulgaria, on the other hand, had fought on Germany's side in World War I and in consequence had lost heavily. Both countries were populated by the South Slav branch of the Slavonic race, and at one time they had even seemed to be gravitating towards union, which would have been a great relief to Europe in general; but their history, so far, was one of continual feuds, jealousies, and disputes of territories. This was a ready field for Hitler's methods. Bulgaria had been liberated from Turkish rule by Russian arms in 1878, and the bulk of the population was still strongly pro-Russian. The Soviet Government had done everything to promote this friendship, and developed every link which occasion offered. Here the tie of Slavonic blood was peculiarly strong, and any anniversary of Slavonic history or culture was celebrated simultaneously in both countries—another proof that the new Russia prized the ties of Slavonic kinship. As usual, Hitler's "friends" were in the ruling class and those of Russia in the mass of people. Bulgaria was somewhat advantaged in the partition of Rumania at Hitler's dictation (August 21). This was followed up by intensive German pressure on King Boris, the entry of innumerable German tourists, and finally by Bulgaria's adhesion to the so-called "New Order" of the Axis

Powers and her admission of German troops on their way to
Greece (March 1, 1941). The Soviet Government openly
expressed its disapproval in a sharp note to Bulgaria, but took
no other step (March 3).

Yugoslavia was a different proposition. Prince Paul, more
than wavering in his choice of "friends," was faced with a
German demand for the use and control of his railways, de-
mobilisation, and adhesion to the "New Order." While the
country was as far as possible kept in ignorance, his Premier
and Foreign Minister were more or less smuggled to Vienna,
where they ceremoniously joined the Axis Powers (March 25).
But no sooner was this known than a common rising of
army and people, skilfully organised, drove him from the
country and replaced him by the young King Peter, who was
shortly due to reach his majority (March 27). The people of
Belgrade showed their hopes and wishes by carrying the British and Soviet flags side by side through the streets. England
at once offered all help. Russia openly showed her complete
sympathy with Yugoslavia and chose this moment to conclude with her a pact of friendship. All the forces of the country were called up, but though the new government avoided all
provocation, the Germans were not long in launching their
Panzer divisions (April 6). Croatia, formerly part of the Austrian Empire, was doubtful, and geographically indefensible.
But that was not Hitler's main road. He passed along the frontiers of Yugoslavia and Bulgaria and struck simultaneously at
Yugoslavia and Greece.

The British Government had kept a keen watch on these
events, countering them when it could. In an improvised crusade by air, our Foreign Secretary and Chief of Staff had done
their best to organise a general resistance. British airmen had
long been helping the Greeks in their successful fight against
Italy, and now our army in North Africa, which had nearly
completed the conquest of Italian Abyssinia, detached a force to
Greece, whose transportation the Italian navy and air force
were quite unable to prevent. British forces were now fighting in
the Balkans, which were of such vital importance to Russia.

But there our successes ended. The time was too short
and the help too small. The Greek right wing was surprised
in Western Macedonia; the Yugoslavs were pushed through
their mountains by vastly superior equipment; the British and
Greek centre was slowly forced back from point to point,
and the Greek left wing was isolated and surrounded. Athens,
the Isthmus of Corinth and the Peloponnese were successively
abandoned. The large island of Crete, where the Greek King

had taken refuge, was invaded by vast swarms of planes and parachutists, and in default of active preliminary measures of defence and the presence of British "fighters," even our Navy was unable to prevent its conquest (June 1). Meanwhile, our weakened forces in Libya were faced by a formidable counter-offensive under German direction, and were driven from nearly all their recent gains—with the exception of Tobruk, which remained like a thorn in the side of the advancing enemy (May 28).

By these successes, Turkey, which lay next on Hitler's advance eastwards, had been prepared for German encirclement. The Turks had been allied with the Germans in World War I, but, like others who had trusted them, they had been disgusted by the way in which they interpreted the alliance. Worsted, like the Russians, in that war, and like them preferring internal reorganisation to the recovery of lost territory, they had forgotten old enmities and formed a close friendship with Russia. England had also had the wisdom to make close friends with the new Turkey of Kemal Ataturk. Here there was another link between England and Russia. In the alliance which Turkey made with England she expressly excluded any thought of hostility to Russia. To complete the historical similarity with the eve of Napoleon's invasion of Russia in 1812, it may be mentioned that in that year England managed to cut short a war between Turkey and Russia, so that Russian forces were released, and nearly cut off Napoleon's retreat on the Berezina.

But Turkey, already exposed to the full force of Hitler, though fully prepared to defend her territory, could not be expected to take the initiative in attack. Soviet Russia did at this time repeat 1812 by assuring the Turks of the security of their rear (March 24). But there were criticisms in Turkey of the smallness and comparative ineffectiveness of the British military help to Greece, and the Germans and Italians were now established in a ring of islands in the Aegean which enveloped all their western frontier. In reply to the usual German pressure, Turkey even concluded a pact of friendship with Hitler, by which the integrity of her territory was presumably, at least for the moment, guaranteed (June 18).

But the threat already extended further to the Turkish rear. In Iraq (Mesopotamia), a country mandated to England by the Versailles treaty and, now in alliance with her, a former Prime Minister, Sayid Rashid, inspired by Germany, raised a revolt which drove the Regent from the country (April 3). British forces from India, enforcing a treaty right, landed in the Persian Gulf and marched towards Baghdad. The Germans, as often, overdid their pressure and demanded control, especially of the oil centres. Rashid's supporters deserted him, he fled the country, and the British position in Iraq was fully restored (June 4). It was the sturdy defence of Greece and Crete that had upset the German time-table and made it impossible for them to send Rashid any effective support in time to save him. It is to be noted that the Soviet Government even renewed relations with Iraq under Rashid's rule, for it was very necessary for it to keep a close eye on the situation there, so near to the Russian frontier; but it refused his request to take up in any way the championship of Arab independence.

Our forces in the Middle East, that is, in the neighbourhood of Russia, had now been heavily reinforced, and our policy had become correspondingly more forceful and effective. The German counter-offensive in Libya had been brought to a standstill. The government of conquered France, yielding to pressure, had allowed the intrusion of German airmen and other agents into Syria. This we challenged vigorously, and in default of any satisfaction we invaded from Palestine and Iraq. Without encountering any great resistance, we ultimately made ourselves masters of Syria (July 12), thus extending our Middle-Eastern front from Egypt to Iraq. This put us in a position to deal with Iran (Persia), with its vast oil resources, where German peaceful penetration was already making much progress, and our success tended effectively to reassure Turkey.

Can the reader follow, through all this rather confused detail, how effectively a common danger was bringing England and Russia into ever closer contact?

But both England and Russia were faced with a common danger on another side—in the Pacific. I have explained in an earlier chapter (No. XII) the origins of German-Japanese alliance. As I showed there, Japan became both Nazi and aggressive before Germany—in 1927, the year which really terminated her friendship with England. Japan had her own *Mein Kampf* in her *Will of Tanaka,* which aimed at universal conquest, and that brought into play on the other side another great potential factor of resistance in China, where, as in Russia, a great process of national transformation was in progress. Soviet Russia had begun her relations with China by renouncing all claims, territorial or financial, of the government of the Tsars. She never wavered in her support of Chinese independence and gave it very material help. Japan was the first Power to defy and leave the League of Nations.

It will be remembered that on November 25, 1936, when Stalin was engaged in winning the support of the peasants and the Comintern had been severely chastened, Hitler had engineered an Anti-Comintern Pact with Japan, later joined by Italy, which was clearly directed more against territory than against communism. In July, 1938, the constantly recurrent frontier incidents between Japan and Russia boiled up into a small undeclared war. The Changkuping Hills, near Lake Hassan, which had been occupied by the Red Army, were taken by the Japanese but retaken with sharp fighting by the Russians, and an armistice was only concluded on August 11. The Russian success continued for a long time to be a matter of frequent and exultant commemoration in the Soviet Press. As a result of the Five-Year Plans, in contrast with the war of 1904-5, the Russian Far-Eastern Front was now self-contained and had its back on much nearer sources of munitions. In the subsequent sharp turn in Russian foreign policy, the one factor which remained unchanged was the Soviet hostility to Japan. Minor difficulties were tackled and some of them were patched up, for instance, the long delay of Japan to settle up on the purchase of the Chinese Eastern Railway in Manchuria and some of the difficulties in the question of the Far-Eastern fisheries; but the quarrel of the frontier remained, and a joint commission to define the boundaries broke up in complete disagreement (January, 1940).

The Soviet Press had for a long time limited itself to reporting news of Japanese reverses in China and complications at home. After the world-shaking events of the summer in Europe, it became remarkably objective in its Far-Eastern news too, and followed closely all developments during the Japanese parliamentary session when, after a momentary outburst of criticism of the Chinese adventure and of economic home policy, the various parties dissolved themselves to make room for a single national party bearing a distinctly totalitarian character (July, 1940). The new and militant Cabinet of Prince Konoye was intently weighing the opportunities for a forward foreign policy. Since the invasion of Holland, it was feeling after the chance of appropriating the petrol and other valuable resources of the Dutch East Indies. This roused the resolute opposition of the United States, which replied by leaving its trade treaty with Japan unrenewed and proceeding to cautionary naval measures in the Pacific. Japanese influence had long been traversing Siam, and a Treaty of Amity was signed on June 12. (Siam was on Japan's road to Singapore.) The fall of France opened a path into French Indo-China.

Japan forced her way in, and imposed concessions of territory to Siam which the Vichy Government was in no position to resist with force. We had closed the Burma Road of Munitions to China for a time; but as Japan only became more threatening, we reopened it and strengthened the defences of Singapore. It looked very much as if the whole Japanese menace was shifting, as had been anticipated, southwards. This new direction was openly and freely discussed in Japan, and Australia was at long last wide awake to her danger.

And now also, on September 28, came the conversion of the Anti-Communist Pact into an aggressive "Tripartite" alliance with Germany and Italy, to set up the boasted "New Order" in Asia, Europe, and, no doubt, Africa. The Will of Tanaka, with its threat to the "Southern Seas," was coming into full operation, and also the alliance of Japan and Germany long before called for by Werner Daya, with the addition of Italy. From Germany came repeated rumours that Russia, of all things, was being drawn into the "Anti-Communist" combination; and to Western eyes, with their interpretation of the Russo-German Pact of 1939 as a masked alliance all things seemed possible. It was perhaps consistent that on this side, as in the West, Russia might evade a conflict and play for time; but there no real place left for her in this new order. She publicly confirmed her policy towards China and Japan, and drew the attention of her people anew to the "capitalist encirclement," which in this case of course meant Germany and Japan.

In March the Japanese Foreign Minister, Matsuoka, paid an exploring visit to Moscow and Berlin, where it appears that he was urged to subordinate Japanese policy to the aims of Germany. He was in time for the ceremonial admission of Yugoslavia to the Axis at Vienna and for its immediate repudiation by Yugoslavia. He proceeded to Rome, and on the appropriate date of April 1, he and Mussolini probably exchanged condolences on the exorbitant demands of their senior partner. Matsuoka returned home by way of Berlin and Moscow, and in Moscow, amidst extravagant expressions of friendship, was concluded a Pact which the Russians might certainly regard as one of reinsurance (April 13). Russia stood aside from any interference with Japan's march southwards and gained not only the usual guarantee of her territory but also Japan's engagement to remain neutral in case of attack on Russia by a third party (presumably Germany). Meanwhile, by the carefully worded Tripartite Treaty, Japan had pledged herself to enter the war on the side of Germany if the latter were attacked by a so far neutral country—a clause obviously directed against the United States. The pact with Russia was ratified by Japan but very variously explained, and soon after his return Matsuoka was discarded, Japanese policy, with no precise pledge of German assistance, and faced by the ever-hardening attitude of America, was an unconvincing mixture of bluster and hesitation. The position was further confused for her by what was to follow so soon after in Europe.

On November 13, 1940, Molotov paid a courtesy visit (or was it a scouting one?) to Berlin, and Hitler announced that the British Empire was finished, and suggested dividing the inheritance. Molotov suggested postponement, but Hitler, proceeding in his own manner, offered Russia the Persian Gulf, which of course meant also the Persian oil fields. Molotov replied that Russia wanted the Dardanelles (as she had since A.D. 865). This Hitler thought quite inadmissable. Russia, continued Molotov, would also like to open a road through the sound at Copenhagen. Intolerable, said Goering and others. Molotov went home saying he would write. Two weeks later Hitler signed the detailed military plan for the invasion of Russia and fixed it for May 15, 1941, which was later postponed to June 22.[1] All this long remained unknown to us.

The economic agreement made on the eve of the war had not worked satisfactorily for either party. Germany had not gained anything like the help that she expected, while America was now sending to England enormous supplies not only of food but of war materials, and was even preparing to join in a common defence of the Atlantic. Hitler was more and more in need of oil, in which he was hopelessly outbalanced by his adversaries. It was becoming clear that he could not hope to get all that he wanted without taking over the production and transport himself within Russia. On the other hand Germany with her own war needs, was in no position to fulfill her part of the agreement, which soon became a subject of criticism in Russia. The agreement was bolstered up by new promises on January 10, 1941.

Over the turn of the year the official Moscow broadcast continued to criticise our rule of India, but it never attacked our Prime Minister, in spite of his prominent rôle in the intervention of 1918-20, and it passed over almost in silence the suppression of the *Daily Worker*. German war news was more sparingly given; the miserable conditions of the occupied countries were exposed; the main attention of the public was

[1] See *Foreign Affairs*, October, 1946, "Light on Nazi Foreign Policy" by DeWitt C. Poole, pp. 130-154.

concentrated on the extensive preparations for defence, and there was a nation-wide glorification in film and play of the greatest general of Russian history, Suvorov, who was noted for his marked antipathy to the Germans. St. Alexander Nevsky, who had beaten the Germans in 1242, shared in this form of homage.

On May 6 a significant event took place in Russia. Stalin, so far, did not occupy any post in the Soviet Government. Since the death of Lenin the post of Premier had been one of only secondary importance; everything was settled by the Communist Party, of which Stalin was General Secretary. He now became Prime Minister in place of Molotov, who remained in office as his deputy. This was a further important development in the identification of Party and nation which Stalin had been pursuing for some years. But as Stalin was always the real ruler, it also greatly enhanced the importance of the post of Premier. No doubt Stalin was impelled to this change by the need to concentrate the whole national authority in his hands at a moment of impending danger. It was another step towards emphasis on the nation.

Both Churchill and Eden warned Stalin of the likelihood of German invasion. Hitler had just practised his bullying process on Rumania, Hungary, and Yugoslavia to complete his domination of Europe with his so-called "New Order," and since then I had been keenly seeking any sign that he would try it on Russia. If so, I felt sure Russia would stand. Availing myself of the frank explanations of Mr. Maisky, which were never belied by the sequel, I took my life in my hands near the beginning of June, 1941, and, apologizing for my bluntness, I put my view that there were two concessions which Russia could not make "without losing her regime." They were really one —a deal over the Persian oil fields and the admission of Germans to the country to look after the provision and transport of oil. I had nothing whatever to go on. Mr. Maisky did not object or change the subject: he simply looked straight down on the ground and I guessed that the question was not yet answered. On June 20, I asked to see him again. As I waited in the lounge, a door opened and some young Russians came out, one of them saying, "Eto bor'ba," which I took to mean, "That will be a fight." Mr. Maisky followed smiling happily. Taking my arm he said, "You'll see we shall be masters in our own house." A day and a half later, Hitler's army had swept into Russia, and the same evening our Prime Minister in one of the greatest of his great speeches offered Russia our full and unqualified alliance (June 22).

XVII

THE SECOND FATHERLAND WAR[1]
(1941-1947)

THIS BRINGS US TO EVENTS OF THE UTMOST PORTENT TO THE whole world. The first major factor for the future was Russia's resistance to the invader, anticipated only by those who without prejudice had closely followed her past and understood her present.

There are certain constant elements in the history of Russian military defence. Russia is always far stronger in defence than in attack, for defence is always the affair of the whole people. With no protective sea frontier or formidable geographical boundaries, Russia has always had to retire before a sudden aggression. Normally it takes fifteen days for her real strength to gather on her western border. But as soon as the enemy passes the frontier, it is not only the regular Russian Army, but the whole people and even the country itself that rise to resist him. This involves vast and uncalculating sacrifices, especially at the outset; and Stalin at once (July 3) ordered a strategy of "scorched earth," by which nothing of value should be left to the invader. The unstinting thoroughness with which this was carried out was the first great surprise to Hitler and to everyone else.

On the other hand, Russia's vast distances are in themselves a great defence. The object of any invader must be to bring the Russian army to a real decision—to encircle it and destroy it. So long as the army is in being and is supplied, Russia is not beaten. It is this that inspired the tactics of Peter the Great against Charles XII and of Kutuzov against Napoleon. But every advance is contested, and in this "back fighting," especially at night, the Russian is a past master. Even the army of 1915, threadbare of all supplies except the bayonet, was never encircled.

This, for the enemy, results in a constant wastage of effective strength. Here the country is almost more important than the army. Napoleon lost more in this way than in any other. Russia, especially in the north and centre, has a greater proportion of marsh than any other country in Europe; in the treeless south, rain churns up the rich black soil into a sea of mud, peculiarly obstructive to mechanised transport; even

[1] This chapter first appeared in *A History of Russia,* copyright, 1947, by Alfred A. Knopf, Inc.

in the initial stages of the new campaign the early autumn
rains brought pitiful complaints from the broadcaster accompanying the German forces. Instead of the metalled roads
and built-up areas of France, the invader was surrounded, in
the north and centre, by vast and mysterious tracts of no-
man's land—forest or marsh or both together—where only
the patient Russian peasant could feel at home or find a way.
This gave abundant cover for guerrilla warfare all along the
German lines of communication, with easy contact, often
by parachute, with the Russian rear. Russian agriculture, almost throughout Russian history, had been collective; and
now, replacing the antique village communes, which were so
effective against Napoleon in day or night warfare at any
point on his road, there were the new collective farms, far
better organised and led, and with a far closer interest in the
soil that they were defending. In World War I peasant hoarding of food was one of the primary causes of the collapse
of the Imperial machine. In the Second it was the Soviet
collectivisation of agriculture that maintained the regular
distribution of food to both army and people.

From the first was vindicated the wisdom of Stalin's long-
considered policy of military defence against a long-anticipated
invasion. By this pact of non-aggression with Germany in
1939,[1] "the pact which was also a duel,"[2] he had put off
the evil day for a year and a half. He had himself recovered
that *glacis* of independent territory—a large part of what
Russia had lost in the preceeding war—that lay between the
two great States, and of which Hitler had been thinking in
Mein Kampf when he spoke of his designs on "Russia and
the border states formerly dependent on her."[3] He had been
able to watch the noveltics of German warfare in France,
tank formations, dive-bombers, and so on, to study in the
most assiduous practice methods of opposing them, and to
turn Russia into an almost wholesale "defence in depth."
The Russian plan was to cut off the advancing tanks from
their supporting infantry, a task requiring signal individual
courage that had not so far been seriously attempted. If one
goes further back, he had eliminated in advance the nucleus
of that "Fifth Column" on which Hitler, largely encouraged
by Russian emigrant advisers, still placed such reliance, and
the sincerity of the Russian resistance showed that this hope
was illusory.

[1] Treaty of Berlin.
[2] Walter Duranty in *The Kremlin and the People*.
[3] *Mein Kampf*, Vol. II, pp. 742-3.

All the same, through those vast spaces the tremendous German machine pounded its way, taking masses of prisoners, but always at a cost that gravely upset the time-table Hitler had announced. The newly acquired *glacis* was quickly overrun, for its defences were recent and incomplete, but it served a purpose in giving time to recover from the first effects of the shock. The passages of the Pruth and Dniester were contested with special vigour, for the country that lay behind them was comparatively open and easy. Kiev in the First World War was not a fortress, but it was now the first town in Europe to hold the dreaded Panzers at bay (August 7 to September 20).[1] It held out long after it had been outflanked; it had to be carried against desperate street-fighting, leaving the ruins of this ancient and lovely city to the conquerors. Every kind of booby-trap was left to the incoming Germans. Odessa, though close to the frontier, held out even longer with the help of the Red fleet (August 14 to October 16), and long after its occupation Russian suicide squads in underground refuges continued to blow up German troops on the top of them. On August 24 the retreating Russians themselves blew up the Dnieper Dam, perhaps the most outstanding achievement of Soviet industry. The defence of Sevastopol was even more memorable than that of the Crimean War; soldiers would buckle grenades to them and throw themselves under the German tanks; the civil population, men, women and children, took the fullest share in the fighting (November 1, 1941 to July 1, 1942). Russian military production had been furiously speeded up in the years preceding the invasion, and measures of which this people would earlier have been thought incapable were largely successful in removing whole factories with their staffs to places far in the rear. Leningrad lay perilously close to the frontier. The neighbouring Finns joined in the German assault on it; but that great hive of war industry held out and continued to function, though almost ringed round by the enemy, fighting off the beleaguerers in incessant and prolonged counter-attacks.

Hitler had challenged comparisons with Napoleon, invading one day earlier in the year, and his main interest was concentrated on the road to Moscow; for it was there that a real decision might be reached. Thither, beside the new metalled track, still runs the old road of Catherine the Great—the "big 'un," as the peasants still call it—with its double line of silver birch, enveloped by forests of birch, pine, and fir. Russia is full of strong local traditions, and at each natural barrier

[1] The dates given in each case include the period of encirclement.

on this road the fighting flared up stronger. The invader was held up for days on the Berezina, which winds in silver streams among a half-mile stretch of peat bog (July 1). Smolensk, with its old walls of Boris Godunov—"the precious necklace of Russia," as he called them—had kept Napoleon at bay till it was all on fire, and it did the same with Hitler (July 17 to August 11). Here in Great-Russia, where peasant patriotism is at its strongest, the advance slowed down until it was brought to a standstill at two historic spots, Mozhaisk and Malo-Yaro-slavets. Mozhaisk is almost identical with Napoleon's battle-field of Borodino, and at Malo-Yaroslavets in 1904 I found a tablet commemorating his other great check after he left Moscow. It reads "End of offensive, beginning of rout and ruin of enemy." The two small towns eventually also stopped Hitler and remained the buttresses of the Russian line (October 19 to January 19).

This turn of the tide came in the early days of December. The Germans had captured the ancient city of Novgorod in the Valdai hill-district (August 26) and had the road from Leningrad to Moscow, occupying Kalinin (Tver) street by street (October 23), and pushing forward a great pincer for the envelopment of Moscow as far east as Dmitrov. They also threatened the capital from the south with another great pin-cer which penetrated past Kaluga as far as Orel. It looked as if Russia was being cut up into pieces, which were to be encircled in turn. On November 23 the enemy reached Rostov, which was occupied only after the fiercest street-fighting; but Timoshenko, with a brilliant flank movement, drove them out in something very like rout and followed them up in swift pursuit. It was at this point (December 6) that on the order of Stalin, as commander-in-chief, Russia, with fresh reserves, launched a great counter-attack in the whole Moscow area, winning back one point after another by desperate fighting, often by-passing the "hedgehog" strong points that the Ger-mans had set up, but gradually pressing their whole line west-wards.

Hitler would have liked to call a halt on his Russian front, but this the Russians did not allow. They continued the most vigorous counter-attacks throughout the winter, making appre-ciable gains at different points of the line and leaving none of it in peace. Zhukov, in turn, threatened Vyazma with two formidable converging pincers. Timoshenko reconquered a large part of the Donets coal and iron region, where sixteen mines were even set working again.

Hitler had failed to supply his troops with the necessary

winter clothing, and this winter was peculiarly severe. Russian energy did not relax, and for the first time the Germans had most to suffer; sometimes whole numbers of men were found frozen stiff at their posts. The long, hard winter culminated in a peculiarly bitter March, when Berlin admitted (March 23) that the invaders were faced with their hardest trials. A promised German spring offensive was anticipated and rendered impossible; Russian initiative was eating up reserves destined for later German attacks, and Hitler had to scour conquered Europe for new unwilling cannon-fodder.

Throughout the winter the guerrilla bands, in which Russian women played a great and fearless part, engaged in enterprises of amazing audacity, cutting off German supplies, destroying isolated detachments, wrecking tanks or aerodromes, and making the German soldier's life a burden to him day and night. Again clear evidence of this occasionally came through in the plaintive accounts of the German field broadcaster to the only less harassed population at home. In May, Berlin announced that, despite the many punitive expeditions, these guerrilla bands kept springing up everywhere again like mushrooms.

In England, it was now evident to all that success both in war and in the achievement of a lasting peace settlement depended on keeping this new-found friend. The initial lead had come from the British Prime Minister. Now he and President Roosevelt, meeting in the Atlantic on August 14, 1941, issued a joint declaration, the Atlantic Charter, which Russia accepted (September 4); indeed, some of these were principles in which she was herself specially interested. At the same time came the offer to Stalin of a joint Russo-British-American conference in Moscow for the pooling of military supply and its distribution according to the most pressing needs of the Allies as a whole. This generous offer was cordially welcomed; and the practical realism with which this business was carried through probably did more than anything else could have done to create an atmosphere of reciprocal confidence. From that time onward a great stream of British and American supplies flowed into Russia past bitter and ever-increasing Axis opposition, with silent but immense sacrifices of the naval forces involved. Later the Russian Foreign Minister, Molotov, himself came to London, and his visit led to the conclusion of a treaty of twenty years between Britain and Russia, for the joint achievement both of victory and of a permanent peace settlement. This was announced on June 12, 1942.

It was just at the time when Stalin was turning the tide in Russia that the scope of the war became world-wide. The United States of America has normally been in friendly relations with Russia. Under the old regime there was one great disturbing factor: Russia's treatment of her minor nationalities, which were strongly represented in America, and especially of her Jewish population, kept under by almost impossibly oppressive legislation. The hideous pogroms or armed attacks on Jews definitely stirred up by the Imperial Department of Police. Nowhere has the new regime been more happy than in its complete solution of this question of nationalities. All of them are now, both in principle and in practice, equal in rights and responsibilities, and this solution was peculiarly the work of Stalin himself, at first as Commissary for the Minor Nationalities, and later as the drafter of the new federal constitution of the Union of Soviet Socialist Republics (1936).

America took relatively little part in the intervention of 1918-21. She barely associated herself with the settlement of Versailles, which Russia has never recognised. She was foremost in the work of relief in the great famines that followed in Russia. She has played a far larger part in Stalin's industrialisation than any other country. Definitely, Russia took her as her model in this whole work of construction and owes to her the most substantial of all foreign contributions, both in machinery and technicians. The sudden rise of English to the first place among foreign languages in the Russian school system is, in the main, a recognition of the importance of industrial collaboration with America. According to Litvinov, it was an American Ambassador, Joseph E. Davies, who has published the most important contribution in English to a sane understanding of present-day Russia.

With the withdrawal of the Russian menace in the Far East and the consistent support which the Soviets gave to China, American and Russian interests in the Pacific became for the time almost identical, and both powers alike stood for peace. To both the threat of danger came from Japan. Japanese policy had led naturally to alliance with Nazi Germany. Japan was evidently not the leading power in this alliance, and she hesitated for a long time to cast the die, but this she did when it was perhaps least expected, with the usual Axis preface of negotiation and deception, by a sudden attack on the American naval base at Pearl Harbor (Sunday, December 7, 1941). War between Britain and Japan followed automatically, for Britain's interests in the Pacific were generally the same as America's. On December 11 Hitler announced the full solidarity of Germany and Italy with Japan; that is, Germany and Italy were now at war with America. Russia still had a non-aggression treaty with Japan, and it could not be expected that she should challenge an extra conflict when her military resources in the Far East were so important for the reinforcement of the defence of her capital. Two events in Russia followed naturally enough in this period of friendship: the dissolution of the Comintern on May 22, 1943 and the restoration of the Patriarchate on September 4, 1943. The Russian Church had convincingly shown both its vitality and its patriotism.

In May and June, 1942, after a tremendous and far-probing effort of German organisation, Hitler was at last able to resume the offensive in colossal force, with thousands of tanks and dive-bombers in a double drive for the lower Volga and the Caucasus. After Sevastopol had at last been taken, house by house (July 1, 1942), it was possible to cross the narrow outlet of the Sea of Azov and push on even into the foothills of the Caucasus. By the fall of Novorossiisk the Russian fleet was deprived of almost its last refuge in the Black Sea. On the road to Baku the Russians were compelled to destroy and abandon the valuable oil wells of Maikop, and Grozny was seriously threatened. At one moment it seemed to be touch and go whether the invader did not secure the master key of the passage through the Caucasus range.

Close northward, Rostov was again outflanked and taken, the Don crossed at the point where it comes nearest to the Volga, and by sheer weight of metal and of numbers, through country that offered few possibilities for defence, the invaders forced their way to the outskirts of Stalingrad. There was no Stalingrad in World War I: this new and immense industrial city, like the Dnieper Dam, was purely an achievement of Soviet industry. Here the Russians of today were fighting for what was very specially their own. If ever in history some vital event was required to fix a new place-name decisively on the map, it was to be found in the weeks and months that followed. The Germans had reached the Volga— in fact, at tremendous sacrifices, they actually held short stretches of its western shore—but this great eastern city remained unconquered. By the nature of things, the German tanks could never have free play in the rubble created by the German artillery, and the dive-bombers were largely hampered by the presence of the attacking battalions, thrown separately or in whole divisions into this death-pit. Always at their best in conditions that call for individual initiative, cour-

age, and resource, the Russians held on to every shelter in
their battered factories and cellars.

It was now that General Zhukov and his Chief of Staff,
Vasilevsky, planned a war of manœuvre which in the end
sealed the fate of the besieging Sixth and Fourth (tank) German Armies. In mid-November, 1942, the British victory of
El Alamein in North Africa and the pursuit of the beaten Germans stopped the flow of reinforcements to the German armies
in front of Stalingrad. The Russians were enabled by the
greatly superior reserves of their manpower to bring into action fresh troops, finely trained, which could change the balance and draw a line behind the besieging armies of von Paulus
in a combined "pincer" action from both north and south.

By November 15 Rokossovsky, supported by Vatutin, was
moving, chiefly at night, from the north across the great bend of
the Don towards Kalach, which is due west of Stalingrad. Towards this point of junction Yeremenko also moved from
the south of the city; he broke the enemy line on November
20 and almost closed the gap. On December 10 a German
relief force under Mannstein came up from the southwest,
but it was successfully held by Yeremenko, and the Russians
now launched a new great thrust from the north directed
against the relieving force. The gap behind Stalingrad was
finally closed, and Mannstein was sturdily driven back. Further
Russian successes opened the way to the west; and in the
south Mannstein was pinned down to a narrow front running
east to west along the Black Sea, with only a precarious connection with the German forces still remaining in the Caucasus. On January 8 an ultimatum was sent to von Paulus; it
was rejected, and on February 2, 1943, after further attacks
grinding down their strength, came the final surrender of the
pitiful remains of the great besieging armies along with twenty-
four generals.

In the Caucasus the Germans were already retreating; the
region of the oil fields was abandoned at the end of January,
and they were hard pressed to hold Rostov. To the north
the Russians cleared Voronezh of the enemy and were pressing
on victoriously westward to attack the line of the Donets, with
its great industrial resources. General Golikov on the road
to Kursk was taking hosts of prisoners. At every turn the great
gaps in the German manpower were becoming more evident.
Kursk fell on February 7 and Belgorod on February 9. The
Donets coal and iron region was recovered and the Germans
were pushed back towards the Dnieper. Even Harkov, industrial centre of Ukraine, fell on February 14. On the same day

Rostov, now far to the east, was finally recovered.

To the south of these new Russian gains Mannstein was organising a fine defence along his far-extended eastward line: the Dnieper was his one road of escape. At last, strongly reinforced, he was able to threaten the flank of the Russians advancing westward through their newly regained territory to the north of him. The speedy successes of the Russians had dispersed their troops, and they were held up by heavy thaws, which made co-ordination very difficult. Mannstein was thus enabled to make considerable gains, and on March 15 he even recaptured Harkov. Meanwhile, on their northern front the Germans had been compelled to shorten their line. Around Leningrad the besieged Russians opened up a corridor ten to twenty miles wide, which greatly eased their communications and supply. The strong German "hedgehog" at Rzhev was at last captured on March 3, and directly afterwards the strong point of Vyazma, from which the Germans had so long threatened Moscow. No recourse was left to them but a rapid retreat to Smolensk.

Floods and marshes caused a long lull at this point. The Germans had by now lost something like half of their original striking force and three quarters of the satellite forces with which they had in 1942 tried to replace the heavy losses of their own regular army. What remained of that army was of noticeably poorer quality. The Russian losses must by now have been some five million men from their army alone, without counting a far greater number of sacrifices both of partisan forces and of civilian population of the vast occupied territory; but with their advantage in manpower, their replacements were far more efficient and better trained than the enemy's; in fact, the general quality was improved.

By now the Germans could do no more than try to forestall the next Russian attack, which, they knew, would come from the watershed district of Kursk. This they attempted on July 5 with half a million men, as compared with the million of the Stalingrad offensive of 1942 or the two million of their original advance in 1941. At a tremendous cost they gained some initial success; but after ten days of furious fighting the Russians were able to counter-attack westward towards the enemy strong point of Orel. On the 22nd, after further desperate fighting, imposed by Hitler's refusal to face events and retreat in time, the Germans began to withdraw from in front of Kursk. This was their only offensive of 1943. Orel, earlier a cornerstone of the German advance on Moscow in 1941, fell to the Russians. Harkov was recovered on August 23, and the road lay open for an advance to the famous Pinsk marshes, which have figured so prominently in every western invasion of Russia, and also to the Dnieper. The German forces were all the more restricted, especially in the air, by the Allied successes in North Africa and Sicily and their new threat to the French coast and to the Balkans, but far the greater part of the German strength was still on the Russian front. There they still had strong points at the extremities of their long winding southern line in Bryansk and Taganrog, but they could hardly hope for a strong offensive by Mannstein from this side.

It was with a great sweep and splendour that the Russian mass now rolled forward. They began their next move with Tolbukhin's capture of Taganrog at the far eastern end of Mannstein's line on August 30; but their main drive was on the Dnieper. Rokossovsky, suddenly plunging southwestward, thrust in the direction of Kiev. To either side of him seven great Russian army groups were on the move. The Germans had no choice but to retreat on the Dnieper with heavy delaying actions. Day by day the Russians swept up more successes: on one single day, twelve hundred towns and villages were liberated. Five army commanders joined in this southern advance: Rokossovsky, Vatutin, Konev, Malinovsky, and Tolbukhin. Poltava, scene of Peter the Great's historic victory over Charles XII of Sweden, fell on September 22. To the north, the formidable German "hedgehog" of Bryansk was abandoned on the 20th. On the 25th, Sokolovsky, entered the key fortress of Smolensk. The Russians were advancing all along the line. On the 24th Rokossovsky's men had reached the Dnieper and sighted the belfries of Kiev, and Vatutin also reached the great river lower down at Cherkasy, with Konev at Kremenchug, September 28) and Malinovsky at Dnepropetrovsk. All eastern Ukraine except the very south was now liberated. Fine summer weather still prevailed, and no respite was given.

Mannstein's tenuous southern line to the Sea of Azov had been heavily entrenched. At its western end it joined the Dnieper at Zaporozhe near the formidable Dnieper rapids. Behind this cover the Germans were hurrying back to the river, pressed hard by Tolbukhin. Mannstein, one of their best generals, might still try to counter-attack the long exposed flank of the Russian advance. Above the rapids, along the high cliffs of the western bank, the German defence was largely entrusted to mobile troops. North of Kiev, where the river is narrower and more exposed, Rokossovsky reached the bank before a bridgehead could be established on it and also occupied an island in midstream. Here the east bank had forest cover, and here Rokossovsky, assisted by excellent repair work on the available railways and by a good supply of motor vehicles, attacked on October 5 and made a surprise crossing in boats and rafts collected under cover on the east bank. More crossings followed south of Kiev. Zaporozhe, the all-important bridgehead, was captured on October 14. On the 17th, Konev, who had already crossed the river, advanced from near Kremenchug westward towards the great iron centre of Krivoy Rog. Malinovsky, with another surprise crossing, captured Dnepropetrovsk. This brought the far-eastern wing of Mannstein hastening back to the river, thus isolating the weak German forces still left in Crimea. Vatutin, with another unexpected advance, enveloped and entered Kiev on November 6 and hastened on westward, but he was himself to die of his wounds in Kiev.

The fall of the Dnieper barrier transferred the next main Russian attack to the marshy district northwards, where the frost had already made advance possible. A Russian thrust here would of itself cut the connections between the Germans to the north and to the south. The whole Russian line was now on the move. First Rokossovsky, who was nearest to Kiev, enveloped and took the hornets' nest of Gomel. North of him Popov, with mobile columns followed by infantry, was penetrating the frozen marsh of White Russia and quickly approaching the old frontier of 1939.

The last German hold on the Dnieper was soon broken by the capture of Kremenchug (December 6), the Kherson bridgehead (December 20), and Kreshchatik (February 5, 1944). Important gains followed: Nikopol with its manganese (February 8) and Krivoy Rog with its iron ore (February 22). On February 14 ten German divisions were encircled and eliminated at Korsun. The lot of the Germans still at Sevastopol was by now hopeless. The Russian fleet was again complete master of the Black Sea, and the German attempt to escape resulted in a terrible massacre. The Russian mass streamed on to the Dniester and entered Bessarabia on March 19. On the 24th the frontier of Bukovina was reached; on the 26th, that of Rumania; and on the 30th Chernovets was captured. On January 3 the First Ukrainian Army reached the Polish border of 1939, and on the 12th it captured Sarny, nearly forty miles beyond. On January 15 the Russians began to break out of beseiged Leningrad. On the 20th they cut off the German corridor to the Gulf of Finland, thus isolating the Finns from German help. On the 27th Leningrad celebrated the end of two and a half years of siege. To the south the last German hold on the railway to Moscow was broken, and on February 2 the Russians entered Estonia.

This was really the end of the Fatherland War, as such; but there was to follow such a manifestation of Russian military power beyond the frontiers as had never before been witnessed in Europe. The Germans were in effect already crushed. They held on much too long on the southern coast of the Baltic in order to keep Finland in the war as long as possible. The powerful northern Russian Armies of Govorov and Bagramyan systematically carved up the coast territory still in enemy hands, and an enormous pocket of German troops was isolated in a corner of Latvia. Next westward came that hornets' nest of European history, home of the old Teutonic Order, East Prussia, with its great fortress of Königsberg. The Russians were evidently out for more than a merely military settlement. The province was traversed by the tank columns of a gifted young general, Chernyakhovsky, who died of wounds at his task, and the great Junker fortress was completely pounded to ruins. While the war still lasted and the going was good, the Russians, as will be seen, were digging the grave of their immemorial enemies, the feudal lords of Prussia, Poland, and Hungary.

Next to the south lay the complex and multi-national realm of the proud Polish landlords. The conquests of Pilsudski, made at the time of Russia's greatest weakness, were for a second time eliminated, and the Russian population of Poland were again liberated from their Polish masters. It was a different story with the Polish capital, Warsaw. Here politics came in; and the central armies of the great Russian mass, those of Rokossovsky, Zhukov, and Konev, were at least partially halted. The fugitive Polish government of 1939, mainly rooted in the landed classes, had taken refuge first in Rumania, next in France and, after the collapse of 1940, in England. While Stalin and Hitler were racing through Poland under the Russo-German Pact, there were voices in England calling for a breach with Russia. With the Anglo-Russian Alliance of 1941 the position of the Poles in England became peculiarly difficult. Churchill's government did what it could to reconcile Russian and Polish interests, and until the Polish Premier, General Sikorski, perished in a plane disaster near Gibraltar (July 27, 1943) there seemed hopes of success. These hopes rose again during the premiership in London of the Peasant Leader Mikolajczyk; but the terms which he obtained in Moscow in August, 1944 were rejected by his more reactionary colleagues in London, and he resigned his office. In Russia there was a Polish "National Committee of Liberation" under the wing of the Kremlin, and this group moved with the Russian troops into Poland and took the title of "The Polish Provisional Government of National Unity," centered at Lublin. The underground forces of the London faction were dominated by General Sosnkowski, a bitter enemy of Russia. There is evidence that he ordered his forces to oppose the incoming Russians as they had opposed the conquering Germans—a policy that was hopeless unless England and America were ever to be persuaded to fight both. It was more than manifest that the liberation of Poland from the Germans could only come from the Red Army.

There followed a period that still requires to be elucidated. General Bor (Komorowski), head of the Polish underground forces in Warsaw, seems to have received orders to rise and drive the Germans out before the Russians came in. The Poles made a very fine attempt in the terribly battered city. The Russians stopped in front of it and waited till the rising was crushed (Aug. 1-Oct. 2, 1944). They even refused their landing-space to planes that came from the west to bring arms and provisions to the insurgents in the city, thus compelling these airmen to make a journey doubled in distance and in danger. It is true, of course, that the Russian way of taking a stronghold was not to batter their heads against it but to by-pass and isolate it by going round it. Nothing could be more formidable than the eastern front of Warsaw, enthroned on high cliffs with the broad Vistula in front of it; in 1831 Paskevich had been compelled to cross the river and outflank it, but now the Russians stayed where they were. After the rising had been crushed, they ultimately took the city; but even now they did not hurry forward on the flat and easy road towards Berlin.

Again it would seem that behind the operations there was a broad and definite policy of more than military purpose, which could hardly have been other than the concept of Stalin and Molotov. Konev, it is true, still following the plain, was advancing to fight his way solidly through the industrial district of Silesia, partly Polish but also one of the greatest centres of the German military industry. But to the south of him Petrov was set the formidable task of following the mountain line that had formerly separated Germany from Austro-Hungarian Monarchy—in other words, the mountain spine of Czechoslovakia. To the south of him Malinovsky fought straight over the eastern Carpathians into the bottleneck of Hungary. It must have been the Russian purpose to settle once for all with those time-honored enemies of Russia, the feudal land-lords of Hungary, by conquering their country, establishing a government of friendly pattern, and distributing their great estates, as it now proved easy to do both in Poland and in East Prussia. Anyhow Malinovsky fought through against bitter resistance into the very heart of Budapest and left it a heap of ruins (February 13, 1945).

To the south of Malinovsky the remaining great army of Tolbukhin evidently also followed a definite purpose. This was to fight its way past Bulgaria, which was never hostile to Russia except for its German dynasty, to the friendly country of Yugoslavia, always devoted to Russia and now awaiting relief from the tremendous underground struggle that it had throughout waged with such gallantry against the occupying Germans. Tolbukhin, following the Danube, was in the end able to join hands wth the Yugoslav leader Tito, which meant in the long run that Russian influence now extended to the Adriatic. It followed of itself that this junction also liberated Greece on the south, from which the occupying forces es-caped as best they might. From Hungary Malinovsky and Tol-bukhin pushed on to the conquest of Vienna (April 13, 1945).

All this cleared the ground for the grand finale at Berlin. Something like three million Russians now stood in front of the German capital on easy military ground, lined up without a break and leaving no weak spot to inspire a counter-attack. Let us imagine what this presupposes. The advance from Stalin-grad to Berlin had proceeded almost uninterruptedly except for weather hindrances and inevitable re-formations; and behind that advancing line every railway had to be changed back from the German gauge to the Russian, factories repaired and again set in action, and almost a miracle of supply carried out, to follow without delay the stupendous offensive. To the south everything was already secure. To the north Rokossovsky had carried the Russian triumph to Stettin, at the mouth of the Oder, thus making the Russians militarily the masters of the settlement of Poland's new western frontier.

And now the end of all things, Berlin. The great mass closed in on the doomed enemy capital. The British and the Ameri-cans, triumphant onward from D-day, closed in on the other side. Berlin did not prove a Stalingrad, and Adolf Hitler was driven to take his life in the cellar of his own chancellery be-fore his victorious enemies stormed in above him. By May, 1945, came the final unconditional surrender of the Nazi realm to the conquering Allies. Was there ever a cleaner finish?

And so, while no one seemed to notice, it came about that Russia achieved an unexpected victory over feudal and militant countries, sometimes called the *cordon sanitaire,* which had baffled her for many centuries. Of course, everyone joined in the cheering and everyone held it an allied victory. This was how the "Iron Curtain" was made, and once Hitler's back was broken—think of it!—the radical destruction of the hornets' nest of East Prussia was an easy task.

EPILOGUE[1]

THIS BOOK, FIRST PUBLISHED IN 1941, HAS ALREADY BEEN TWICE brought up to date. Now I have to make a beginning of a difficult chapter on the peacemaking. This new chapter will be long, and I can at present only touch the fringe of it. It would be profitless to dwell on the wearisome and inconclusive meetings and conferences. The only guidance one can offer is by trying to get behind the slow progress of events, to give some idea of what is blocking the way.

It is far harder to make peace than to make war. War is the simplest and most primitive of human activities, and the highest qualities of devotion to one's community come out spontaneously. The more dangerous the enemy, the greater is the compulsion to a collective loyalty. And how often do the combatants realise what they are going to lose in loyalty with the removal of the one bond that holds them together? But peacemaking and peace-keeping demand a thousand special requisites that are neither simple nor common—in the first place a full understanding of the claims of one's allies and a forbearance towards their ideas.

This was of course foreseen; and in the days of the greatest danger the Allies tried to make such provision as they could for the future. England and Russia made a treaty, announced on June 12, 1942, by which they agreed to hold together for twenty years. The war tasks, of themselves, imposed the necessity of frequent conferences—of the Foreign Ministers of the "Big Three" (Russia, England, and the United States) at Moscow on November 1, 1943, and of the Heads of State themselves at Teheran on December 1, 1943, and at Yalta

[1] Part of this Epilogue first appeared in *A History of Russia,* by Bernard Pares, copyright, 1947, by Alfred A. Knopf, Inc.

on February 3, 1945. The last named was the last activity of that supreme world statesman President Franklin Roosevelt, who died on April 12, 1945. A standing committee of all three powers was set up in London. What could be settled in advance at the time of common unity of purpose was, however vaguely, foreseen. The Big Three promised cooperation in peacetime.

But thinkers all over the world called for something more. After the first overthrow of Napoleon in 1814 his principal enemy, Alexander I of Russia, found to his dismay that at the peace congress of Vienna Talleyrand, the brilliant representative of conquered France, had split up the conquerors and had carried off a treaty of offensive and defensive alliance of France with England and Austria, directed against Russia and Prussia, an experience that in changed conditions could happen again. After Waterloo he rose from his bed one night, in deep distress, to draft a sacred engagement between sovereigns called the Holy Alliance. After the first World War the same passionate world urge to peace produced the League of Nations. The wish is father to the thought—the burning wish that a world of savagery shall be transformed straight off into a world of angels.

No signatures on a piece of paper can of themselves give a permanent guarantee of peace. Bismarck who certainly had experience enough in treaty-making, writes:[1] "International policy is a fluid element which under certain conditions will solidify, but on a change of atmosphere reverts to its original diffuse condition. The clause *rebus sic stantibus* (things standing as they were) is tacitly understood in all treaties that involve performance. The Triple Alliance (his own treaty) is a strategic position, which, *in the face of the perils that were imminent at the time when it was completed,*[2] was politic, and, under the prevailing conditions, feasible. It has from time to time been prolonged, and may be yet further prolonged; but eternal duration is assured to no treaty between Great Powers, and it would be unwise to regard it as affording a permanently stable guarantee against all the possible contingencies which is the future may modify *the political, material and moral conditions under which it was brought into being;* . . . it does not dispense us from the attitude of *tourjours en vedette.*" The reason, as he gives it, is that the world is not static and cannot be stopped from moving on; and the record

[1] *Reflections and Reminiscences*, Vol. II, p. 280 (English edition of Smith & Elder).
[2] My italics.

of treaty after treaty confirms him to the full.

The improvisation of "the United Nations," which came into being at San Francisco on June 25, 1945, as the answer to the world urge for peace, suffered from the first from the contrast between principle and practice. The thinkers sought for a world of equality, which in practice does not exist. Ethiopia and England, Holland and Russia, Rumania and the United States, alike count for one vote each, which is simply ridiculous. Who will suggest that one Rumanian is as important a pillar of world peace as ten Americans? But this fantastic arithmetic, of course, could be no more than window-dressing. In reality, each of the great powers had its train of followers, whether they were to be called good neighbours or satellites. England, in all, had a train of six, including India, to which she was soon to offer independence. The United States, thanks to the Monroe Doctrine and the Good Neighbour Policy, could ordinarily muster more than twenty. Russia, after an unwilling admission of Ukraine and White Russia (and when was White Russia ever independent?), still has no full recognition of nearly two hundred millions of population, whcih are in themselves a kind of League of Nations. With all this, everyone knew that there could be no peace, least of all for the smaller states, without agreement between the Big Three; each of these therefore was armed with a veto, which could bring all debates to a standstill. Even China, which is more of a commitment than a power, has the same privilege.

This was all that was left of the idealising of "democracy" and the magnifying of the "small powers," and more was not to be obtained, without the rupture of the whole organisation. Certainly UN is a great step forward in providing a forum of debate, some kind of articulation of a "world opinion," and even the Russians would not wish to be left out of it; but as a promise of a world state, it means nothing at all until the big powers are ready to accept the new arithmetic as a substitute for their sovereignty, which not one of them can be expected to do.[1] That is the whole point of the veto, which is in practice the most substantive part of the entire organisation. And the Russians are well aware that, even with the reservation of real authority to the Security Council, on which they have insisted, they are at best likely to be outvoted there every time, say by seven to four. That is why they remain with one leg in and one leg out, and fight every little detail till the moment might come that they would prefer to leave altogether. The mere fact that they are still half in is some kind of evidence

[1] Apparently, not even South Africa.

that they wish to be in if they can get what they think essential inside, and therefore of a relative success of UN.

For myself, I can see no wisdom in winding up a great coalition by breaking up the world of authority into as many small units as possible or by a series of clamorous meetings ("quack, quack, quack, quack, quack")[1] to find out what holes you can pick in each other. For that to be anything else but disastrous, it would be necessary, first of all, to shut off some of the noise (quack, quack) and then for there to be an understanding by each and all of us of everyone's affairs, which at present simply does not exist and will take a very long time to acquire. There is still wisdom in the famous judgment of Solomon who ingeniously suggested a different arithmetic; or, to take a more recent illustration, an Englishman must still have a poignant memory of the time when he was left alone to face the common enemy with such remnants of resources as pacifism and idealism had left to him.

This, in the rough, is the framework within which the Russians have had to act, and I must say that here, at least, I have much general sympathy with them. Here were the main points that Molotov had to drive home to a hopelessly uninformed world; they will be self-evident to anyone who studies the record of fact contained in *A History of Russia*.

That there was a Russia before 1914, whether we knew it or not, built up by centuries of effort;

that Russia had no hand in the settlement of Versailles, which marked the most humiliating defeat and the greatest loss of territory in her history;

that this is not to be the first war in history after which a return is automatically made to the entirely bankrupt settlement of the war before;

that this time Russia is a major winner: that she does not for instance, acquiesce in an eternal deprival of the principal lifework of Peter the Great in opening her sea road to Europe, which she lost at a moment of chaos in 1918;

that so far most of the sharp debates in the UN concern some territory or some title that Russia had before the last war and now insists on recovering;

that as one of the major winners, she has just the same right to preach her ideas as we have to preach ours, though we have an equal right to say that we disagree with them.

The methods chosen by Molotov to teach these simple les-

[1] Quotations from Mr. W. S. Jordan, delegate from New Zealand to the Peace Conference in Paris.

sons, so obvious to any one who knew anything about Russia before 1914, naturally seemed irritating, and the Russians will have reason to regret later that they paid far too little attention to the loss of good will which these tactics have cost them. Nevertheless, they have met with considerable success. Molotov, it will be remembered, replaced the Russian advocate of co-operation with the Western democracies, Litvinov, in the spring of 1939, when England quite failed to realise the implications of a frank alliance with Russia against Hitler and expected to limit Russian co-operation to military aid to Poland. Molotov was appointed to talk "plain Russian" to us. I picture him now as having in his portfolio a number of "poker points," designed to correct Western misapprehensions. We talk of free elections in Bulgaria, a country liberated by Russia from Turkey at a time of intolerable oppression in 1878, a country that settles her political questions in other ways, where, to quote a Balkan diplomat, "the minority does not accept the verdict"; and Molotov suggests that Russia is interested in Argentina and in democracy as practised in South Carolina or, he might say, Mississippi or Georgia. We go back to the old traditional English policy of keeping Russia from the Straits, by which England insists on placing an international watch on Russia's main outlet to the sea, and Molotov suggests that Russia might be interested in participating in an international control of the Panama Canal.

Unfortunately, nearly all the sharpest debates in the UN are challenges to a Russian recovery of what she had before 1914 or to questions that are to be solved on her doorstep. And what a ground to choose for the next quarrel—just where it is least possible to challenge her with success! As has been pointed out in the last chapter, Russia went out of her way to settle such questions in her own favour while war conditions still prevailed and the going was good; and "possession," we are told, is "nine points of the law."

It is quite clear that Russia is succeeding in the tasks she has set herself and is replacing our own earlier idea of a *cordon sanitaire* with a ring of "friendly" neighbours on her western frontier. It is also clear that she has met the claim to set up "one world," an Anglo-Saxon one, backed by the flimsy franchise of the United Nations, by direct attack on the revived English policy of keeping Russia from the sea. This was the policy of England from 1801 to 1907, interrupted only by the alliance of 1812. Even Lord Salisbury, one of the chief authors of the blocking policy of the Treaty of Berlin in 1878, lived to declare that England, in supporting Turkey, had "backed the wrong horse"; and later, both the Conservatives and the Liberals supporting him, Sir Edward Grey reversed this policy by the Convention of 1907 on Persia (Iran), which left the northern zone of influence to Russia. This led up to the British alliance with Russia in the first World War. And in December, 1916, both England and France publicly agreed that the Tsar should acquire Constantinople. Two world wars in which both England and America were allied with Russia brought home to us the difficulties of carrying help to her which our own blocking policy had set up. But what we were willing to grant to the tottering Tsar we would not allow to the Bolsheviks; for them we had the cordon sanitaire, or policy of blocking off Russia from Europe, which lasted until a new war forced on us a new alliance.

Now less than ever can England keep Russia from the sea. In Iran her summons to stop is an empty pistol, even if the United States were ready to save for Britain her old colonial system, which she has no right to expect. To have continued on the lines of Sir Edward Grey might have saved all this trouble. It is on the seas themselves, and not on the approaches to them, that Britain may still count on holding her own. For it will take much more than the emergence of Russia at a given point to make her a great naval power.

And we are still faced by the greatest danger of all in the unfinished peace work for a settlement of Germany; and the protagonists of the "peacemaking," Molotov, Byrnes (and then Marshall), and Bevin, have all plainly shown that they have recognized this.

When I started serious work in Russia in 1904, my apprehension was that, if Germany and Russia were united in a world war against England, they would be invincible. I found that a large number of the key posts of mastery there were held by Germans—whether at court, in the administration, in trade and industry, or even with the stewards of absentee landlords on country estates—and that they fully shared the unpopularity of the government. It followed that the masters of the moment in Russia were mortally anxious not to offend Imperial Germany and feared before all things anything that would bring the Russians themselves into the management of their own affairs. This meant that any movement in the direction of reform was inevitably accompanied by one of friendship for Britain, France and America, if only as an alternative to a German monopoly of their country. This was an arithmetic that has never failed me in all my work in Russia. From the danger I have indicated, of a united Germany and Russia, we were only delivered by Germany herself, when she was so foolish as to exchange a successful peneration for sheer domination, by invading in 1914 and again in 1941. But we have no right to count on the same mistakes, should the old motto of "Germany and Russia," at one time popular in the higher command of both countries, be exchanged for a new motto of "Russia and Germany"; and we have already reached the moment when Germany, with her population of some sixty-six millions, including so many efficient potential agents of policy and commerce, is coming back right into the middle of the picture, with the split that is developing so fast between her recent conquerors.

It appears that the only solution to be found is in a direction very different from that so far followed by the United Nations. The United Nations in the long run, and with patience all round, can be very useful in reducing the margins of disagreement. There is no doubt that it gained greatly in prestige with the mutual exchange of Christmas presents at the close of 1946. But instead of two divergent ideologies seeking each to win a purely formal "majority" for its own conception of "one world," safety is often only to be maintained by agreement, where necessary, to disagree, which is surely the test of any ordinary friendship.

It would have been far better if, while the fighting was common and the spirit was most comradely, plans had been undertaken by the "peace loving peoples," for the simple reconstruction of all that had been cast down by the common enemy without any introduction of differences; indeed, there was a beginning of a consideration of such a program at the time. This might have been an uncontroversial edition of a "Marshall Plan." We never got to anything so simple.

The beginnings of the United Nations was a period in which Molotov tried to see whether the new institution could be turned into something which Russia could accept, and he showed infinite patience and great restraint in a brilliant effort to make others realise what Russia held to be indispensable. In many instances he confronted his colleagues with examples in which they could find that they had only to look at home in order to answer their own criticisms of Russia.

This situation could not last forever. Soundly defeated in England for causes which Englishmen do not find any difficulty in understanding, Mr. Churchill embarked on a crusade to engage the United States in the championship of British imperial interests, and he and Mr. Truman in doctors' gowns at Fulton, Missouri (March 5, 1946), set going the "Truman

Doctrine." "The "Truman Doctrine" is identically the policy of the most distinguished of British imperial statesmen, Benjamin Disraeli, at the Treaty of Berlin in 1878 when, after a complete victory of Russia over Turkey, the other Great Powers tore up her treaty and substituted a law of exclusion of Russia from an approach to the seas, founded on British fears of a Russian conquest of India. Mr. Churchill's Fulton speech didn't meet with a good reception in Washington and his second speech at New York (March 15, 1946) was less confident. On the very same day his triumphant successor as Premier in England, Mr. Attlee, announced the independence of India. Later the swollen proportions of the anti-Communist scare in the United States gave Mr. Churchill a better chance, and the "Truman Doctrine" reappeared as essentially linked with the Marshall Plan (Joint Session of Congress, March 12, 1947). This was entirely inacceptable, whether to a Tsarist or a Communist Russia.

That, so it seems to me, is where the break came, and at 3:17 in the morning on July 3, 1947, Molotov almost furtively packed up in Paris and disrupted the best instrument for the achievement of peace, the Conference of Foreign Ministers. The peak of promise was definitely passed when the Western powers went on their way and organised Western against Eastern Germany. Every step that they advanced on this road took the world farther away from a real settlement; for the treaty with Germany, the major task of the Allies, had yet to be agreed.

This leads on to the mysterious drama of Zhdanov. The present is an epilogue and in no sense can it be history. But so long as this is made quite clear, the issue is so important that we may see whether we can find a picture by piecing together what we do actually know which could give us a reasonable explanation of the mysterious background.

The war in Russia was attended by costly losses. For the task itself was destructive. We know of the conventional five million men out of the line and fifteen million within the conquered portion of Russia, but few were the families in the whole country that were not robbed of a near kinsman. So the Germans themselves, for the second time, had chosen!

And the loss was of course heaviest in spirit, for that is exactly where a country suffers most. To the end, much the greater proportion of the German troops was in Russia, and there was nothing like it in the homeland of most other countries—in America nothing at all—so that it is impossible for other nations to understand the enormous encouragement to Russia to further victory; and to Russians it would almost seem that there was nothing at all which could defy conquest to the flag of Communism, under which they had marched.

And proportionately the heaviest portion of the Russian loss fell upon the Communist Party. At the front it was the Party men who gave the inspiration. Many of the best were soon gone, and others of a lower level were brought in to take their place. In the end there was a general fall of merit all along the line down to the country posts in the rear.

And possibly the most serious loss of all was still impending in the disappearance, by the laws of nature, of the leadership of Stalin, who had seen his way clearly through the whole story.

From now onward it becomes more and more impossible to know what was happening in Russia. That a very great deal was going on behind the scenes was evident. Its chief feature was clear. Amid the varying voices there was more and more emphasis on those which called for a clash and a break, and a renewed attempt at world revolution. Russia had little chance at this time, or at any other within sight, of making good such a program. According to Mr. Churchill, she seemed to be seeking to win the spoils of war without the war. In a word, she had now to find how much could be won by bluff.

One day, on his way with his secretary to his daily work in the United Press in Moscow, Harrison Salisbury was halted by an unusual gathering of people before a life-size picture of Stalin. A dark-haired man with flashing eyes had been replaced by a grey-haired old man. No doubt Stalin had beeen grey for years, but this hadn't been made clear to the common folk, and now everyone was staring at it. It was an altogether new picture. Certainly this change could hardly have been made without a direct vote of the Politburo, the mysterious rulers of Russia, for this is how Russia is told what to expect. It didn't mean "Stalin is gone," or even "He doesn't count for so much as before," but it definitely did mean "Stalin is not necessarily with us forever, and our decisions must from now on be corporate and subject to discussion and disagreement." This made it a period like that before Stalin had consolidated his power. Even retirement isn't easy for a man who has done so much killing. Stalin seemed to be tempering and timing his own withdrawal. It appears that he was away from his desk of Premier for three months of 1946, and for five of 1947.

Two candidates for leadership were in training—one, Vyacheslav Molotov, for the country, and one, Andrei Zhdanov, for the Party. The more important of the two was the second. After the fighting, the losses and, in general, the national ex-

cursion into Europe, as soon as the fighting had stopped, when
the reaction from war to peace was sharpest, and the Russian troops, like many others, broke all bonds of discipline,
evidently it seemed to Zhdanov that discipline must be sharply brought back as near as possible to the initial level of the
Party, when it was small and conquering. More than that, it
must have seemed, from the amazing Party success in Germany and elsewhere immediately after the war, that there was
nothing that could not now be attempted and that those were
cravens who would not attempt it. Zhdanov was not like
Stalin, the plain man, the opportunist who looked round on
all sides first, he was the Intellectual, the pure theorist, a man
with a mission who insisted that the fighter should see no
good in his adversary, that the main fortress of the past should
be carried by storm. His name, made memorable by his leadership of Leningrad, besieged in vain for over two years from
August 21, 1941, stood for extreme measures.

Marxism, except for its attraction for a herd of desperates,
had lost its driving power and was beginning to wear rather
thin. And indeed it was from Zhdanov's own fears that his
action must have started. Above all there was a great wave
of purely national pride in a superb and unprecedented victory, and a stirring to stretch oneself and to find greater freedom
of action.

Zhdanov went back to the first lessons of the Party, to the
tightest discipline. A great new region had now been brought
within the Soviet field, a great advance towards the goal of
the World Republic of Soviets, and it must be absorbed without
delay. For this purpose was instituted under Zhdanov and
Malenkov of the Politburo the new "Cominform," the school
of the future World Republic, intended for the general familiar-
ising of the new scholars with Soviet life (made known on
October 5, 1947). Like the procedure of other builders of
empires in the past, all was to be done without delay, according
to a preconceived pattern. The small but more advanced
peoples of the "Iron Curtain" were not prepared for a retreat
from their standard of common civilisation and independence.
They had looked forward to a time of greater liberty, and now
they were scheduled for less. This began to show itself on all
sides.

This is an all-round challenge to something real—something
which the born empire-builder of Rome or Britain would have
been careful to respect. We may add that the same question
may arise if the Politburo takes it for granted that it can itself
run a Communist China. In Bulgaria, Dimitriev, who has

enormous international prestige, could certainly, if he cared, find ways of resistance. In Poland it has to be recognised that anything coming from Russia is, to start with, under a discount. Russian empire builders there in the past sometimes came to the conclusion that sheer compulsion stood a minimum chance of any effect. I have known the Tsar's official "Messenger" write that Russia would do better if she parted company altogether with Poland. In Czechoslovakia, where, unfortunately for herself, life is far in advance of her neighbours, sheer oppression may prevail for a time. But with a traditional circumspection the oppressed will still be able to choose ways of resistance and of circumvention, and the spirit has lived on through centuries. Finland, though generally in the past unable to make good her full independence, has always known how to make a solid defense of her local liberties and to save them through dangerous crises. The Yugoslavs and especially the Serbs have been famous in history through their passion for independence, especially against Hitler's New Order. When Zhdanov called on Tito to clear out (June 28, 1948), and his country to toe the Moscow line, he dared a challenge which he could not make good; and every day that Tito stayed on was a further strain on the Moscow prestige.

Russia had always despaired of reaching any peace settlement except through direct negotiations with the major powers. The last big four Foreign Ministers Conference on a German peace treaty ended in complete failure in London on December 15, 1947. From this time on, the door was completely shut down in Russia. That, of itself, opened up, in the conditions of the time which we have examined, the question of Russian intentions on the burning subject of world revolution. Of course the Communists believe in world revolution. The question is, how and when it can be achieved. It has not been fully realised that with the perfection of modern weapons of destruction power has gone back to the hands of the few. Marxism is without scruple and the question left is who controls the Politburo. There is certainly a variety of views until a new chief becomes absolute.

The story of the blockade of Berlin is, on the face of it, an absurdity. Nothing could be more disastrous than that conflicting victors should fight out their differences over Germany's dismembered body, even at her heart. And nothing could do more to bring back the Germans as a major factor in these differences. My own guess is that a great enterprise was in preparation, of which the blockade was to be a very brief preface, and indeed that was what the Berliners were told when they were warned against collaborating with the West, in view of the "unavoidable withdrawal of the Allies which will come about very suddenly within the near future" (March 15, 1948). The Western powers had begun to integrate their zones into a Western state, which was seen by the Russians as a violation of the Potsdam Agreement (July 17-August 2, 1945). Of this Agreement for a joint administration of a conquered Germany there are totally different interpretations, but it is evident that the decision to act separately carried matters further away from any prospect of a common settlement.

The Russians walked out of the Allied Control Council (the commanders of the four powers governing Germany) in Berlin the middle of March, 1948, and from that time onward they began to tighten all travel controls. The Allies replied by increasing air activity, and on April 5 there was a collision between a Soviet fighter and a British passenger plane with fifteen casualties, including the attacker.

On June 16, the Russians walked out of a meeting of the Berlin Kommandatura (the four power body created to govern Berlin). The Western powers began currency reform on June 18. Immediately thereafter the Russians clamped down a tight economic blockade, following with their own currency reform on June 23. (So far both sides had used the old Reichsmarks and now each had a currency of its own.) By middle and late June only air transport remained to link the Western sectors of Berlin with the West itself, and there were reinforced guards along the frontiers of the British and American zones.

The airlift, which was now the only road to Berlin for the Western powers, was the answer of the Allies to the challenge of the blockade, but it could not of course be permanent.

In September crowds under Communist direction broke up the meetings of the Municipal City Assembly situated inside the Russian zone. The Assembly majority moved to new quarters in the British sector. In October the Assembly, minus the Communist minority, announced elections for December, at which the Social Democrats, whose sympathies were with the West, polled the largest vote. Earlier the Communists had elected a city government of their own in the Russian sector.

On July 6, 1948, the Western powers, in an effort to settle the Berlin question, had urgently asked to see Molotov, At first he put them off with his deputy, Zorin, but a meeting with Molotov took place on July 31. There followed other meetings in Moscow during the next weeks. At the meeting of the four powers in the Kremlin on August 2, Stalin himself took part, and it seemed that agreement had been reached on a suggestion of his which promised a full consideration of all questions, including even the settlement of a peace treaty with Germany. But this agreement, when drafted respectively by both sides, contained, in the Soviet draft of Molotov, a number of implications of the Soviet rights in the matter previous to the discussion, which the other three powers, on the communication of his draft, seriously challenged. The four powers determined that agreement should be reached between the four military governors in Berlin for the practical implementation of what had been decided. Also the Foreign Ministers were to get together in the near future to discuss any outstanding questions regarding Berlin and any other outstanding problems affecting Germany as a whole.

Though the directive to the military governors was agreed and dispatched, Molotov still held up his final confirmation. The four commanders met on August 31, but evidently Marshal Sokolovsky was not prepared to honor the understandings reached in Moscow—for instance, on the Allies' claim to a full share in the control of the use of the Soviet mark as the sole currency in Berlin, and of that of the Western trade of Berlin. He even suggested the imposition of some new restrictions. No working agreement was reached. His action was confirmed by an *aide memoire* of the Soviet Government communicated to the Allies on September 18. This the three Allies regarded as nullifying what agreement had been reached—a view shared by the Soviet Government in a note of September 25. Always in the background was the question of the monopoly of the Ruhr by the West. The talks came to an end, and we were where we started.

Andrei Zhdanov, it seems, did not take part in these Moscow talks which were conducted by Molotov, but the two must have conferred throughout. It appears that Zhdanov was the member of the Politburo entrusted with the direction of the blockade of Berlin.

And then, as I picture it—though I have no evidence whatever, but it is the only thing that seems to me to fit in— Molotov says to Zhdanov, "I'm sorry, but we can't follow you further now." And Zhdanov finds his own way out. Anyhow he died during the Kremlin talks, (August 31st, 1948). And they gave him a grand state funeral. And then there follows a retreat of a sort, accompanied by every kind of face saving.

And now comes a new big chapter—namely, China, and the collapse of Chiang. There is plenty to come on this side. The best judges have for quite a time past been convinced that

Russia was preparing for a clear-out on the European side, and a concentration in the East and certainly the situation there offers great opportunities. But after all, will not the same snag face them there? Mr. Marshall could tell us quite a bit about this, for he has been at close quarters; but everyone who knows something of the Chinese Communists—for instance that first-class expert Mr. Owen Lattimore—will tell you that there is no real likelihood that they will just tail along according to the dictates of the Politburo, that they are Communists of a kind of their own, very different from the Russians, that though they have moved before now in the same directions as have been suggested to the opportunism of Stalin, they will choose a way which is their own; and indeed did they not do that after the first dazzling successes of Borodin before the period of Chiang?

It was a bluff to be called. For the one thing crystal clear is that Russia, which is still living in hovels and short of men, is in no condition to engage in a third world war. I have just heard from inside that "the people simply thirst for peace."

And was not Zhdanov right if he felt that Marxism itself, for an early promise of a real success, had need of new resources and a renewed spirit? In his best-known translated pamphlet, he harks back to Lenin's insistence that "philosophy" should be pugnacious towards all thinkers before Marx. This was Lenin's hallmark before the Revolution, which made him so unpopular with rival revolutionaries. It is assumed that Marxism is the beginning and end of all things. Marx instituted a new era, before which nothing was any good, and Zhdanov blamed the official Party propagandist and Communist historian, G. F. Alexandrov, for suggesting otherwise. (Alexandrov has, by the way, since Zhdanov's death, received another good appointment.) Further, Marx was absolute and laid down the law for all time. A revolution has always two sides, the constructive and the exterminative, the "Thou shalt not"; and, as in the great example in France, the second tends to get the better of the first—that is, more emphasis is put on what you are not to think than what you are. Carl Becker has put it, "Marx leads us to the threshold of truth, and there commits suicide." Nothing could be more sterilizing, for instance, to real study or to real literature than this constant official prohibition of thinking in certain ways.

We are told at the start that the State is ultimately to disappear. On the contrary, although a first class liberal constitution with all the famous "liberties" of the Russia of 1905 was stored up in 1936 for the future, ordinance, police and compulsion are intensified to preposterous proportions. No wonder Marx himself, who was much better than his followers, lived to say, "I am not a Marxist." Of course, he was a thinker of the first order and his emphasis on the economic, and the form which he gave to it, are come to stay. But he must allow to others the right of thinking for themselves. And Russian philosophers before him and the spirit of nearly all the greatest Russian thinkers and writers was idealist. One can say, if one likes, that there is no explanation of anything that is not purely and absolutely materialist, but it is as easy to say the opposite. And it remains, in any case, a simple assertion.

And is Marx the only prophet? Stalin himself said that Marx could not tell us what was to happen a hundred years after he was dead, that Marxism, if it is a live doctrine, has got to conform itself to the conditions of the time. For myself, I have always regarded Stalin as a loyal student of Marx who with excellent good sense was trying to see which of his various lessons was most suitable for adoption in Russia—and there are plenty, for the community has always been the stamp of Russian thought—where in radical ways this industrial doctrine, imported from Germany, found greater challenges to meet than anywhere else; for I would say that there is no country where it is more impossible to shut out the other world. And then I read dutifully my *Pravda,* reporting, as evidence of the non-existence of God, the two airmen who went up to heaven and couldn't find Him.

If one had gone to Russia, as I did in the four years just before World War II, one would have thought Zhdanov very optimistic. In 1936 the railway men listened to a young member of the government who explained, as the newspapers frequently did, how the country would pass from socialism, which was already achieved, to communism, which was not, and what was the difference between the two. The workmen asked plain, critical questions such as might have been asked in Newcastle or in Pittsburgh. Can we keep marriage? Will there still be over-time? And can you really equalise different workers' abilities? An average non-party Soviet citizen in 1936 would speak of Communism as a distant goal to be achieved, as Christianity might be with us, but no one believed that it would be attained at all.

Vladimir Gsovski's [1] article on family and inheritance in Soviet law (*The Russian Review* for Autumn, 1947), shows

[1] Vladimir Gsovski is Chief of the Foreign Law Section, Library of Congress and Head of Russian Department, Georgetown University, School of Foreign Service.

how vastly the novel and alarming professions of the government on these subjects have exceeded the importance of its legislation on them, and how various have been the changes, as they have also been with reference to the profit motive.

They began by saying that "a dissoluble marriage, and not a lifelong union," was the first principle of the new legislation. According to the Code, "Birth itself shall be the basis of the family. No differentiation whatsoever shall be made between relationships by birth, whether in or out of wedlock" (1918). Divorce at first could be obtained freely by either party and we were told that "the family, creating a series of rights and duties between the spouses, the parents and the children, would certainly disappear in the course of time and would be replaced by government organisation of public education and social security." But a reverse trend began about 1935, and on May 28, 1936, *Pravda* wrote: "So-called free love and loose sexual life are altogether bourgeois and have nothing in common either with Socialist principles or ethics. . . . Marriage is the most serious affair in life." And again we read, "Marriage basically and in the spirit of Soviet law is in principle essentially a life-long union." Now the Russians have gone further than many non-Soviet countries. We read that "all children born after July 8, 1944 outside of a registered marriage have no succession rights to the father's property and may not claim the father's name, and that he is not even liable for their support." Divorce is now given only for reasons which the courts hold to be serious and the fees for petition range from 500 to 2000 roubles.

Inheritance was at first simply abolished outright (April 27, 1918). It was soon found that a nexception had to be made for a property under the value of 10,000 roubles. This restriction had also later to be evaded, and later still every sort of provision had to be made, licensing various categories of heirs according to blood relationships. "At present," writes Gsovski, "there exists the possibility of unlimited accumulation of private wealth in money and securities in Russia, if deposited in certain government banks." The latest edicts in that direction date from March 14, 1945, and June 2, 1945. Very large encroachments on the original Soviet rigidity were due to exceptions in favour of the usual peasant practice. And this and other departures were thus explained in the press: "Succession appears to be one of the stimuli for the development of personal ownership—for increasing the productivity of labour, and for fortifying the Socialist family."

There has been a vast deficiency in the world threat.

And who did all this? The peasant sense of Russia. When the old serfdom was abolished root and branch in 1861, the gentry became a dying class. Till now at least the interests of masters and serfs were in a sense corporate. Then, in 1861, they became economic enemies. The land of the old community, now divided roughly in half between masters and serfs, became ripe for revolution. Whenever the police should withdraw, the peasants on one side of the economic barrier could simply walk across and take the rest. This they tried to do in the last hectic three months of 1905. And this they did wholesale in 1917 before the Bolsheviks ever came into power on November 7. So that all the government had to do was to ally itself, first, with the Socialist Revolutionary Party, and on the first day of its existence declare the settlement good. But the peasants had taken the land in their own way not for the possession of the State but for that of the existing village community. From the first I always felt that from now on the real opposition was the peasantry. And it is they who have done so much to radically transform the original program of the dreamy Communists, who possess all the machine guns, so that they are still in power today.

I should like to quote, as I very often do, as parallel to the Bolshevik creed and practice, an analysis of Russian history by a Volga peasant in 1908, which is far more accurate than any Party formula: "There is a community, and that's why there's a State, and that's why there's a Church. (Both are only facets of the communtiy, and not the other way around.) The State has got wrong with the community, and it has dragged the Church with it. (How true!) We are going to put the State back right with the community, and when we do that, we shall put the Church right back, too, and then you'll see we'll all be orthodox." (Of course, orthodox to the community, which is the real basic thing.)

Or again take a definition of the Siberian co-operators of 1919, when uncontrolled whether by the Reds or by the Whites. They were with neither, they explained, and they would do nothing to break their connection with their brother co-operators on the other side of the line, and there could be no better guarantee for the integrity of Russia. "We," they said, "are a pyramid resting on the village. Bolshevism is a pyramid upside down, trying to rest on its point." They were the one constructive organisation in the public life of the country at that time and they were the representation, in modern turmoil, of the original system of the *Mir,* which means the old peasant world of the community which has existed all through Russian history as the specialty of Russia, and is the original source of Russian inspiration and of the ideal of Communism. These modern cooperators took their ideal not from Moscow but, as they explained to me, from Rochdale in Lancashire, that is, from the originators of the world co-operative movement. And when I came to them, they sent me back to Holyoke House in Manchester with plans for close and friendly contact with England.

Or if we look back through Russian history, especially through the centuries of serfdom, when nothing was left to the under-dog population except to emasculate the alien authority imposed on them, we shall find that there was a vast underworld which, wherever it had a chance to speak past the parties of "the masters," of which the Bolsheviks of course are one, voiced the simple principles of democracy just as they are understood by us. "The intelligentsia," said Alexander Kerensky, "debates democracy, the peasants practice it." The very essence of the *Mir* was justice. All through serfdom the village community was the corporate owner of all its landed property, and therefore it was the essence of authority for all the peasants in it. They debated everything in common, even when to go haymaking. They held immediate meetings on all subjects of public interest. The *Mir* was meant to be the essence of justice. In the division of their common property the first requirement was that all things should be fair. Every man's strips had to run right through the property so that all should get an equal value. When two-thirds majority required, everything could be redivided on the basis of the existing number of workers. "The land belongs to those who work it." This was the motto of the Russian peasant party, the Social Revolutionaries who, in the first period of Soviet rule, shared authority with the Communists. It was a beginning of modern Socialism. In fact the peasants, though enslaved, were the only class that, during serfdom, possessed such a system.

In 1776, when Catherine the Great wanted to learn the true facts of her subjects' life, she called a kind of vast critical committee of other than her officials, to which she summoned also representatives of the Crown peasants. For their direction as to what principles laws should follow, she herself took a year and a half to write a Nakaz, or Instruction, filled with the maxims of Montesquieu, Beccaria and the other encyclopedists. These peasants, adopting her title, Nakaz, wrote their own instructions to those whom they chose. (The peasant of Archangel, Chuprov, brought with him as many as 195.) They were the simple principles of local self-government. "The principal refrains of these instructions," we read, "were absence of any definite right, the miserably bad provisions of justice, the uncontrolled arbitrariness of government officials, their corruption, and the hopelessly overpowering burden of taxes."

The peasants who were elected to the two really representativ Dumas of 1906 and 1907, of which I attended nearly all the sessions, again used the word Nakaz for their instructions to their members, and enjoined them to visit regularly the meetings of all the parties of "the masters," and to write home regularly as to which was likely to do most for "the people," which at that time meant before all things, the peasantry. At the elections to the second Duma it was only the peasants who understood the principles involved in the famous question of the Wilkes election in Middlesex, England—namely, that the government could not choose the member for a constituency but only the constituency itself. And when they were told that Aladin, the peasant's champion, was excluded, they simply elected him as long as they were called upon to elect. To prevent any "faking," they often set watchers to guard the urns (1907). They showed more of political instinct than any other section of the population. Stolypin, the Prime Minister, had offered them the bait of many solid reforms in a parliamentary vacation. They intended to give him a qualified answer, in no sense approving of the sudden dissolution of the first Duma. The electoral law set free a member of the Duma who had been sent to prison without trial. This had happened to many revolutionary champions and the peasants now elected them, so that they had to be set free as long as this Duma existed, warning them meanwhile to make this period of holiday as long as possible in order to put to good use the exemption of the Duma debates from the censorship.

During the so-called "New Economic Policy," in the relaxation of Bolshevik rule, from 1921 to 1928, for a brief time the peasants of the Soviet Union got the same opportunity and were able to put forward their own policy. It was the reversal of Bolshevism—a free market, no taxation on thrift, restoration of the ballot (which had then been abolished by the Bolsheviks), no dictation of choice by the Communist Party (which was the habit of sending down the names to be chosen) and the equalization in value of a peasant's vote with that of a townsman (at that time it took five times as many peasants to elect the same number of members). This is the actual spirit of the history of Russian peasant protest. I do not know of anything like it in any other country. Most of these concessions were granted later in Stalin's new Constituition of 1936, when he was preparing to meet Hitler in the field.

We do not know what (perhaps nothing) is yet to come from below, but we can imagine the strain that is put on such an authority as that of the Marxist so long as it is successfully challenged, and that was the situation which existed at the moment of Zhdanov's death.

The real gap between the two camps in the world is one of knowledge. England, after many long tussles with Russia, has far less excuse for the lack of it. An America in isolation had no urge to study Russia, and it is intelligible that she should start her study from the moment when she first fixed her eyes on the subject, which probably dates from 1914. While America took no action of her own, her criticisms, well or ill founded, were not necessarily taken as serious politics. The amazing achievements of American landings, first in North Africa and then in Normandy, have radically changed all that; and now the poverty of knowledge is in pathetic contrast with the might that waits on it for its direction. Irresponsible criticism is generally self-confident; but no one cares to be told: "I am holier than thou," especially by anyone who doesn't know his facts. The Russians, on their side, are themselves responsible for the unintelligent secrecy with which they cover all their moves. Till they find the sense to open their doors to foreign inquiry, they cannot expect to be understood. Many are the journalistic reputations that have been ruined by the senseless prohibitions of the Soviet censorship, which is like a sore that poisons Russia's foreign relations at the source. And even more important is the senseless exclusion of foreign students. It is a terrible sign of weakness. Triumph for the Soviet conception of the world is not to be won by a policy of closed doors. On the other side, the newspaper chains in the Western democracies, which can control what news and views they will pass on to the public, are thus enabled to live on sensations instead of facts, and malignity to everything Russian becomes a profitable profession. Thus on both sides is precluded the one remedy: namely: constant and objective study.

And a little knowledge will tell us that in the actual course of life, as contrasted with word-slinging, things are not necessarily at all as bad as they are painted. It will tell us that the original fantastic experiments of the militant Communism of 1917 were abandoned in 1921, for the simple reason that they did not work and led of themselves to a colossal and devastating famine; that the authors of those wild experiments have all been eliminated by the present holder of power in Russia; that he publicly countered Trotsky's program of "permanent revolution" with one of common-sense construction at home and, to use his own words, of "working relations with any foreign government, even capitalist, which is friendly to the Soviet Union"; that he definitely preferred to a foreign policy of revolution the association of the Western democracies against Hitler (especially during the Spanish Civil War) and that it was more our fault than his if they did not accept his proffered hand up to 1939 (when Litvinov was replaced by Molotov); that the present product of his rule is not a generation of world revolutionists, but a new race of technicians, each with a vigour of purpose that was new to Russia in her work of home construction; that with this program he not only outmanned but, with plentiful Allied aid, even out-equipped Hitler's Germany and carried his country to such a complete triumph as Russia had never known before; and, lastly, that anyone there, official or unofficial, who will maintain that Russia, herself, has actually adopted that system of Communism which she is so freely credited abroad with seeking to impose on the rest of the world.

If we go back to the facts, there is much to comfort us. The main fact in the world is the crying demand for world peace, and nowhere more than in Russia. The main opportunity now is in cooperative reconstruction of a broken world.

For us, the high road to peace with Russia is equally simple; it is study. World opinion, to have its effect on Russia, as on others, must be frank, but it cannot afford to be ignorant. Cannot we pay to that immense and to us unknown country the very small compliment of crediting her with a separate and individual life of her own, with a course of development which she alone can determine for herself? That is the real subject for our study, and it is a task that we have hardly begun.

And knowledge alone is not enough without understanding, which is much more hardly won. To no country does this apply more than to Russia. Some things are so very hard to guess; and others, which often do not express themselves at all, are so abundantly clear. One can always see at once whether anyone talking of Russia has really lived there; it is a kind of freemasonry, entirely independent both of class and of views. It is that real knowledge which we have got to win. At present we are far away from anything of the kind.

This gap has to be filled, or it will cost us dear.

SOME BOOKS ON RUSSIA

FLETCHER, GILES. *The Russe Commonwealth* (in Hakluyt's *Principal Navigations*, 1598). Dutton, 1927, An enthralling Elizabethan picture of medieval Russia.

WALLACE, D. MACKENZIE. *Russia* (2 Vols.). Cassell.

WILLIAMS, HAROLD. *Russia of the Russians*. Pitman. By the greatest of British students of Russia.

MAYNARD, JOHN. *Russia in Flux*. Gollancz, 1942; Macmillan, 1948.

MAYNARD, JOHN. *The Russian Peasant*. Gollancz, 1942;; Macmillan, 1948.

MIRSKY, D. S. *A History of Russian Literature*. Knopf, 1934.

MIRSKY, D. S. *Modern Russian Literature*. Oxford, 1925.

BARING, MAURICE. *Outline of Russian Literature*. Holt, 1915.

BARING, MAURICE. *What I Saw in Russia*. Heinemann.

MURPHY, JOHN THOMAS. *New Horizons*. Lane, 1941.

PARES, BERNARD. *The Fall of the Russian Monarchy*. Knopf, 1939.

MIRSKY, D. S. *Lenin*. Little, Brown, 1931.

CHAMBERLIN, WILLIAM HENRY. *The Russian Revolution* (2 vols.). Macmillan, 1935.

KARLGREN, ANTON. *Bolshevist Russia*. Macmillan, 1927. The best picture in English of the peasantry in 1921-28.

HARPER, SAMUEL N. *Civic Training in Soviet Russia*. Chicago University, 1929. By the foremost American authority on Russia.

HARPER, SAMUEL N. *Making Bolsheviks*. Chicago University, 1931.

LENIN, V. I. *Imperialism the Highest Stage of Capitalism*. International Publishers, 1933.

LENIN, V. I. *The State and Revolution*. G. Allen & Unwin, 1919.

TROTSKY, L. *Our Revolution: essays on working class and international revolution, 1904-17*; biography and notes by M. J. Olgin. 1918, New York.

TROTSKY, L. *The Revolution Betrayed*. Doubleday, 1937.

HINDUS, MAURICE. *Broken Earth*. International Publishers, 1926.

HINDUS, MAURICE. *Red Bread*. Random House, 1931.

LITTLEPAGE, JOHN D. AND BESS, DEMAREE. *In Search of Soviet Gold*. Harcourt, 1938.

DAVIES, JOSEPH E. *Mission to Moscow*. Simon & Schuster, 1941.

PARES, BERNARD. *A History of Russia*. Knopf, 1948 (5th edition, revised and enlarged).

ANDERSON, PAUL B. *People, Church and State in Modern Russia*. Macmillan, 1944.

CRANKSHAW, EDWARD. *Russia and the Russians*. Viking, 1948.

INDEX

Other MENTOR Books of Interest

The Statesman *by Henry Taylor.* A wise and witty handbook for politicians, written over a hundred years ago.
(#MD250—50¢)

The True Believer *by Eric Hoffer.* A provocative analysis of the nature of mass movements and the fanatics who give them power.
(#MD228—50¢)

American Diplomacy: 1900-1950 *by George F. Kennan.* A trenchant appraisal of U.S. foreign relations by a distinguished diplomat.
(#MD80—50¢)

The United Nations and How It Works *by David Cushman Coyle.* The only book in the paperback field covering the United Nations, its agencies, and their work throughout the world.
(#MD220—50¢)

The Public Philosophy *by Walter Lippmann.* A penetrating and challenging analysis of the changing state of Western democracies, by an influential American commentator.
(#MD174—50¢)

The Prince *by Niccolo Machiavelli.* The classic work on statesmanship and power, the techniques and strategy of gaining and keeping political control.
(#MD69—50¢)

Books That Changed the World *by Robert B. Downs.* Histories of epoch-making books, from Machiavelli's *The Prince* to Einstein's *Theories of Relativity.*
(#MD229—50¢)

Rebels and Redcoats *by George Scheer and Hugh F. Rankin.* A powerful eye-witness account of the American Revolution taken from letters, diaries, journals, and battle reports.
(#MT249—75¢)

A Short History of India and Pakistan *by T. Walter Wallbank.* This comprehensive and readable history is a revised, abridged, up-dated edition of *India in the New Era.*
(#MD224—50¢)

The American Presidency *by Clinton Rossiter*. A clear account of the history and evolution of the Presidency and the President's current duties and responsibilities.

(#MD267—50¢)

Arms and Men *by Walter Millis*. A history of the American Army, its strategies, weapons, tactics, current problems.

(#MD208—50¢)

Democracy in America (abridged) *by Alexis de Tocqueville*. The classic critique of freedom and democracy in 19th century America by a brilliant Frenchman. (#MD161—50¢)

A Documentary History of the United States (revised, expanded) *edited by Richard D. Heffner*. Important documents that have shaped our history. (#MD78—50¢)

The United States Political System and How It Works *by David Cushman Coyle*. A key to national, state and local politics, and theories of democracy. (#Ks303—35¢)

This Is the West *edited by Robert West Howard*. A true and colorful account of the building of the American West, by experts in the field. (#S1424—35¢)

A Brief History of the United States *by Franklin Escher, Jr.* A convenient guide to American history outlining the events and trends that make our heritage. (#K304—25¢)

American Skyline *by Christopher Tunnard and Henry Hope Reed*. An illustrated panorama of American civilization as shown in the growth of our cities. (#MD175—50¢)

The Mentor Philosophers

The entire range of Western speculative thinking from the Middle Ages to modern times is presented in this series of six volumes. Each book contains the basic writings of the leading philosophers of its age.

50 cents each

THE AGE OF BELIEF: The Medieval Philosophers *edited by Anne Fremantle.* (#MD126)
"Highly commendable . . . provides an excellent beginning volume." —*The Classical Bulletin*

THE AGE OF ADVENTURE: The Renaissance Philosophers *edited by Giorgio de Santillana.* (#MD184)
"The most exciting and varied in the series." —*New York Times*

THE AGE OF REASON: The 17th Century Philosophers *edited by Stuart Hampshire.* (#MD158)
"His (Hampshire's) book is a most satisfactory addition to an excellent series." —*Saturday Review*

THE AGE OF ENLIGHTENMENT: The 18th Century Philosophers *edited by Sir Isaiah Berlin.* (#MD172)
"(Sir Isaiah) has one of the liveliest and most stimulating minds among contemporary philosophers." —*N. Y. Herald Tribune*

THE AGE OF IDEOLOGY: The 19th Century Philosophers *edited by Henry D. Aiken.* (#MD185)
". . . perhaps the most distinct intellectual contribution made in the series." —*New York Times*

THE AGE OF ANALYSIS: 20th Century Philosophers *edited by Morton White.* (#MD142)
"No other book remotely rivals this as the best available introduction to 20th century philosophy." —*N. Y. Herald Tribune*